THE COLLECTIVE VOICE

THE COLLECTIVE VOICE

Modern Literature and the Politics of Speech

MATTHEW TAUNTON

STANFORD UNIVERSITY PRESS
Stanford, California

Stanford University Press
Stanford, California

Library of Congress Cataloging-in-Publication Data
Names: Taunton, Matthew author
Title: The collective voice : modern literature and the politics of speech / Matthew Taunton.
Description: Stanford, California : Stanford University Press, 2026. | Includes bibliographical references and index.
Identifiers: LCCN 2026020827 (print) | LCCN 2026020828 (ebook) | ISBN 9781503642300 cloth | ISBN 9781503648494 paperback | ISBN 9781503648500 ebook
Subjects: LCSH: Literature, Modern—20th century—History and criticism | Oral communication in literature | Collective behavior in literature | Politics and literature
Classification: LCC PN771 .T38 2026 (print) | LCC PN771 (ebook)
LC record available at https://lccn.loc.gov/2026020827
LC ebook record available at https://lccn.loc.gov/2026020828

Cover design: Bob Aufuldish / Aufuldish & Warinner
Text design: [designer] if new design
Typeset by [typesetter] in [text size/leading and face]

The authorized representative in the EU for product safety and compliance is: Mare Nostrum Group B.V. | Doelen 72 | 4831 GR Breda | The Netherlands | Email address gpsr@mare-nostrum.co.uk | KVK chamber of commerce number: 96249943

For Benjamin Kohlmann

CONTENTS

ACKNOWLEDGMENTS

In the course of writing this book I have benefited from many forms of support, both institutional and personal, and I would like to record my thanks here.

I am most grateful to the British Academy for funding this research with a Mid-Career Fellowship (grant number MCFSS22\220014). In addition to precious time to read, write, and think, this award provided me with the means to conduct archival research in the United States and to work with arts organizations and practitioners around the topic of the collective voice. The University of East Anglia (UEA) generously funded research time over many years, and the Faculty of Arts and Humanities granted two periods of study leave that enabled me first to do some initial groundwork and then later to complete the book.

As well as keeping the lights on, UEA has provided me with a brilliant range of colleagues, in the School of Literature, Drama and Creative Writing, in the Faculty of Arts and Humanities, and beyond. A surprising number of them have been happy to listen to me talk about collective vocalization and then have said intelligent, well-informed, and sometimes testing things in return. I have learned in particular from Sola Adeyemi, Tim Anderson, Karina Aveyard, Stephen Benson, Birgit Breidenbach, Sophie Butler, Clare Connors, Katherine Cooper, Alan Finlayson, Richard Hand, Joel Halcomb, Katherine Hunt, Claire Hynes, Ben Jones, Tommy Karshan, Duncan Large, Anshuman Mondal, Jeremy Noel-Tod, David Nowell Smith, Rachel Potter, Tom Roebuck, Will Rossiter, Karen Schaller, Jos Smith, John Turnpenny, Georgia Walker-Churchman, Steve Waters, Nonia Williams, James Wood, and our much-missed Peter Womack. It has been a difficult period for UEA, and this book feeds on the collective experiences of the picket line and the redundancy pool that I shared with these extraordinary current and former colleagues.

In the course of the writing of this book, I have had the opportunity to present work in progress at the Rothermere American Institute, University of Oxford, the Department of English Language and Literature, University College London, the "Interwar Women Writers: Politics, Citizenship, Style" symposium at King's College London, the School of English and Drama at Queen Mary, University of London, two connected symposia at the Institut für Anglistik und Amerikanistik, Universität Regensburg, and at several meetings of the Modernist Studies Association and the British Association for Modernist Studies. I thank the organizers of these events and all those who discussed and responded to my work.

At these events and elsewhere, I have benefited from many discussions with brilliant and knowledgeable people who have (whether they realize it or not) helped me to write this book. I thank in particular Elizabeth Anderson, Rebecca Beasley, Matthew Beaumont, Kasia Boddy, Katharina Boehm, Beci Carver, Daniela Caselli, Steve Connor, John T. Connor, Ben Dawson, Finn Fordham, Nick Gaskill, Francis Gooding, Helen Hackett, Dan Hancox, Ben Harker, Ken Hirschkop, Janice Ho, Suzanne Hobson, Peter Howarth, Matthew Ingleby, Jeanne-Marie Jackson, Ann Marie Jakubowski, Julia Jordon, Peter Kalliney, Nicole King, Caroline Levine, Ramesh Mallipeddi, Liz Miller, Michael McCluskey, Scott McCracken, Colin MacCabe, Douglas Mao, Elizabeth Miller, Tiziana Morosetti, Anindya Raychaudhuri, Nicole Rizutto, Richard Osborne, Anthony Ossa-Richardson, Sonali Perera, Laura Salisbury, Laura Scott, Luke Seaber, Akshi Singh, Dave Stelfox, Lyndsey Stonebridge, Matthew Stratton, Elinor Taylor, Pam Thurschwell, Daniel Trilling, David Trotter, Anna Vaninskaya, Nathan Waddell, Jasmine Wallace, and Kiron Ward.

I am of course particularly thankful to the people who have read and commented on drafts of various sections of the book. These include Tim Anderson, Katherine Cooper, Clara Jones, Natasha Periyan, and Anna Snaith. Benjamin Kohlmann in particular has been an unstintingly generous and insightful reader throughout the writing process. My graduate students past and present have been a continuing source of inspiration and fresh thinking. I would like to thank in particular (and in chronological order) Dr. Charlotte Hallahan, Dr. Joseph Williams, Dr. Matthew Mullett, Anna Devereux, and David Strong, all of whom have discussed various aspects of collective voicing with me and have enriched my understanding of it through their own work.

The British Academy provided the impetus and funding to bring the collective voice to the public and out into the streets. I thank the Whitechapel Gallery, and in particular Jane Scarth, Luke Gregory-Jones, and Sam Williams, for hosting an event, The Voice of the People, that grew out of this project. The speakers, Alan Finlayson, Ananya Kabir, and Rory Pilgrim, provided insights into collective speech that have stuck with me, as did Rory's film of collective speech and action, *The Undercurrent* (2019), which we screened that day. With generous additional financial support from Helen Lindsay and from the AHRC Impact Accelerator Account held at UEA, I was also able to take part in the Declamations! Project, which brought the collective voice to the streets of Norwich. Working in the tradition of the mass declamations of Helen's father, Jack Lindsay, we commissioned four new political choral works from UEA students, which were performed in promenade in Norwich on 27 April 2024. I am grateful to Helen, to Steve Waters who acted as dramaturg, to Simon Floyd who directed the shows, to the Common Lot Theatre Company, and to the wonderful cast of amateur actors. The writers Jose Socrates Delos Reyes, Chloe Yates, Merlyn Haycroft, Phoebe Segal, and Mae Milburn brought energy, creativity, and political commitment to the work, and they are a testament to the vitality of the script-writing program at UEA. I had the privilege of working closely with Bartek Dziadosz of the Derek Jarman Lab as he directed, shot, and edited a film called *Declamations!* about this project (now available on YouTube). I am grateful to Cinema City, Norwich, and to Birkbeck Cinema, for hosting screenings of the film, and to those who attended and contributed to stimulating Q&A sessions. Collaborating with practitioners illuminated for me in a new way some practical and affective dimensions of collective vocalization.

I am grateful to the librarians and archivists who have provided invaluable assistance over the course of this project. I thank the staff at the Beinecke Rare Book and Manuscript Library, Yale University; the British Library; the Church of England Record Centre, Bermondsey; Lambeth Palace Library; Lilly Library, Indiana University; the Special Collections Research Center, Southern Illinois University Carbondale; and the University of East Anglia library.

The section of chapter 3 on Katharine Burdekin is derived in part from an article published in *Women: A Cultural Review* (2020), copyright Taylor & Francis, available at https://www.tandfonline.com/doi/full/10.1080/09574042.2020.1843246. I thank the editors for permission to reuse this material. It has been wonderful to work with Stanford University Press on this book. I am above all grateful to my editor Erica Wetter, whose initial enthusiasm for the book was followed with wisdom and patience. I also thank Caroline McKusick, Larkin Paddack, and my assiduous copy editor Katherine Faydash. I am particularly grateful for the supportive, detailed, and probing reports I received from Stanford's anonymous peer reviewers—the book is much better for the careful attention they gave to the manuscript. All remaining errors, misapprehensions, and deviations, are my own.

I thank my wife, Doris, and my sons, Albert and Oscar, for their patience, love, and good humor, especially in the inevitably painful final stages of writing this book. I am lucky to live with such lovely, caring, and clever people. My parents Peter and Gloria and my sister Kate have been wonderfully supportive throughout the process. The greatest debt I incurred was to Benjamin Kohlmann, and I dedicate this book to him in friendship.

INTRODUCTION

THE COLLECTIVE VOICE

WHEN TWO OR MORE people say, chant, or sing the same words at the same time, there is a collective utterance. The reasons for making such an utterance are many and various, ranging from prayers to oaths of allegiance, from football songs to chants at political rallies, to the various forms of the theatrical chorus. These practices are disparate and apparently randomly distributed through modern societies, but they also share family resemblances. As Steven Connor has put it, "Choric utterance is almost always concerned with the establishment of solidarity."[1] This type of speech invokes collective presence and group belonging, and it is usually heard as oral expression, although it is often underpinned by written or printed scripts. It breaks down the boundaries between speech and music, and between speaker and listener. It challenges theories of language premised on one-to-one communication, suggesting, for Fred Cummins, "a larger view of just what language is, and how the vocal activity of humans works and how it matters."[2] This book investigates the various relationships between collective speech and politics. It follows Connor and Cummins in suggesting that, while different types of collective vocalization can be identified and taxonomized, these can nevertheless be treated coherently together as a multifaceted single object. While seeking to map a formidably various field, this book wears its definite article with pride: *the* collective voice.

Compared with the spontaneous, improvisatory, and individual utterances found in conversation, collective vocalization seems to echo through the ages. To say the Lord's Prayer is to commune not only with an embodied congregation speaking synchronously in the present, but also with the generations who have spoken the same words across many centuries. Collective spoken rituals are often associated with the distant past. The influence of evolutionist anthropology is still strong, and with it the tendency to divide human history into progressive cultural stages.[3] The collective voice is frequently linked with earlier, "primitive" forms of life, and it is thought to have declined under pressure from the individualism of capitalist modernity, existing only as a residue of an earlier more communal social formation. But while the places one might expect to hear collective speech are now, as always, highly dependent on historical and cultural context, a simple narrative of decline misses the mark. The collective voice is still very much audible today.

In fact, *The Collective Voice* is conceived partly as an answer to a particularly brash form of contemporary collective speech. The idea for this book took hold as I watched (on television, from the United Kingdom) Donald Trump's rallies during his first presidential run in 2016. Large crowds—apparently frenzied by Trump's anti-immigrant rhetoric and his misogynistic derision of Hillary Clinton—chanted "Lock Her Up," "Drain the Swamp," and "Build the Wall." Such chants have become emblematic of a certain kind of contemporary populism, which imagines "the people"—usually conceived in ethno-nationalist terms—speaking as one. Judith Butler's *Notes Toward a Performative Theory of Assembly* (2015) acknowledges some of the disturbing resonances of such speech: "It would be odd, if not terrifying, to imagine every member of the group called 'the people' together and speaking in unison [. . .] Usually, we associate the event of everybody speaking the same things at the same time with fascism or other compulsory forms of conformity."[4] Embedded in Butler's "usually" is a long intellectual tradition of crowd pessimism that runs through Gustave Le Bon, Sigmund Freud, José Ortega y Gasset, and Elias Canetti.[5] These thinkers share a view of the crowd as a phenomenon that short-circuits the rational, individual self and taps into primitive, aggressive drives. When Joseph Goebbels posed the question "Do you want total war?" to the crowd in front of the Berlin Sportpalast in 1943, they answered together, enthusiastically, "Yes!" This tradition of crowd pessimism would see this fascist populism as typical of collective speech as such.

However, recent works such as Hans Ulrich Gumbrecht's *Crowds: The Stadium as a Ritual of Intensity* (2021) and Dan Hancox's *Multitudes: How Crowds Made the Modern World* (2024) have critiqued the arguments of this tradition to celebrate the crowd's liberating potential.[6] Gumbrecht and Hancox see the crowd as a supplement to individuality, rather than as a threat to it, and emphasize its utopian charge. The question faced by all those who recoil from fascistic collective utterances is, How might we answer them? Writers like Gumbrecht and Hancox imply that mass vocalizations from the left have an important role to play.

What might this sound like? The question is explored in Spike Lee's 2018 film *BlacKkKlansman,* based on the true story of Ron Stallworth, a Black police officer who infiltrated the Ku Klux Klan in 1970s Colorado Springs. Like many of the literary and dramatic works I discuss in this book, *BlacKkKlansman* imagines several different roles for collective speech. There are the confrontational slogans at a Kwame Ture rally that Stallworth attends, shouted by the audience: "Hell no, we won't go!" (i.e., to Vietnam) and "All power to all the people!" In a brilliant montage, Lee puts a veteran civil rights activist's account of the lynching of Jesse Washington into dialogue with Stallworth's initiation into the Klan (Stallworth himself interacts with the Klan over the phone; a white cop plays Stallworth in person). These intercut scenes both culminate in collective utterances initiated by the leaders: a chant of "Black Power!" is juxtaposed to the Klan's "America First!" chant, initiated by David Duke, who leads the ceremony. These are bubbles of solidarity on opposite sides of a political divide, but both seem to imagine the collective voice operating on a much larger scale, the country divided along racial lines into two opposed choruses.[7]

The film's ending segues to the recent past, in Trump's America, using found footage from the Unite the Right rally that took place in Charlottesville, Virginia, in 2017, and that led to murderous violence as a man drove a car into a crowd of antifascist protestors, killing one and injuring thirty-five. Chants of "Black Lives Matter!" are met with "White Lives Matter!" and "Jews will not replace us!" In a powerful reading of *BlacKkKlansman,* Amelia Saunders has argued that the chants at the Kwame Ture rally also descend into a "depersonalizing unison" and an "automatism."[8] Lee's film—which alternates between comedy and melancholia—sees the political field as fundamentally constituted by the noisy clash of chanted slogans, left and right, fascist and antifascist. Such an understanding of the contemporary political scene is partly corroborated by the fact that the chant "Jews will not replace us!" developed from "You will not replace us!" which in turn seem to have originated as a subversive inversion of "He will not divide us." It was one of the responses solicited by Shia LaBeouf, Nastja Säde Rönkkö, and Luke Turner's live streamed durational artwork HEWILLNOTDIVIDE.US.[9] This piece invited passing members of the public to recite or to respond to this progressive, anti-Trump slogan, facing a camera that was mounted initially on a wall outside the Museum of the Moving Image, New York. The work had to be moved, as it became a magnet for rival groups of protesters and counterprotestors, including groups of far-right thugs, inspired by the "great replacement theory," who chanted, "You will not replace us!"

Collective voices that interact in this way are not involved in a conversation or a debate. Such a ramping up of verbal antagonism, in which slogans are simply inverted and shouted back, cannot readily be situated in a framework of discursive liberal dialogue. Such displays lead Cummins to enquire whether "joint speech" (as he prefers to call it) is in fact "the inane and shouty little brother of dialectic and reasoned argument."[10] These forms of verbal performance expose the limitations of a purely liberal approach to understanding political communications and seem more appropriate to Chantal Mouffe's theorization of our "populist moment." From the 1980s onwards, Mouffe and her erstwhile collaborator Ernesto Laclau have argued that traditional socialist parties (whether descended from the reformist Second International or the revolutionary Third) have struggled to adapt to the changing political scene. Collective vocalization was also important to those older movements, and socialist hymns such as "L'Internationale" are part of a nineteenth-century collective speech inheritance whose history is traced in this book. But the emergence, since 1968, of "resistances against various forms of domination which could not be formulated in class terms" has opened the space, and created the necessity, for forms of solidarity that reach beyond the working class.[11]

Concurrently, as Mouffe points out, a mood of "post-politics" set in among centrist parties, which offer limited change via the ballot box, even while they insist that it is the only legitimate channel for political expression. During the 2024 US presidential election, Kamala Harris's campaign sought to capture some of the energy of the rallies which had energized Trump's successful 2016 run. Goading the Republican candidate by boasting that her rallies were bigger than his, Harris seemed to accept the premise that the election would be fought and won through live events that generated crowd noise and chants. She developed some call-and-response lines to counter Trump's. Do we believe in the promise of America?" Harris would ask, and the crowd cheered, "Yes!" And Harris: "When we vote . . ." And together with the crowd: "We win!" In some of the rowdier moments, Harris's audiences broke into spontaneous chants, in some cases directly mirroring those from Trump's rallies. "Lock him up!" they chanted (Trump had recently been found guilty on thirty-four counts of falsifying business records). But Harris shut them down: "The courts are going to handle that; we're going to beat him in November."[12] During the same campaign, Barack Obama, acting as a surrogate for Harris, implored a crowd, ecstatic in its hatred of Trump: "Don't boo: vote!" The most succinct summation of the campaign's approach to the collective voice came in a line Harris repeated in the days before the election: "Your vote is your voice, and your voice is your power." In some respects, the campaign was typical of a form of liberal constitutionalism that recognizes both the power and the danger of the collective voice. In this view, collective vocalization is a populist intoxicant which must be handled with care, and with a view to substituting in the safer action of voting. Harris would have struggled to make the same point in German, where the word for "voice" (*Stimme*) also means "vote": the idea that voting and voicing are in some way interchangeable is built into the German language itself.

For Mouffe, the centrist attempt to exclude the rowdier forms of popular political speech ends up presenting an opportunity to the far right. Left populism is a political strategy designed for these times: "To stop the rise of right-wing populist parties, it is necessary to design a properly political answer through a left populist movement that will federate all the democratic struggles," she writes.[13] In advocating for a left populism, Mouffe grants that contemporary politics will as a matter of course be dominated by those who shout loudest. She would therefore see a tactic of uniting large groups of speakers around simplified slogans and demands as an indispensable political strategy for the left. The challenge for Mouffe, then, becomes one of how to articulate a genuinely inclusive version of the collectively speaking mass: a dilemma that confronts many of the writers discussed in this book.

Writing about collective speech is often concerned to explore how popular voices may interrupt or override established political hierarchies and processes. This can be illustrated using a passage from *God's Bits of Wood* (1960), by the Senegalese writer and filmmaker Ousmane Sembène (whose work I examine in more detail in the bridge that joins Chapters 1 and 2). Set in the dying days of the French colonial regime, and in the ferment of a strike in which industrial action meets anticolonial resistance, the novel dramatizes a scene in which the colony's governor-general and his deputy address a fractious crowd from behind a "battery" of microphones. But the restless crowd decide to "shout until they can't even hear the loudspeakers," demanding that Bakayoko, one of the strike's leaders, be allowed to speak: "*Baillika mou vahe, baillika mou vahe!* Let him speak, let him speak!"[14] The governor-general eventually has to concede and allows Bakayoko to address the crowd. The collective voice in the twentieth century has to contend with a media revolution in which machines can amplify, reproduce, synthesize, and multiply the human voice. Coming together to sing, chant, or pray in unison often pushes back against this technologization of the voice. In *God's Bits of Wood,* the microphone is a tool of colonial domination. The collective voice becomes one of resistance.

This form of choral speech evokes an embodied and de-hierarchized collectivity as a popular challenge to established status hierarchies. Leftists often cite the "human microphone" at the 2011 Occupy protests—where a speaker's unamplified words were repeated by groups in the audience, rippling outwards until everyone has heard—as a nonalienated and democratic form of collective utterance. Judith Butler was one of those whose voice was amplified by the human microphone during their visit to the Occupy Wall Street in 2011. So, as well as noting the potentially fascist overtones of collective speech, Butler celebrates its potential to advance progressive causes, for example, in protests and solidarity marches. Butler focuses attention on the "assembly" as a small and temporary gathering with specific demands. "There are many examples of people coming together, forming a way of speaking as a collective, and demanding a change in policy," they write. Distinct from any conception of the people as unified by language, nation, culture, or ethnicity, Butler's conception of the assembly is predicated on agonistic conflict: "No one popular assembly comes to represent the entirety of the people, but each positing of the people through assembly risks or invites a set of conflicts [. . .] about who the people really are."[15] The formation of an assembly constitutes a performative democratic claim—"we, the people"—that cannot be understood in descriptive terms: "The people" is not a sociological category, but an assembly created by a collective speech act. Speech act theory has—from J. L. Austin onwards—tended to focus on individual speech acts, like the "I do" in the marriage ceremony. Butler suggests that the collective utterance "we the people" is a performative in Austin's sense, because it brings into being a speaking group—and furthermore that all collective speech (regardless of its semantic content) has this primary perlocutionary effect. Butler's performative theory of assembly grants an inaugurating power to any self-selecting group that may decide to go out into the street and speak in unison.

Butler's work around this topic, then, has acknowledged the troubling presence of "bad" (fascist, exclusionary) collective speech, but it has tried to distinguish from it some forms of "good" (democratic, inclusive) collective speech. The philosopher Adriana Cavarero recently went further than Butler in attempting to pin down the specific formal qualities that distinguish good collective vocalizations from bad ones. To see how she got there, it will be helpful to set the context in her earlier work. In *For More Than One Voice* (2005), Cavarero stressed the unique individuality of every voice. Philosophy has tended to think of language as an abstract and disembodied system of signs, she argues, as a result of a process she calls the "devocalisation of logos."[16] The embodied pneumatic process of voice production, with all its "sonorous materiality," has been left out of philosophy, Cavarero claims.[17] "The typical freedom with which human beings combine words is never a sufficient index of the individuality of the one who speaks," she writes. Focusing on language as communication will inevitably foreground the repeatability of the semantic units that make speech intelligible: "The voice, however, is always different from all other voices, even if the words are the same."[18] For Cavarero, the voice is an audible fingerprint, an index of the distinctive individuality of every human being.

In *Surging Democracy* (2021), Cavarero turns explicitly to collective vocalization and explains its fascist potential via the specific sonority of what she calls the "mass" voice, in which "individuality—and even more so uniqueness—vanishes into the indistinct unity of the collective subject."[19] The critique is already familiar from the tradition of crowd pessimism mentioned above. But Cavarero wants to distinguish this "voice of the masses" from a form of collective vocalization which is more in touch with "the Arendtian category of plurality . . . which, far from agglutinating individuals, exalts precisely the embodied uniqueness, distinctive and exhibitive, of those who compose it."[20] To illustrate this, Cavarero reflects on an anecdote in one of Arendt's essays in which the dissident poet Boris Pasternak returns to the Soviet Union in 1946. He begins reading one of his poems but accidentally drops his script, at which point the crowd gradually takes over and begins to recite the poem in unison and from memory: "The poem is recited in unison, but [. . .] the dynamic of this choral performance, is not the typical fusional effect of speaking in unison, but rather the adding, one after the other, of singular voices. Put another way, the voices unite with the choir as unique voices and, independently of the effect of reciting in chorus, remain plural."[21] This models for Cavarero a form of antitotalitarian collective speech. In effect, she makes a moral distinction between the "voice of the masses" and the "voice of plurality." Bad collectivities—the "masses," the potentially totalitarian ones—are those in which individuals are compressed into a singular, collective subject; good collectivities, or "pluralities," are ones in which the uniqueness of every individual (which still resides above all in the voice) is preserved.

Beyond Good and Evil: A Positional Schema

As useful as I find Cavarero's close attention to the sonorities of collective vocalization, I am less persuaded by her tidy-minded moral categorization. No analytic razor is sharp enough to separate the "masses" from the "plurality." On a purely formal level, as the range of examples explored in this book tends to demonstrate, it is not consistently possible to *hear* the difference between fascist and antifascist collective speech. The chants of "Yes we can!" at Obama's rallies in 2008 were metrically identical to the Trumpian "Build the wall!" In fact, they both echo the three-beat pattern (/ / / —) heard at North American professional sports events (and often effectively mandated by the amplified beat on the jumbotron). Even close semantic analysis can be misleading. Ultimately the meaning of a collective utterance, including its political charge, is lost without a historically informed sense of the context of that utterance and its position in relation to hegemonic political structures.

Speech act theory has elaborated thoughtfully on what are sometimes called "felicity conditions": in J. L. Austin's words, "the things which are necessary for the smooth or 'happy' functioning of a performative."[22] In Austin's example, saying "I do" can render you married if you say it in a church, at the right point in a marriage ceremony, and in the presence of an ordained minister, but not if these very specific felicity conditions are not met (in fact, the Book of Common Prayer mandates "I will"). How and what collective speech acts *do* depends not only on their semantic content, or on the tone, manner, pitch, or rhythm of the delivery. The recovery of the context of specific collective utterances is therefore an important aspect of this book's method, in which formal analysis of specific collective utterances is complemented by detailed historical scholarship. In this way, the felicity conditions that make specific collective utterances effective as speech acts are revealed to the reader. Rather than seeking to refine a set of formal criteria that could finally separate good collective utterances from bad ones, *The Collective Voice* builds its argument, and its structure, around positionality.

My three main chapters therefore explore three different relationships between the collective voice and political power, which I refer to as the polis.

Chapter 1 investigates collective utterances that are, or are seen as, insurgent, primordial, Dionysiac, racialized, emanating from outside the polis and even beyond the boundaries of "civilization" itself: here, the collective voice occupies a position of refusal or exile. Chapter 2 looks at the ways in which the collective voice has been reframed as the voice of the people (or some subset of them) and imagined as protesting, politically engaged, or otherwise democratically active within the polis. Finally, chapter 3 turns to forms of collective utterance in which the collective voice is, or seems to be, in a position of hegemony or power, being promoted (and in some cases imposed) by sovereign power, or by political, religious, and civic institutions. The structure I am proposing can be expressed diagrammatically (fig. 1).

As figure 1 shows, the three chapters model the movement of the collective voice from an insurgent position on the margins, or even outside of civilized society, to a dominant position in which collective utterances are endorsed or even mandated by the state and its institutions.

There are two "bridge" sections, linking the chapters, which show how the collective voice can turn from refusal to political engagement, and from protest to hegemony. And there is a coda, which shows how hegemonic and

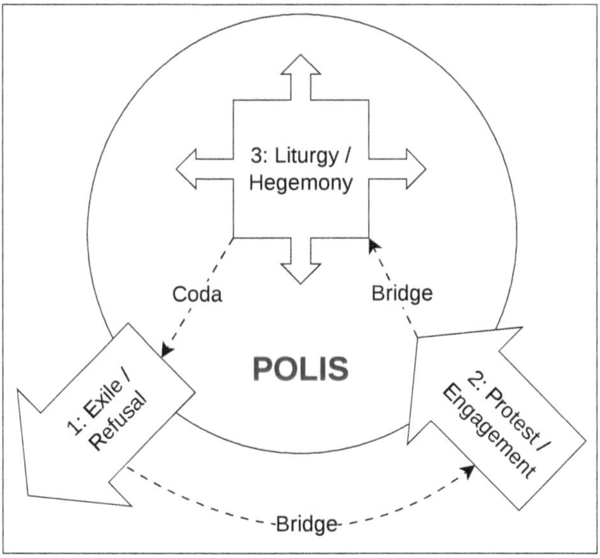

FIGURE 1: Diagram of chapter structure

liturgical forms can produce refusal as a response, completing a circular movement between the three different positions my book delineates. This movement is conceived as a conceptual rather than a historical trajectory, and it is not intended to point fatalistically to any inevitable outcome. It should not be taken to imply that any one expression of fugitive refusal will inevitably turn into a protest chant or that any one protest chant will become institutionalized as state liturgy. Neither is it a mechanism for sorting fascist collective utterances from antifascist ones: examples of each can readily be found in each of the three positions on the diagram. *The Collective Voice* does not aim to steer readers into any particular position in relation to the polis. Such decisions have become increasingly context-dependent when the threat to the liberal state and its norms comes more often from the far right than from the left. I propose this positional schema to promote deeper understanding and reflective discussion of the varieties of collective speech and the ways they join cultural expression with politics. This book is not a rallying cry, but a map.

Like any diagram this is an abstraction, whose function is to propose a temporary reduction of the messy complexity of the many different collective utterances (and their contexts) discussed in this book, like an "X-ray of a concept." Schematizations should not be seen as the final distillation of an argument: on the contrary, as Fredric Jameson has argued, they "interrupt . . . discursive thinking" with "a visual moment that claims its own rival intelligibility."[23] My diagram immediately suggests some problems that will need to be teased out discursively in the course of this book.

At the center of the diagram is the polis, serving as an abstract figure for political power, in ways that will prove fruitfully problematic. The term "polis" is used most frequently in the liberal tradition that flows from Hannah Arendt, and such usages can be accused of idealizing the Athenian city-state, referring to it as a "political community."[24] Such a vision of "community" downplays the violently coercive dimensions of state power emphasized by Marxist and Weberian theorists of the state. While thinkers such as Butler, Cavarero, and Bonnie Honig view collective speech as a potential means to amplify the voices of excluded groups and to assert their place within the political sphere, many of the Marxist writers and activists discussed here would resist any suggestion that the state is a venue for such renegotiation, seeing it instead as a mechanism of class domination destined for revolutionary overthrow.

Yet Marxists have also long debated how state institutions might be used to effect social change, from reformist and gradualist traditions influenced by

Hegel and Gramsci to avowedly revolutionary models of the "dictatorship of the proletariat" articulated by Marx, Engels, and Lenin, culminating in the announcement of "the State of the whole people" in Stalin's Soviet Constitution of 1936.[25] The Marxist writers I discuss in this book, such as Jacques Roumain, Sembène, Jack Lindsay, and Langston Hughes, were formed as much by the history of communist parties in and out of power as by the Marxist critique of the state. So while their staging of collective vocalization can in some cases be seen as antistate revolutionary praxis, at times they also activated collective expressions that imagined a closer relationship with political power. Rather than wading into theoretical discussions about the nature of the state, this book works at a slightly lower level of abstraction, showing how literature grapples with the practicalities of political speech and collective expression. It acknowledges that political power is understood at different scales: as a nation-state, as a transnational empire, as a specific government, or as capitalism or governmentality in general. I am willing to risk using the idea of the polis rather loosely, because such an abstraction is a necessary precondition for a coherent mapping of the political possibilities of the collective voice.

My map both builds on and modifies the model suggested by Bonnie Honig's *A Feminist Theory of Refusal* (2021). Honig describes a politics of intransigent refusal, which she links to the bacchants in Euripides's *Bacchae*. This is the archetype of that Dionysiac form of choral speech that I discuss in my first chapter. In the play, the worship of Dionysus has been outlawed by the king of Thebes, Pentheus, but the chorus of bacchants (including Pentheus's own mother, Agave) disobey his command and persist in performing their frenzied Bacchic rites, leaving Thebes for Mount Cithaeron. The conditions of this departure from the polis resonate with an ambiguity that I have tried to capture in the title of my first chapter, "Exile/Refusal" (although the arrow on my diagram rightly points outwards, it is also a schematic simplification, too crude on its own to illustrate all the internal push and pull dynamics that emerge in the analysis of my case studies). The bacchants have been outlawed, and their exile is imposed on them by Pentheus as king: as bacchants—and indeed, as women—they have never been allowed to participate fully in the life of the polis. At the same time, they joyfully (and in rhythmic choral chanting) celebrate their separation from the strictures of the polis and adopt a deliberate stance of refusal.[26] Exile/refusal.

Honig links this refusal with an exilic tendency in contemporary Black studies, according to which "fugitivity is embraced as the only way for Black life to flourish."[27] While Honig makes Saidiya Hartman the primary representative of this tendency, it is Fred Moten's work that is perhaps most closely associated with the celebration of Black cultural expression as "fugitive sociality," understood as entailing a refusal of politics.[28] Moten sees the latter as a kind of trap: "Politics, insofar as it is predicated upon the exclusion and regulation of difference, will have always been the scene of our degradation and never the scene of our redemption, redress, or repair."[29] For Moten, as George Shulman puts it, "*any* effort to politicize (black) sociality is inherently self-defeating."[30] Moten reverses Arendtian political theory by elevating the social over politics: Black sociality is self-sustaining as a source of creativity and a site of endurance, and as such it flies by the nets of citizenship, nationhood, and democratic representation.[31] Moten's argument tends to be descriptive rather than normative: these are the conditions under which Black life *has* flourished.

In answer to such arguments, Honig's *A Feminist Theory of Refusal* presents the normative case for a return to the polis and a reengagement with the state. Honig illustrates her critique of fugitivity as a model for Black politics via a new reading of the end of Euripides's tragedy. The key moment for Honig's argument comes after Agave leads the chorus of bacchants in a frenzied hunt and slaughters the animal. As she proudly holds the dripping carcass, Cadmus, her father, talks her out of her frenzied state and brings her to the awful realization that what she is holding in her hands is not an animal, but the dismembered head of Pentheus, her son and king.[32] Honig encourages us to read this as an "agon of fabulation," in which two possible meanings of her murderous act are genuinely at play—both the tragically accidental filicide and the revolutionary regicide.[33]

The scene therefore suggests two contradictory readings of the dramatic action which must be held in tension. The first, tragic reading sees the Dionysiac rites as a form of delusion for which Agave is inevitably punished by the death of her son. The second sees the chorus as embracing a life-affirming collective rejection of the polis that ultimately leads to fundamental change, symbolized by the death of the king. For Honig, the first reading has tended to be prioritized over the second. By recovering this second reading, Honig suggests that the bacchants' return to the polis at the end of the play can be seen as a renegotiation of their position within it. Their "arc of refusal" sees them move from a complete refusal of the polis into something more like political engagement: they turn to the state in a claim for recognition, and also for redistribution (in Nancy Fraser's terms).[34] In figure 1, this arc traces the line from chapter 1 to chapter 2 of this book, encapsulated in my first bridge. The trajectory Honig opens up by emphasizing the return to the polis is not only descriptive but also normative: she acknowledges the power of Dionysiac refusal (and implicitly of Moten's account of antipolitical, fugitive sociality), but she recommends that it ought to be transformed into political engagement.

By adding a third stage to Honig's schema, my book explores how collective speech patterns associated with political liberation can themselves become hegemonic formations. The most obvious examples are the national anthems of postrevolutionary societies. The "Marseillaise" was, in the nineteenth century, "unambiguously synonymous with liberty and . . . was taken up by almost every imaginable freedom cause."[35] Also, it is the state anthem and a central element in the secular liturgy of a major European power. "L'Internationale" was composed on the barricades in the Paris Commune in 1871: mere decades later it was being sung in Stalin's honor in Red Square as the tanks rolled past. Of course, hegemonic and liturgical forms of collective speech do not always originate from outside the polis, or in radical and subversive hymns! Established power structures also express themselves through anthems, set prayers, oaths of allegiance, and in massed shouts of "Sieg Heil!" Regardless of their origins, hegemonic collective speech forms often aspire to a condition in which politics and its agonistic struggles are suspended, and in which consensus reigns. In this position they can be viewed skeptically as elements of the ideological apparatus that generates feelings of national and spiritual belonging, and also legitimates state power. At times of crisis, these liturgical forms of collective utterance can become more explicitly compulsory, even violently imposed, as Catholics found out during the English Reformation, when they were burned at the stake for refusing to speak the Anglican liturgy set out in the Book of Common Prayer. While acknowledging that hegemonic collective speech forms are often seen in this skeptical light, my aim is to map, rather than to condemn them.

With this end in view, Michael Hardt and Antonio Negri's *Assembly* (2017) has proved helpful. Hardt and Negri delineate three modes of engagement with the state—a "three-faced Dionysus"—that broadly mirror my chapter structure. They call these "exodus," "antagonistic reformism," and the "hegemonic strategy." Their schema has considerably less normative force than Honig's. Where Honig exhorts that exodus ought to be converted into antagonistic reformism, Hardt and Negri propose a more open-ended analysis: "It is not a matter of debating which of these three is correct," they say, "but rather finding ways to weave them together."[36] Hardt and Negri's book has a different kind of limitation; it only considers left-wing or progressive movements: the three positions are conceived as "strategies," differing approaches to some shared egalitarian goals. My book analyzes collective speech forms that have quite different political alignments, to show that their relationship to the polis can be understood in terms of the three positions I have described. The book is a symptom of my recoil from the fascist tendencies I see in Trumpism, but working on it made me aware that the potential for fascism exists in all three positions I have described: in separatist groups that withdraw from the polis as "sovereign citizens" (exile/refusal), in insurgent political movements vying for power by electoral and other means (protest/engagement), and in the state apparatus itself (hegemony/liturgy). For Hardt and Negri (though not for theorists of fugitivity like Moten and Hartman), all three "strategies" are legitimate and potentially fruitful routes for socialist and anti-racist projects.

Voice, Literature, and Representation

As well as referring to political rallies and demonstrations, I have already invoked literary and dramatic texts to exemplify various political functions of collective speech: *BlacKkKlansman,* Pasternak's poem, *God's Bits of Wood,* and the *Bacchae.* Works like these supply the primary archive for *The Collective Voice.* Modern literature and drama provide me with a vast range of collective speech forms, and my book works by analyzing the relationships between these forms and political life. I have selected the texts I focus on because I find them deeply perceptive in the ways that they stage, represent, and critically analyze collective speech. But this book makes no claim for literature itself as a special way of accessing the collective voice. It is, to take a felicitous term from Old English, a "wordhord." The texts I draw on constitute an expansive and various archive of things supposed, or imagined, to have been said, simultaneously, by more than one speaker.

Nevertheless, it might be said that "literature" in its modern sense of published works of imaginative quality, generally designed to be read alone and in silence, is a funny place to start looking for collective speech. Musical culture might have been a more obvious candidate. Indeed, to look closely and carefully at the collective voice—always rhythmic, often melodic—is to be confronted with the "inextricable mingling of the fields of speech and music" to the extent that "any firm boundary between the two becomes invisible."[37] Still, while *The Collective Voice* has a lot of music in it—from the folk music of the US South to the operas of Richard Wagner and Benjamin Britten—it is not a work of musicology. The historical development of choral music is largely left to one side: it is beyond my expertise, well rehearsed elsewhere, and only peripherally important to my argument.

Literary critics have struggled to reckon with collectivity, Caroline Levine argues, and when they try, their methods have often led them to "favor the small scale." The "traditional novel" is a central form for literary studies, and yet it is structured by an "overarching plot and a small number of protagonists," with the result that it has "serious limitations when it comes to the project of politics on the large scale."[38] This book often catches literature in the act of trying to stop being literature—reverting to speech or music to activate more collective forms of social and artistic practice, or innovating within the form of the "traditional novel" to open spaces for collective life on a larger scale. Marxist literary critics have designed cunning mechanisms for extracting a collective essence from texts that often seem resolutely individualistic in their thematic preoccupations and in their contexts of production and consumption. Reflecting in 2022 on the legacy of *The Political Unconscious* (1981), Fredric Jameson wrote that his work "was designed to demonstrate that the life and value of a text lay in the hidden kindling of a collective spark in its representations."[39] The texts I examine are generally explicit about the fact that they are trying to represent or even embody collectivity (sometimes for the purposes of critique). *The Collective Voice* is interested in statements such as "from eight thousand throats rang out the royal salute of '*Koom*,'"[40] which appears in H. Rider Haggard's *King Solomon's Mines* (1895). I did not have to work very hard to find the "hidden kindling of a collective spark" here, because it is not hiding: the sentence simply tells us that a collective utterance has taken place. However, I did not hear this utterance, and I cannot be confident that it ever took place: the text it appears in is fictional, and even if it were presented as reportage, we might doubt the author's account. Because *The Collective Voice* bases its analysis primarily on literature, and on textual evidence about live performances, it deals largely with second-order representations of collective speech.

To try to account for this theoretically, I propose a distinction between "primary" collective speech, where two or more people are present in a single location uttering the same words at the same time, and "secondary" collective speech, where the collective utterance (not actually present) is indicated by a secondhand oral report, a written notation ("they chorused"), a recording, a visual image, and so forth. This seems useful because it clarifies that while primary collective vocalization is in fact quite common (in church congregations, football crowds, political rallies, birthday parties, theatrical and musical performances, and so on), the minute one starts to analyze the phenomenon critically, one becomes aware of, and drawn into, the even larger realm of secondary collective speech. Though we have all done it, or at least have heard it done, primary collective vocalization proves difficult for the scholar to access except through a tissue of secondary quotation. This book is therefore as much about people mentioning, describing, or imagining collective speech as it is about the thing itself. The kind of self-consciousness about representational questions that is often found in literary and dramatic makes these a rich resource.

The book is free-ranging in its choice of examples: as will already be clear, it is not an in-depth study of one local or national context, but brings together a relatively diverse range of texts from different countries and continents. The book engages with (though obviously it could not hope to cover) writing from Europe, North America, Africa, and the Caribbean: the Atlantic sphere. This range is important to what this book is trying to achieve. In exemplifying my argument with a geographically and temporally diverse range of texts I echo Levine's work on the power of forms to move across geographical contexts and historical periods.[41] But where her work is programmatically formalist, *The Collective Voice* seeks to reconcile an interest in the transhistorical portability of the three positionalities I have described, with a historical-materialist approach. Position, after all, is only partly a formal quality: as I have already stressed, it is also determined by the ways in which collective utterances are rooted in given cultural and institutional structures, even when they are striving to assert autonomy from them.

A word more about the specific content of the chapters. I have already explained the structure of the book from a conceptual point of view: this is the generalizing, schematic map of what follows, and readers should keep it in mind. I am committed to generalizing about this topic, which is why I insist on referring to *the* collective voice. But such generalizations on their own would hardly be convincing. In an illuminating essay on German idealist philosophy's discussions of the Greek dramatic chorus, Simon Goldhill reflects: "There are barely any analyses either of individual odes or of the action of any chorus within a play. *A* chorus is of minimal concern, only *the* chorus deserves attention."[42] This book tries to avoid this pitfall by keeping both the general and the specific in view, and indeed trying to connect them: it presents readers with a map and leads them on an expedition into some striking but characteristic bits of the territory.

The case studies discussed in each chapter could well seem recondite when placed next to the schematic map I have offered. The first chapter's exploration of the collective voice in a position of exile and refusal is done with a focus on so-called voodoo. One of my claims is that collective vocalization is often understood through the lens of race, projected onto Black and other racialized peoples, and seen as primitive, becoming associated with indigenous groups who are the objects of the anthropological gaze. At the same time, many collective speech practices that are now associated with Black culture (to take that example) preceded slavery, colonialism, capitalism—and the polis itself. Chapter 1 begins its exploration of the apparently primordial quality of the collective voice by connecting Nietzsche's argument about the chorus in *The Birth of Tragedy* (1872) with brazenly racist representations of African-derived religious chanting by H. Rider Haggard, Jean Rouch, and H. P. Lovecraft. After a critical account of these ethnographic projections, I turn to the Harlem Renaissance, which often mobilized so-called voodoo as a vehicle for the expression of Black ethnic particularism, and as a powerful force for the refusal of white political institutions and norms. I look at Orson Welles's "voodoo Macbeth" and several works about the Haitian Revolution (by Langston Hughes, C. L. R. James, and others). Finally, I turn to Zora Neale Hurston, whose creative output was so intertwined with her ethnographic work, and whose embrace of "Black joy" has been persuasively linked by Lindsey Stewart to a politics of "refusal," rather than "resistance."

The first bridge shows how elements of folk culture, so often the object of racializing anthropological condescension, can be turned towards the polis. I focus first on the work of the Haitian writer and anthropologist Jacques Roumain, who studied Haitian vodou and collected its distinctive chants, but also—as the founder of the Haitian Communist Party—looked forward to the day when "even the tom-toms will have learned / the language of the international." Then I turn to Roumain's Senegalese acolyte, Ousmane Sembène, whose work evolves a "counterethnography" of West African collective speech forms, conjugating these with Marxist and anticolonial ones. Both write novels about strikes, where the refusal of work is the starting point of political engagement.

In chapter 2 I turn squarely to debates about the Greek chorus, and the ways that these were mobilized (especially on the left) to model forms of popular political engagement. Here I explore the influential debate about the Greek chorus within German idealist philosophy—from Schlegel to Hegel, Schiller to Nietzsche—which sought, in the wake of the French Revolution, to reimagine the chorus as a collective, rather than seeing it as Aristotle had done, as essentially a character. Richard Wagner was the artist who brought such theories to bear most fully in his drama, and I read *Lohengrin* through his own contributions to chorus theory. I then turn to twentieth-century left-wing attempts to make the collective voice politically active: first, the fashion for mass declamation poetry in the British Popular Front, spearheaded by the poet, historian, and classicist Jack Lindsay, whose thinking about collective voicing I put into dialogue with that of Jane Harrison. I then look at ideas about the collective work song, as the origin of art and even of language, that were shared between the British left and Black writers in the United States. Langston Hughes's radio plays, for example, seek to animate work songs—above all, "John Henry"—as a resource for bringing together a country divided by racism in an international antifascist war effort.

The second bridge then examines nationalism as a frame for the collective voice: moving from the protest chant to the national anthem. I focus on "L'Internationale," and its use in mass spectacles in the wake of the Russian Revolution (notably Evreinov's Storming of the Winter Palace), as well as George Orwell's ironic rewriting of that hymn as "Beasts of England" in *Animal Farm*. I draw on the work of the sociologist Ernest Gellner to help theorize the homogenizing aims of such national anthems, before turning to Wole Soyinka's uses of the chorus, which often celebrate the expression of African ritual practices while lampooning their cynical uses by postcolonial nationalist rulers.

In the final chapter, the Anglican liturgy is the central example of a form of collective speech that yokes acts of religious devotion to hegemonic state power. For obvious reasons, the chapter is mainly grounded in British literature and culture, just as chapter 1 finds its center of gravity in the US South and the Caribbean, where voodoo, vodou, and hoodoo circulated. I explore how reformation debates about set prayers, which were established in the Book of Common Prayer, resonate in twentieth-century literature. I look at T. S. Eliot's attempts to fuse the Greek chorus with the Christian liturgy, both in his drama and in his own engagement with liturgical reform. Where Eliot saw liturgy as a binding force that could bring together a nation stratified by class and segmented by region, many others felt it as a repressive force. In this vein I examine works by Benjamin Britten, Ngũgĩ wa Thiong'o, and Katharine Burdekin, whose *Swastika Night* rewrites the Book of Common Prayer as a Nazi rite.

The coda looks briefly at those dissidents who refuse to join in with liturgical collective vocalizations they view as repressive. Following in the path of the NFL players in the US who took the knee rather than stand for a national anthem that they had come to view as symbolic of white supremacy, the coda tracks the path away from the liturgical impositions of the polis. My suggestion is that a circle is hereby completed as the seeds of collective exile and refusal are newly planted.

Voodoo, Greek chorus, Anglican liturgy: I admit, it is an unusual itinerary through modern culture. Without the map, it would be easy to get lost in a proliferation of seemingly disconnected examples: we need the map. But on its own—a set of abstract generalizations about collective speech—it would be tendentious and boring. So we will not tarry with the map any longer. It is time to light out on our first expedition.

ONE

EXILE/REFUSAL

THERE ARE TIMES WHEN the collective voice turns away from political power, refusing to acknowledge it. In this position, choral speech taps a raw collective energy that refuses political negotiation. Nietzsche channels this kind of collective speech in his discussion of the chorus in *The Birth of Tragedy,* where he casts the speaking or singing group as the original "primal drama" from which Greek tragedy later emerged. He scorned the notion that this group operated on stage as a "constitutional representation of the people," through which we might perceive the "moral intelligence of the masses."[1] On the contrary, the chorus represented the forces of a Dionysiac nature, such that

> the Greek man of culture felt himself annulled in the face of the satyr chorus, and the immediate effect of Dionysiac tragedy is that state and society, the gulfs separating man from man, make way for an overwhelming sense of unity that goes back to the very heart of nature. The metaphysical consolation . . . that . . . life is at bottom indestructibly powerful and joyful, is given concrete form as a satyr chorus, a chorus of natural beings, living ineradicably behind all civilisation, as it were, remaining the same for ever, regardless of the changing generations and the path of history.[2]

The attempts by earlier German theorists of the chorus, Schlegel and Schiller, to make the chorus a functional part of the polis, were derided by Nietzsche as laughably misguided. Here was no "voice of the people": Nietzsche's "chorus of natural beings" is an undifferentiated and primordial mass that stands outside of all historically specific institutional or political structures.[3] Dionysiac art pointed to a "higher community" and a "primal Oneness" that served (for

Nietzsche) as a valuable corrective that the best art could offer to civilized humans.[4] Civilization, and in particular the political formation of the state, put people at odds with one another. The chorus offered an image of primitive, natural unity, that cannot be assimilated into the political sphere but which lies beneath and behind it as a site of primal being.[5]

In this book I maintain that most, if not all, human societies feature collective speech at least in certain contexts, and that such utterances continue to play important roles in modern societies. But it is also true that some intellectuals, fixated on what they see as the excessive individualism of Western societies, have associated collective speaking with earlier stages of civilization, or with the exotic and the primitive. For this reason, in the twentieth century, the sound of people speaking, singing, or chanting in groups has often been framed by the language of racism.

The racialization of the collective voice goes along with a particular relationship to political life. This relationship can be characterized as one of *refusal*. Honig explores in *A Feminist Theory of Refusal* how the chorus of bacchants in Euripides's *Bacchae* enacts a refusal of the polis. A reading of the *Bacchae* that celebrates the chorus as a Dionysiac rejection of patriarchy and politics can also be used to dismiss the women as "mad." Sometimes, the act of refusal leads choral speech to be pathologized, and marked with gender and race. Honig also emphasizes that the bacchants "return to the city with a set of demands," suspending their Dionysiac rituals in order to renegotiate their place within the polis.[6] In chapter 2, I follow that latter part of Honig's "arc of refusal" and show how collective vocalization can function in politically engaged ways.

In this chapter I will not mainly concern myself with those collective utterances that try to intervene in or reshape the political sphere, like those of the civil rights movement, for example. I focus on a set of speech forms that are functionally and positionally distinct from anything of this nature, being premised instead on what Saidiya Hartman calls "the rejection of a politics of recognition."[7] For Lindsey Stewart, refusal needs to be distinguished from resistance in similar terms. "Resistance locks us into a life-and-death struggle with our oppressor for recognition," she writes. "In contrast, refusal withholds recognition of the oppressor's power or authority to define our lives."[8] When collective speech occupies a position of refusal, it may take a mysteriously cryptic form, in a language unknown to its hearers, perhaps making utterances that are untranslatable or nonsemantic. But it does not always do so—even familiar phrases can express a fugitive sociality when uttered collectively in the right context.

This chapter therefore explores forms of collective speech that are positioned outside the polis, that do not seek recognition in it, and that do not see themselves primarily as forms of resistance to its mechanisms of power or domination. This refusal of the polis—of politics, and sometimes of civilization—exists in a dialectical relationship with racialization. Collective speech that adopts the position and attitude of refusal can appear as the ritual expression of exotic racial others, or as a disturbing, magical utterance that evokes witchcraft and the dark arts, often also in gendered terms. The witches in Shakespeare's *Macbeth* are a case in point: their spells, and their visions of the future, are sealed by some of the most memorable collective speech on the early modern stage:

> Double, double, toil and trouble
> Fire burn and cauldron bubble.[9]

The witches represent a malign and irrational force whose collective utterance has the power to influence and infect the speech of the play's protagonist. Macbeth is not on stage in the first scene of act 1 to hear the witches say, in unison, "Fair is foul and foul is fair," but he unconsciously picks up their language two scenes later, remarking to Banquo: "So foul and fair a day I have not seen."[10] Macbeth's witches are not called a chorus and could not possibly be described as a "constitutional representation of the people." Their collective vocalization seems irredeemably alien, closely aligned to Nietzsche's "satyr chorus," living "behind all civilization."

The form of collective speech that this chapter is concerned with is part of an archive of racist tropes. The same tropes that link Blackness and Africanity to primitive violence, rhythmic dancing, and exotic sexuality also frequently associate them with collective chanting. You will not be surprised to learn that writers such as H. Rider Haggard, T. S. Eliot, and H. P. Lovecraft indulged in racist tropes about Black people: my interest here is not simply to expose racism (where it seems all too obvious), but to describe the cultural dynamics that help to construct Black subjects as an undifferentiated collectively speaking mass. As we will see, prominent Black writers including Léopold Senghor, Jean Price-Mars, Zora Neale Hurston, and Jacques Roumain at times and in different ways made associations between Africanity and the rhythmical, primitive, and exotic. This chapter explores how collective vocalization in the position of exile and refusal exists both as a racist trope and as a vehicle for the expression of ethnic particularity and identity.

Exotic Sounds

Nietzsche's argument that the chorus is a primitive and primal force that speaks from outside politics and civilization is genealogical rather than anthropological. That is to say, he is speculating about a prehistory for choral singing in ancient Greece, rather than collecting evidence about the collective speech practices of contemporary indigenous peoples. However, in seeing the chorus as the antithesis to modern civilization, Nietzsche's argument resonates with popular representations of the collective speech practices of tribal societies. Ethnographic film has often seen chanting in a similar way, casting indigenous rituals as moments of collective embodiment that are charged with pagan magic. Where *Macbeth* locates the collective voice in Scotland's primal past, the makers of ethnographic film looked for evidence of such primitive and magical utterances among their contemporaries in Africa, the Americas, Australia, and the Arctic.

Jean Rouch's colonial-era documentaries about West Africa, for example, are often structured around a contrast between the narration of an individual European observer (speaking French), and the collective chanting of the indigenous tribe. His *Yenendi: Les hommes qui font la pluie* (1951) shows a traditional ritual in Niger (then in French West Africa), intended to bring rain after seven months of drought. Rouch's narration provides context and interpretation, while the songs and chants of the Songhai people, which form part of the ritual, are not subtitled or translated and act as an atmospheric background of collectively produced sonic texture. The Songhai people, in Rouch's film, seem to exist entirely within the bounds of a stable and essentially timeless *ethnos*. Rouch's voice is that of the secular individualist, fascinated by a people who live by a ritual pattern, shared in common with all living members of the tribe, and inherited from previous generations. For Rouch, and perhaps for the anthropological imagination in general, collective chanting is symbolic of a fundamentally collective life based on shared, unchanging, and unquestioned rituals and beliefs.[11]

Like Rouch's films, H. Rider Haggard's African fiction mobilizes a counterpoint between the individualism of his cunning English protagonist Allan Quartermain and the collective behaviors of the natives he encounters on his travels. The fictional tribe at the center of *King Solomon's Mines* (1885) is the Kukuana, thought to be based on the Matabele tribe.[12] The Kukuanas are often to be found speaking in unison, and in ways that make them vulnerable to being controlled, duped, and dominated, both by their own rulers and by the wily colonialists. In his first encounter with the tribe, Quartermain tells a group of Kukuanas that he and his friends are supernatural beings "from the biggest star that shines at night." Haggard portrays the group responding in unison: "'Oh! oh!' groaned the chorus of astonished aborigines," and "'It is so, it is so,' said the chorus."[13] This racialized, collectively speaking other is marked by a high level of obedience and credulity.

Over the course of the novel, Quartermain and his companions encounter a number of remarkable rituals in which collective speaking creates a sense of a heavily hierarchical and authoritarian social structure. This plays into what David Pocock describes as the "received view of African political societies—which were derived from Hollywood and Conrad and Kipling and Rider Haggard most particularly—of abject slaves being ruled by a chief with three feathers in his head . . . and a bone through his nose."[14] In the scene in which we first encounter the king of Kukuanaland, he raises his spear before the massed ranks of the tribe:

> Instantly eight thousand spears were lifted in answer, and from eight thousand throats rang out the royal salute of "*Koom.*" Three times this was repeated, and each time the earth shook with the noise, that can only be compared to the deepest notes of thunder.
>
> "Be humble, O people," piped out a thin voice which seemed to come from the monkey in the shade, "it is the king."
>
> "*It is the king,*" boomed out the eight thousand throats in answer. "*Be humble, O people, it is the king.*"[15]

The thunderous might of this sound, which shakes the earth by multiplying the "throats" of the speakers, appears more than a little ominous to the English characters in the story. And indeed, like the other examples I discuss in this section, the racism of the depiction is part of a reflexive cultural response to the real dangers posed by Black collectives, as they came together to oppose colonialism and white supremacy.

Rider Haggard's "Koom" thus bears a family resemblance to later representations of Black collective speech, discussed by Rachel Blau DuPlessis, that invoked the nonword "hoo." Tracing its use in poems by Vachel Lindsay, Wallace Stevens, and T. S. Eliot, DuPlessis argues that "hoo" is "a racialized syllable" that suggests a "vibrant, aggressive threat."[16] The male chorus of "HOO / HOO / HOO" that concludes Eliot's *Sweeney Agonistes* is infused (DuPlessis argues) with an implicit Africanity: wild, de-individualized, sexual, and primal.[17] For DuPlessis, the sound "draws on black agency and autonomy, which, because mysterious, inexplicable, and frightening to Euro-American writers, is paradoxically affirmed and denied."[18] Rider Haggard's "Koom!" shares its long and resonant vowel sound with "hoo," as well as some of the same racial connotations: it is the untranslatably exotic core of a collective utterance that the narrator otherwise seamlessly mediates into English from the Kukuana ("an old fashioned form of the Zulu tongue").[19] Sounded by "eight thousand throats"—decoupled from heart or brain—it is the speech of a single compound organism in thrall to its master. DuPlessis places helpful emphasis on the fact that such racist representations are a reaction to "black agency and autonomy." Black collective vocalizations do sometimes respond to white supremacy, but they are not made or determined by it.

The assembly at a witch-finding ceremony, designed to root out disloyal "wicked ones,"[20] is an even larger and more terrifying affair, with twenty thousand present. A lone voice intones: "What is the lot of man born of woman?" And then: "Back came the answer rolling out from every throat in that vast company—'*Death!*' "[21] Haggard invokes the witches from *Macbeth,* who prophesy (via an apparition) that no man "of woman born" (or "born of woman" as Macbeth later puts it) shall do him harm.[22] Haggard incorporates a number of other allusions to *Macbeth* in his novel, cementing an implied link between the Kukuanas and the weird sisters, and figuring their shared propensity for collective speaking as demonic and otherworldly.

The racist lens through which Rouch and Haggard viewed African collective speech practices also extends to those of the Black diaspora, including chain-gang songs, carnival chants, the call-and-response sermons of the Black church, rain dances, and all manner of religious and spiritual rituals. There is perhaps no form of collective speech ritual that is more enmeshed in racist discourse than voodoo chanting, and this will form the focus of the present chapter's investigation of the collective voice in a position of exile and refusal. Together with related terms such as "vodun," "vodou," "voudoo," "vaudou," "vaudoux," "hoodoo," "root work," and "conjure," the term "voodoo" brackets a heterogeneous ensemble of ritual, magical, and religious practices predominantly of Afro-Creole populations in the American South and in the Caribbean, particularly Haiti.[23] The relationships between these terms are complex, and the practices they name are extremely various. They are contested, sometimes controversial terms with long histories of racist use. Ahmad Greene-Hayes, for example, has shown how lurid and sensationalist conceptions of voodoo ceremonies that "recapitulated longstanding tropes of African peoples as barbaric ritualists" led to the framing of a series of axe murders in Louisiana as "voodoo murders."[24] Greene-Hayes argues that " 'white race makers' . . . promoted the erroneous idea of a monolithic Black religion, often haphazardly characterised as 'Voodoo.' "[25] As DuPlessis notes, the racialized "hoo" deployed by Lindsay, Eliot, and Stevens (mentioned earlier) is an "allusion to, or a resistant version of, the words *hoodoo/voodoo*," and Haggard's depiction of African religious practice clearly resonates with popular representations of voodoo in the US and the Caribbean.[26] Adam McGee goes the furthest, arguing that while Haitian vodou is a real religion that is subject to racial prejudice, "voodoo" is in fact an "imagined religion" that is "principally an invention of Hollywood," with "no basis in fact." For McGee, "voodoo" has no reality other than as an archive of racist tropes linking Black people with exotic and Dionysiac ritual behaviors: "voodoo is a meme."[27]

Questions of classification have animated historians' attempts to recover and describe the ritual practices of the African diaspora. Albert J. Raboteau's field-defining 1978 work *Slave Religion: The "Invisible Institution" in the Antebellum South* (revised 2004) announced in its title its project to give those practices the dignity of a religion, and Raboteau asserts that "no discussion of Africanisms in the religious life of black Americans could be complete without reference to voodoo." But he also points out that "the movement from *vadou* to hoodoo"—for Raboteau, that means from a ritual cult to a system of magic—"can serve perhaps as a paradigm of the larger history of African religion in the United States." It exemplifies the ways in which "bits of African faith and practice persisted in folk beliefs and customs, though their original meaning had been lost."[28] More recently, scholars such as Judith Weisenfeld question the applicability of the term "religion" itself, asking us to reflect on the "implications of naming certain things religious, or denying the label of religion, within particular racialized frameworks."[29] Tomoko Masuzawa has launched a powerful critique of the process by which, in the course of the nineteenth century, a suite of around twelve "world religions" emerged as way of understanding a putative "non-Western" world that was "thoroughly in the grip of religion, as all aspects of life were supposedly determined and dictated by an archaic metaphysics of the magical and the supernatural."[30]

Well-meaning liberal efforts to elevate collective vocalizations to the status of a "religion" might be part of the mechanism by which "European universalism was preserved in the language of pluralism" (to quote the subtitle of Masuzawa's book).

The Haitian Revolution was a key moment at which voodoo seemed to have an impact upon the history of European colonial expansion from the outside, and for interwar intellectuals it became, as Stuart Hall noted, a "means to imagine afresh the possibilities of black liberation and black self-creativity."[31] The first anticolonial movement to put a dent in the French Empire has often been associated with voodoo practice. C. L. R. James's classic account in *The Black Jacobins: Toussaint L'Ouverture and the San Domingo Revolution* (1938) has sometimes been accused of a Eurocentrism that tended to underplay "the relative place of African cultural retentions and continuities in shaping the consciousness of . . . resistance and rebellion."[32] James's text makes Toussaint L'Ouverture the tragic hero of the revolution and presents him as a man of the Enlightenment who "could find the language and accent of Diderot, Rousseau, and Raynal, of Mirabeau, Robespierre, and Danton."[33] Toussaint, as James portrays him, engages forcefully with existing European political institutions and languages, demanding recognition and respect from his French allies (from the polis), and therefore belonging in chapter 2 of this book, according to my schema. Yet James does dwell on one particular voodoo chant, which formed part of Haiti's revolutionary ferment:

> One does not need education or encouragement to cherish a dream of freedom. At their midnight celebrations of Voodoo, their African cult, they danced and sang, usually this favourite song:
>
> Eh! Eh! Bomba! Heu! Heu!
> Canga, bafio té!
> Canga, mouné de lé!
> Canga, do ki la!
> Canga, li!
>
> "We swear to destroy the whites and all that they possess; let us die rather than fail to keep this vow."[34]

James associates the chant in particular with what is known as the "Bwa Kayman" (or "Bois Caiman") ceremony, which Crystal Nicole Eddins describes as a "free space where participants assembled outside the scope of colonial surveillance to draw upon spiritual power, strengthen oppositional consciousness, forge solidarities, and incite rebellion."[35] The chant itself has been important to discussions of how a refusal of slavery and colonialism developed. It was one of a number of "cultural artifacts that . . . helped build solidarity by encoding information about the power of spirits to end slavery."[36] That position "outside" of colonial power is significant here: like Honig's bacchants, these celebrants engage in collective speech acts that are entirely their own and that refuse the prevailing codes of political engagement and representation.

"Eh! Bomba!" first appeared in print in Moreau de Saint-Méry's 1797 survey of the island of Saint-Domingue, where no translation was provided.[37] James could offer only a mistranslation, which seems to result from his confusion of this song with another that was translated (itself probably erroneously) in a French source he was using. In the wide variety of sources Alasdair Pettinger surveys in a wonderful essay on "Eh! Bomba!" there is no scholarly consensus on the semantic meaning of the chant, nor even on what language it is in. Pettinger floats the possibility that Saint-Méry made it up: perhaps it was at its very origin a racialized projection by a colonial observer about collective utterance, a more elaborate "hoo" or a "Koom!" But where "Koom!" was symbolic of subservience, James's use of "Eh! Bomba!" and his possible mistranslation of it as a vow to "destroy the whites" makes it emblematic of a culture of refusal, positioned as a primordial will to freedom outside and regardless of any "education or encouragement" that the Enlightenment might offer.[38] "Destroy the whites" is not a bid for recognition or an attempt at engagement, but an expression of a complete autonomy from colonial institutions.

James offers no source for his claim that, "for over two hundred years the slaves sang it at their meetings, as the Jews in Babylon sang of Zion, and the Bantu today sing in secret the national anthem of Africa."[39] But perhaps this is part of a tendency, identified by Pettinger, to make this kind of collective singing "a privileged signifier that captures a whole culture in miniature or condenses fundamental social forces."[40] Jean Price-Mars, the Haitian intellectual, ethnographer, politician, and leading light of the "indigenist" movement, anticipated some of these arguments in 1928. Having encountered the same translation of "Eh! Bomba!" as James did—"We swear to destroy all the whites"—he decided: "I consider this translation to be somewhat suspect."[41] Price-Mars even speculated that those chanting did not know the meaning of the words: "It is highly probable that the forms of incantation, of chants, of prophesy in which the same words often were repeated, engraved themselves on the minds of the sect followers as much as on those of the occasional spectators; that these forms have lost their peculiar meaning little by little in past ages to the point that those who repeat them in the present time are totally ignorant of their original sense." Price-Mars suggests, however, that the religious observations of the slaves took on a political dimension because of the social context in which they were performed and the ways in which they were observed: "the colonial world . . . did not begin to take umbrage at the religious demonstrations of the slaves until they seemed to become the symbol of revolt around 1740–1750."[42] The voodoo song fuses prayer, ethnic identity, and the politics of refusal in its mysterious and potentially untranslatable phonemes.

Of course, in James's account, it was Toussaint L'Ouverture who was the leader and the tragic hero of the Santo Domingo revolution, and James emphasizes that his critique of slavery—his whole analysis and program for action—derived from the ideas of the French Revolution. David Scott argues that James's Toussaint operates as an embodiment of Enlightenment values and as a "conscript" of modernity: this is where the accusations of Eurocentrism derive from.[43] But James's picture of the social and political forces at work in the Haitian Revolution has a dialectical quality. While Toussaint spoke for the Enlightenment and forbade the practice of voodoo, *Black Jacobins* contrasts him with other leaders such as Dutty Boukman—a *houngan* or papaloi (high priest) of voodoo who led the first slave rebellion—and Jean-Jacques Dessalines, the first emperor of Haiti, known for ordering the massacre of all the white inhabitants of the island. Far from symbolizing all that the Enlightenment must reject, the voodoo chant becomes an inflection point at which the objectives of both sides of this dichotomy become aligned. "Voodoo was the medium of the conspiracy," as James wrote suggestively of Boukman's rebellion, but—as Pettinger glosses it—"its message was clearly that of the Enlightenment and the Age of Revolution."[44] The obsession with trying to translate "Eh! Bomba!"—as if one would thereby decode the true meaning not only of the chant but also of the culture it came to stand for—is caught up with an anthropological desire to make certain chanted rituals or even single phrases into the generalizable expression of a whole *ethnos*.[45]

Toussaint does not even step onstage in Langston Hughes's play about the Haitian Revolution, *Emperor of Haiti* (1936). This play makes Dessalines the defining figure of the revolution, chosen because "no one hates the French like he does" (as one slave puts it). Hughes's Dessalines expresses the view that "we have no choice but to kill . . . wipe out all the whites on this island."[46]

Toussaint's literary skill and his elegant command of written French is often praised by James, while Hughes goes out of his way to underline Dessalines's illiteracy.[47] Compared to James's *Black Jacobins*, Hughes's play sees voodoo as a much more central element of the insurrectionist social pressure that produced the revolution. In Hughes's version of events, the voodoo drums will start the violence: Boukman will "beat out a signal that'll roll from hill to hill, slave hut to slave hut, across the cane-fields, across the mountains, across the bays from island to island, until every drum in Haiti throbs with the call to rise and seek freedom."[48] When the papaloi and mamaloi come onstage in the buildup to the revolt, Hughes's stage direction reads: "a crowd . . . clusters, chanting, about the high priest and priestess of voodoo, who chatter in an African tongue, calling on the gods." The papaloi and mamaloi invoke voodoo deities, including Legba and Damballa.[49] The semantic content of the chanting and the general "chatter in an African tongue" is not specified, nor is it important: the exotic foreignness of the sound, along with its capacity to invoke an embodied collectivity *outside* colonial political institutions, is the dramatic meaning of these vocalizations.

When Dessalines gives a compelling speech to an increasingly riled up crowd who speaks in unison, as a chorus on the stage, Hughes explicitly mixes voodoo chants with the refusal of slavery. Dessalines describes a moment of political epiphany that struck him as he was being whipped by his overseer.

> DESSALINES: I cried out, he struck again. Then I lifted up my head and looked him in the eyes, and I knew I was a man, not a dog! I wanted to be free!
> VOICES: Free! Free!
> Want to be free!
> Free!
> DESSALINES: Not I alone—thousands of slaves like me wanted to be free! All over Haiti! Now, we're ready. We will not fail! Our time has come!
> VOICES: Come! Come!
> It's come!
> *(Cries of "Legba! Legba! Legba!" from the women, and the chanting of the mamaloi and papaloi grow ever louder as Dessalines continues)*[50]

As this scene suggests, the shared experience of the violence and pain of slavery brings the voices together, and the presence of voodoo implies a spiritual and cultural cohesion which links them to an African past. Hughes uses the material impact of this cacophony of chanting voices to suggest a power of refusal, rooted in folk religion. This power is enough to precipitate the revolution: the ideas of the European Enlightenment, and Toussaint as their avatar, are unimportant here.

But if voodoo appears symbolic of social cohesion along racial lines, that cohesion does not survive the establishment of the Black Haitian state. Dessalines, as emperor, loses the support of his people because of his "growing alienation from African-derived cultural practices and beliefs."[51] Adopting the titles, the bugles, and other trappings of French colonial power, Dessalines effectively bans voodoo from his court: "Drums in the Court!" he exclaims. "The idea! Suppose we had guests from abroad, what would they think of us? They'd think we were all savages, that's what. Savages!"[52] In Hughes's play, voodoo drumming and chanting are part of the revolutionary self-expression of the Black people of Haiti, but they do not produce a unified Black state. As Hughes observed later, "It was in Haiti that I first realized how class lines may cut across color lines within a race, and how dark people of the same nationality may scorn those below them."[53]

Already in James and Hughes, it is clear that the depiction of voodoo chanting invokes a complicated racial politics. Nowhere was this clearer than in the Federal Theatre Project's production of *Macbeth* at the Lafayette Theatre in Harlem in 1936, directed by Orson Welles. The production was set in nineteenth-century Haiti, included an all-Black cast, and became known as "The Voodoo *Macbeth*."[54]

In Welles's version—revised into a three act play for the production—the witches were joined by "a dozen women dressed as Voodoo priestesses" and delivered their prophecies to the sound of "voodoo drums."[55] Brooks Atkinson noted in his review of the production for *The New York Times* that Welles had managed to "crowd the stage with mad and gabbling throngs of evil worshippers."[56] The production was an enormous popular success, initially among a predominantly Black audience, during a ten-week run at the Lafayette in Harlem, before it moved downtown to the Adelphi, where it played to mainly white crowds for a further two months.[57]

Welles clearly saw that a number of interesting effects could be achieved with the use of voodoo drumming and chanting, which are linked to their primitive and prepolitical associations. Richard France suggests that Welles's use of these musical forms "created a primitive aural violence that went beyond mere ethnicity to speak of an immemorial evil that has existed since the fall of man."[58] France asks us to observe the primordial atemporally, without the lens

FIGURE 2: Production still from the "Voodoo" Macbeth, dir. Orson Welles (1936). From the Federal Theatre Project Archive, Library of Congress, https://www.loc.gov/resource/music.musftpnegatives-12210159/?sp=33&q=macbeth&r=-0.105,-0.033,1.334,0.796,0.

of race. Consider Welles's stage direction, which comes a little while after the murder of Duncan, and as Macbeth contemplates killing Banquo:

> (Macbeth is left alone in the courtyard, brooding on his throne. Pause. Then through the air, queer and faint, comes the chant of the voodoos; "ALL HAIL MACBETH! HAIL! KING OF SCOTLAND!" Macbeth starts.)[59]

Then in the soliloquy:

> Our fears in Banquo stick deep;
> *(The voodoo music is heard again. Softer than ever, mostly drums, Macbeth looks up at the sounds)*
> He chid the sisters
> When first they put the names of kind upon me,
> And bade them speak to him: then prophet-like
> They hail'd him father to a line of kings;
> Upon my head they placed a fruitless crown
> And put a barren scepter in my grips.[60]

The chanting acts as a supernatural force driving Macbeth on to murderous acts, as well as terrifying him. And the odd spectacle of voodoo celebrants hailing the king of Scotland is one of many places where the function of Scottishness in Shakespeare's original play—as a timeless and barbaric precivilization—becomes intertwined with the Africanity of the voodoo chants in Welles's version.

Critics remain divided about the racial politics of the "voodoo" *Macbeth.* Marguerite Rippy, for example, argues that Welles's "primitivism retained the romantic association of blackness with dark passions and the supernatural" and sees the production as "unambiguously eliciting white fantasies of race."[61] The fact that, for several performances during a touring run in Indianapolis, after the lead actor took ill, Welles took to the stage in blackface, is taken by Rippy as evidence that the whole enterprise (despite its 137-member-strong, all-Black cast) was tainted with minstrelsy.[62] Michael Denning, by contrast, argues that the production successfully "embodied the black radicalism that took the Haitian revolution as an allegory of African American uprising."[63] And more recently, Benjamin Hilb has sought to redeem the production from accusations of racism, praising it for "contributing to a thriving interest in Haiti and Vodou among US Blacks by staging authentic Afro-Haitian religious rituals under the direction of a renowned African dancer."[64] Hilb even proposes to rename the production the "Vodou Macbeth"—to indicate that the chanted rites were an authentic portrayal of a real religion that faces persecution and prejudice, and that ought not to be dismissed as a white fantasy.

The tension between these two analyses is not merely post hoc critical hand-wringing: it is also deeply ingrained in the production history of the "voodoo" *Macbeth.* The voodoo drumming, chanting, and dancing, for example, was (as Hilb stresses) performed by a troupe from Sierra Leone that was led by the leading choreographer of African dance, Asadata Dafora. Speaking in 1955, Welles remembered: "The witches translated terribly well into witch doctors—voodoo witch doctors. And these witch doctors were specially imported from Africa because the governments in the West Indies took the view that there was no such thing as voodoo, so we had to go all the way to the Gold Coast and import a troupe." On the one hand, this lends weight to Hilb's argument that the thing that Welles's critics saw as an exoticizing, racist *depiction* of African chanting was, in fact, African chanting. On the other hand, it is clear that Welles knew the effect he wanted from this chanting, and when Haiti itself would not supply it, he looked elsewhere. Indeed, the internal dynamics of the production replicate this intriguing dynamic between the wants and preferences of the troupe themselves, and Welles's preconceptions about what voodoo chanting ought to sound like.

According to Welles, the troupe requested twelve live goats, which he obtained from the federal government, and which were sacrificed in the theatre to sanctify the drums.[65] Then, when Dafora first demonstrated the voodoo chanting to Welles and Houseman, they felt it "wasn't really frightening" and encouraged Dafora to make it more so.[66] Arguably, the supernatural elements of *Macbeth* need to be frightening for a production to be effective—but did Welles nudge the troupe to perform in a way that fed popular fears about the demonic character of voodoo chanting? According to a "Broadway legend" recounted by both Welles and Houseman, the Africans decided to put a voodoo curse on the critic Percy Hammond, who had published an unfavorable and plainly racist review in *The New York Herald Tribune*.[67] Following some "unusual drumming" in the basement, and some "chants weirder and more horrible than anything that had been heard upon the stage," Hammond took ill and died the next day.[68]

What are the preconditions for making a causal link between Percy Hammond's death, and the chanting of the troupe? It is plausible enough—although there is now no way of knowing—that the troupe chanted a curse and believed in its efficacy. Looking back, Welles viewed the assumed connection between the curse and Hammond's death with wry humor. He insisted that the story was "circumstantially true," however apparently unbelievable, but also reassured viewers that "I don't advocate voodoo—I don't even believe in it."[69] What is forced into view by this anecdote is the complex interplay between the actual belief system and ritual practice of the Sierra Leoneans and the racist tropes that circulate around Black religious practices. These tropes have become a pervasive way of looking at, or listening to, the collective voice.

This is well illustrated in H. P. Lovecraft's "The Call of Cthulhu," an esoteric mystery story which has an uncanny chanted phrase at its center. The phrase first emerges into the story through the investigations of Inspector Legrasse, who has conducted a raid on a "supposed voodoo meeting" somewhere in "the swamps south of New Orleans."[70] It is clear that they have stumbled upon "a dark cult . . . infinitely more diabolic than even the blackest of the African voodoo." But in his quest for explanations, Legrasse attends the American Archaeological Society, where he meets William Channing Webb, a professor of anthropology at Princeton University, who has encountered strikingly similar rituals in a very different context. In Greenland, Webb studied a "cult of degenerate Esquimaux whose religion, a curious form of devil-worship, chilled him with its deliberate bloodthirstiness and repulsiveness." Webb and Legrasse discover that the "two hellish rituals so many worlds of distance apart" share an identical chanted phrase. "Both the Esquimau wizards and the Louisiana swamp-priests had chanted to their kindred idols" the phrase: "Ph'nglui mglw'nafh Cthulhu R'lyeh wgah'nagl fhtagn." Pursuing their investigation of the Cthulhu cult, the New Orleans police venture into a region "of traditionally evil repute, substantially unknown and untraversed by white men," where they observe another ritual, which is described in these terms:

> Only poetry or madness could do justice to the noises heard by Legrasse's men as they ploughed on through the black morass toward the red glare and the muffled tom-toms. There are vocal qualities peculiar to men, and vocal qualities peculiar to beasts; and it is terrible to hear the one when the source should yield the other. Animal fury and orgiastic licence here whipped themselves to daemoniac heights by howls and squawking ecstasies that tore and reverberated through those nighted woods like pestilential tempests from the gulfs of hell. Now and then the less organised ululation would cease, and from what seemed a well-drilled chorus of hoarse voices would rise in sing-song chant that hideous phrase or ritual: "Ph'nglui mglw'nafh Cthulhu R'lyeh wgah'nagl fhtagn."

The ritual is represented as extraordinary and animalistic, and yet its sheer wildness can be allocated to some racial categories that are near at hand. The narrator has a particular fixation on the perceived dangers of miscegenation, describing "nearly a hundred mongrel celebrants . . . of a very low, mixed-blooded, and mentally aberrant type."[71] The policeman and the anthropologist in Lovecraft's story are presented as rational, civilized individuals, charged with unpicking a series of interconnected, barbaric, and collective rites.[72]

What interests me here is precisely the translocal character of the collective utterance at the heart of the story. Cast in Lovecraft's fictional language of Cthuvian, the chant itself (in praise of an "awesome cosmic entity") is unmoored to any specific geographical region and is not the property of a single ethnic group.[73] It is found in the swamps of Louisiana, as well as in western Greenland and China, and seems to have existed unchanged for millennia. The chant itself is eventually translated as "In his house at R'lyeh dead Cthulhu waits dreaming," but the translation explains nothing.[74] The cult of Cthulhu resembles Nietzsche's primeval "satyr chorus," positioned outside of history and politics. Indeed, Lovecraft seems to invoke Nietzsche's *Beyond Good and Evil* (1886) when Castro (one of the Cthulhu cultists) points to a future time "when mankind would have become as the Great Old Ones; free and wild and beyond good and evil, with laws and morals thrown aside and all men shouting and killing and revelling in joy."[75] This reflects Lovecraft's general commitment to a philosophical "cosmicism," according to which "one must forget that such things as organic life, good and evil, love and hate, and all such local attributes of a negligible and temporary race called mankind, have any existence at all."[76] Supposed ethnic differences within the already negligible human race seem irrelevant indeed at this cosmic scale. Yet part of the interest of the story is that Legrasse, Webb, and the narrator cannot help but explain the chanting through the lens of their local racial categories. Wherever the Cthulhu cult be found, its chanted rite is perceived anthropologically, as a typical expression of the diabolical customary rituals of whichever ethnic group haunts the woods nearby.

The structure of feeling that Rider Haggard and H. P. Lovecraft embody is one that has also shaped the way Black writers have been read. Jeanne-Marie Jackson has written critically of the "too-easy binary of Western individualism versus African communalism" that has shaped understandings of African literature. This is frequently embodied in a tendency to read African texts as a repository of "ethnophilosophy," that is, "a conceptual essence as indicated by traditional practices, proverbs, religious beliefs, and the like."[77] Jackson's argument speaks to the "anthropological fallacy" identified by Henry Louis Gates Jr., according to which "all African art is collective and functional."[78] By emphasizing the tradition of the African novel of ideas, Jackson shows that individualism and philosophical reflection are a key strands of African culture. Yet the characterization of indigenous African, African-diasporic, and Black people as tribal, with a propensity to chanting and other forms of ritualized collective utterance, is not only the imposition of colonial, white anthropologists and literary critics. While Lewis R. Gordon argues persuasively that "the word 'tribe' is a colonial slur," it is also the word used in classic works of anticolonial African fiction, such as Ngũgĩ wa Thiong'o's *The River Between* (1966) and Chinua Achebe's *Things Fall Apart* (1958), to describe communal African societies under threat from individualistic European colonialism.[79]

Some African literature deliberately upholds and even strategically deepens the opposition between white European individualism and African communalism. Achebe himself argued influentially that the collective vocalizations of African subjects were the focus of racist representation, famously condemning Conrad's evocation of a "black and incomprehensible frenzy" as an undifferentiated mass of Africans "howled and leaped and spun and made horrid faces."[80] In *Things Fall Apart,* Achebe imagines a form of African collectivity that is actively valued in the tribal world he depicts. As one of the elders of the tribe contemplates the arrival of white Christian missionaries in the village, he addresses a junior member of the tribe who seems in danger of neglecting their traditions: "I fear for you young people because you do not understand how strong is the bond of kinship. You do not know what it is to speak with one voice. And what is the result? An abominable religion has settled among you. A man can now leave his father and his brothers. He can curse the gods of his fathers and ancestors."[81] The breaking up of the collective clan that can "speak with one voice" coincides with the arrival of European colonists, with their more individualistic religion and way of life. In this context, to reflect on the persistence of collective life, and collective utterance, is a powerful act of refusal.

Black writers, artists, dramatists and filmmakers have in a rich variety of ways worked to harness the power of the collective voice for all sorts of reasons. Some, like the call-and-response chants of a civil rights march, point towards the polis and seek representation and recognition within it. But when it turns away from the polis to engage in the politics of refusal, the collective voice is often linked with forms of primitivism. It has often been argued—perhaps more often, assumed—that primitivism is intrinsically racist: a patronizing and exoticizing means by which white artists and writers view and represent nonwhite peoples, accompanied by the "appropriation," "plagiarism," or "theft" of their artworks and traditions.[82] Critics are starting to question this view. As Ben Etherington argues in *Literary Primitivism,* primitivism has tended to be seen as "a unidirectional ideological projection from the colonizer onto the colonized." It has become "habitual simply to dismiss any artistic attempt to affirm the primitive as an act of essentialism."[83] Etherington argues, though, that we cannot understand primitivism properly if we rely on "a fixed separation of 'West' and 'non-West,' " and he argues that it was Black writers—particularly from the "New Negro, negritude, nativist, and indigenist movements of the global peripheries"—who embraced literary primitivism most fully.[84] Primitivism, for Etherington (at least in its "emphatic" form) is not primarily about reviving a lost past or projecting a racial "Other." Rather, it is a speculative attempt to imagine a future space outside or beyond a capitalist imperialism that was expanding to encompass the whole globe. As we have already seen, the collective voice sometimes strives to speak from outside the polis, even from outside civilization as such. Etherington encourages us to look past the ways in which such a positioning evokes racist discourses in order to grasp the utopian possibilities of primitivist refusal.

Zora Neale Hurston's Ethnography of Collective Speech

Zora Neale Hurston's work as a writer and dramatist builds on her ethnographic investigations of the collective speech forms of Black folk culture. Having grown up in the South, Hurston developed a more academic interest in its music and folklore in the intellectual ferment of New York and as a student of anthropology at Barnard College, at the height of the New Negro movement. She undertook extensive ethnographic research in the South, which she documented in her book *Mules and Men* (1935) and elsewhere. In 1936–37, she continued her anthropological work, focusing on voodoo practice in Jamaica and then (funded by a Guggenheim fellowship) in Haiti. She wrote her most celebrated novel, *Their Eyes Were Watching God* (1937) while in Haiti, and she also worked on *Tell My Horse: Voodoo and Life in Haiti and Jamaica* (1938). While at Barnard, Hurston had studied anthropology under Franz Boas, the most prominent anthropologist of his generation, affectionately known to her as "Papa Franz."[85] Boas was a prominent critic of racial essentialism who had argued (against the grain of contemporary anthropological opinion) that "the weight of evidence is, on the whole, in favor of an essential similarity of mental endowment in different races."[86] Boas had secured for Hurston a fellowship that funded her work in the American South, and when she published the fruits of that research in *Mules and Men,* he wrote the preface. My purpose here is to show how Hurston both critiqued essentialist ideas about the collectivity of Black culture and also held up some of its collective speech forms as resources for the refusal of the racist politics of Jim Crow, and for repair and renewal away from the purview of the white supremacist state.

Hurston's accounts of voodoo and hoodoo are informed by an awareness of the racialized stereotypes that exist around these practices. In *Mules and Men,* for example, where she describes her own initiation into a number of hoodoo cults, she makes the point that hoodoo is an essentially private practice, distinguishable from the sort of public rituals of dancing, singing, and drumming beloved of the anthropological imagination: "believers conceal their faith," she notes. "This is why the voodoo ritualistic orgies of Broadway and popular fiction are so laughable. The profound silence of the initiated remains what it is. Hoodoo is not drum beating and dancing. There are no moon worshippers among the negroes in America."[87] It would be a mistake to view Hurston's work on Black cultural expressions only as a reaction to racism. The representations of "Broadway and popular fiction" are in the end just "laughable"—by taking us inside the rituals, Hurston intends to give us a deeper understanding of the redemptive and creative resources of Black culture.

The hoodoo practitioners Hurston speaks to in *Mules and Men* are also conscious that their rituals are being seen through the lens of racism. Luke Turner, a hoodoo doctor, tells Zora about Marie Laveau, who had a reputation as "the queen of conjure."[88] Turner tells her: " 'Now, some white people say she hold hoodoo dance on Congo square every week. But Marie Leveau never hold no hoodoo dance. That was a pleasure dance. They beat the drum with the shin bone of a donkey and everybody dance like they do in Hayti. Hoodoo is private. . . . The white people come look on, and think they see all, when they only see a dance.' "[89] Hurston herself later reinforces this distinction, participating in a hoodoo dance which she says is "not a pleasure dance, but a ceremonial." This dance is rarely performed, she says, and only for a purpose: "it is always a case of death-to-the-enemy that calls forth a dance."[90] Only the initiated may witness such a dance, and these are inherently secret affairs, conducted behind closed doors to curse an enemy.

Hurston's ethnographic work offered an empirical challenge to the racist fantasies of Broadway, echoing critiques that were being aired within the academic discipline of anthropology and that were well embedded in the circle around Franz Boas where Hurston trained. Boas had set himself apart from the previous generation of "evolutionist" anthropologists who were "under the spell of the idea of a general, uniform evolution of culture in which all parts of mankind participated."[91] Edward Burnett Tylor—Oxford's first professor of anthropology—is symptomatic of this view, the singular noun in the title of his *Primitive Culture* (1871) implying that all primitive societies have a fundamentally similar, even a shared culture. Boas criticized this conception of the "sameness of customs and beliefs everywhere," which implied that any observed phenomenon could be understood in terms of a "slow advance from savagery to civilisation." While Boas politely acknowledged the influence of these "bold generalizations" in building anthropology as an academic field, he also inaugurated a process that would break them down by the accumulation of empirical data.[92]

Known for inaugurating "cultural relativism" and "historical particularism," Boas critiqued the teleological "evolutionist" narrative that would allocate ritual behaviors such as collective chanting to a "primitive" past, that would inevitably be superseded by rational and individualistic "civilization."[93] Instead of situating all cultures as evolutionary stages on the way to the telos of Western modernity, they would be seen as historically situated, unique, and independently valuable. Anthropology "has outgrown the systematizing period, and is just now entering on the empirical revision of its theories," Boas wrote: it was the detailed empirical fieldwork that would allow ethnographers to see beyond the (easily generalizable) spectacular and ceremonial, to grasp the discursive specificity of the everyday.[94]

Hurston praised this quality of Boas's approach: "He outlines his theory, but if the facts do not agree with it, he would not warp a jot or dot of the findings to save his theory."[95] Hurston's work, as an ethnographer, novelist and dramatist, embodies a similar drive to understand ceremonial, ritualistic and religious practices in relation to the everyday, as elements of a distinctive way of life. In his preface for *Mules and Men,* Boas praised Hurston's ability to "penetrate through that affected demeanour by which the Negro excludes the White observer effectively from participating in his true inner life."[96] Hurston and Boas shared a sense that detailed ethnographic study could explode such generalizations and enable the cultural practices of Black people in the South to be understood in their own terms, in relation to their own history, and as a form of collective life and culture whose value was independent of white institutions and of the polis.

Part of the impetus was, for Hurston, to reassert the underlying individualism of Black culture. Much of *Mules and Men* is dedicated to recording folktales, which share things in common with collective speech acts, forming as they do part of the repository of shared scripts in a traditional, predominantly oral society. "We want to set 'em down before it's too late," Hurston explains in a preservationist spirit, when someone asks her the point of this exercise. "Before everybody forgets all of 'em."[97] However, these tales are not spoken in unison, and Hurston inserts them into passages of dialogue in which different speakers trade stories and respond to them critically, implying that she sees them as elements of a discursive culture of debate and contestation rather than as a quasi-liturgical element of a communal religious practice. Her treatment of these stories accords value to the distinctive perspectives of individual speakers. Hurston's ethnographies attempt to rescue a distinctive, discursive, and often individualistic culture from the "bold generalizations" of an evolutionist anthropology that would treat it as a window onto a more communal, primitive past.

This orientation can also be found in Hurston's ethnographic explorations of the private spaces of hoodoo. *Mules and Men* includes some "formulae of hoodoo doctors" in an appendix: these are not large-scale public ceremonies but guides to individual action: "Put an egg in a murdered man's hand and the murderer can't get away. He will wander right around the scene."[98] Hurston's accounts of her initiation into a number of New Orleans hoodoo cults also tend to allocate a very precise space and location to the rites. The initiation ceremony itself acts as a barrier between the public spaces a wandering anthropologist may easily observe and the private rites reserved for the initiated: Hurston's participatory ethnography enables a view inside these private ceremonies. Her initiation by Luke Turner has multiple elements, including drinking his blood and sacrificing a black sheep. As the sheep is led into the circle of congregants, they raise a chant: "He stood there dazedly while the chant of strange syllables rose. I asked Turner the words, but he replied that in good time I would know what to say. It would not be taught."[99] The semantic content of the chant, if any, is impossible to determine—it may be drawn from an African language, or it could be a set of syllables whose meaning is untranslatably tied to the specific context of Luke Turner's initiation ceremony (Hurston undergoes several, and they are all completely different). This is part of a class of collective utterances whose meaning seems fully connected to the fact that the hearer —and sometimes the speaker—does not recognize or understand the semantic content.

We have already seen in relation to the voodoo chant "Eh! Bomba!" that the experience of hearing a collective utterance in an unknown language can play into the exoticizing tendency to view cultural others as an undifferentiated mass, who express their shared ethnic identity through sung or chanted ritual. This sense of an encryption can act as an intransigent refusal of the dominant linguistic order. But in the passage under discussion, Hurston records something a little different, where the hearer is invited to join in (at least in due course). With reference to "Eh! Bomba!" Pettinger notes—given the polyglot composition of the Haitian slave population—that it is quite possible that the voodoo celebrants themselves may not have known the semantic content of their chant. But this only goes to show that "a semantic analysis of a chant . . . cannot tell us much about what it does for those who actually give voice to it: we are not any closer to appreciating it as part of an absorbing physical activity that emotionally binds the participants together but does not necessarily 'communicate' anything at all."[100] When collective speech refuses to speak back to power, semantics are subordinated to embodiment. If I do not understand the language of a collective utterance, that does not prevent me from joining in. I could look up what "auld lang syne" means, but what would that unlock? The dictionary is a key to an empty chest.

Also reflecting on the limitations of translation in understanding collective rites, Kwame Anthony Appiah turns to a moment from Gore Vidal's *Julian*—about Rome's last pagan emperor—which describes "those temples at Rome where certain verses learned by rote are chanted year in and year out, yet no one, including the priests, knows what they mean, for they are in the early language of the Etruscans, long since forgotten."[101] Appiah writes: "But that doesn't render the rites meaningless . . . many of us have witnessed the power of ceremonies in a language we do not know. . . . Whatever that's about it's not about doctrine: for doctrine, by definition, survives translation from one language to another."[102] Such moments of collective utterance should not be cast as translatable *expressions* that communicate a cultural identity, understood in terms of its "doctrine." Appiah is interested here, instead, in ephemeral moments of coalition, when speakers are bound together emotionally and physically by the act of saying the same words in parallel.

The general thrust of *Mules and Men*, then, is to cut through preconceptions about the collectivity of Black folk culture, and to explore, through participant observation, the importance of private social practices that are highly individualizing. The role of voodoo and hoodoo in Hurston's fiction and drama also often reflects this fact, as the private practice of hoodoo is expressive of social discord and disunity. In Hurston's first novel, *Jonah's Gourd Vine* (1934), for example, the protagonist John's second wife, Hettie, secretly uses hoodoo conjure against him, concealing "a miscellany of weird objects" (including small pieces of his clothes) in the mattress and around the house, intended to bring him bad fortune. Joe is told that to break the spell he must "draw her wine" (beat her until she bleeds), which he duly does.[103]

Hurston's short story "Spunk" (1925) also includes hints of hoodoo, but no ritual is staged for the reader: apparently supernatural events are reported as rumor and supposition. In the story, Lena and Joe's marriage is thrown into jeopardy when Spunk, a "giant of a brown-skinned man" arrives in town and takes an interest in Lena.[104] When Spunk pursues Lena in spite of her marital status, Joe attacks him, and Spunk kills Joe in self-defense. However, he then seems to be haunted by a black bobcat that might be Joe "sneaked back from Hell."[105] And when he is fatally wounded in an industrial accident, he claims in his dying words that it was Joe who pushed him onto the circular saw (he works a dangerous job at the saw mill). At the wake, Joe's father Jeff "stood leering triumphantly down upon the fallen giant as if his fingers had been the teeth of the steel that laid him low."[106] If Jeff has used hoodoo to precipitate Spunk's demise, this happens out of the view of the reader, in a concealed private realm: what we know about it emerges through the speculations and secondhand reports of other characters. There is no collective vocalization reported in the story.

By contrast, when Hurston came to adapt "Spunk" for the stage ten years later, she used similar plot elements but gave prominent place to a fascinating hoodoo ritual that includes choric incantations. She also included in the play a variety of work songs, a chain gang, and folk music—so that the "conjure scene," as she calls it, is part of a tapestry of overlapping and contrasting collective speech forms. Perhaps the anthropological and folkloric fieldwork she had undertaken in the ten years since she wrote the short story had an influence on the play. Hodge Bishop is the master of ceremonies, as well as the father—the "meddlesome old root-working papa," as Lina puts it—of the Joe character (called Jim Bishop in this version).[107] Bishop's hoodoo practice is a prominent topic of discussion in the play, and one character suggests that Lina had agreed to marry Jim only because Bishop cast a spell: now Lina has run off with Spunk, perhaps Bishop is "losing his stroke."[108] The ceremony that Hurston imagines on stage—designed to bring about the death of Spunk in revenge for his killing Jim—is thus framed by skeptical conversations about whether hoodoo practice has any efficacy. Spunk even asks, "If these hoodoo doctors can do so much why don't they conjure these white folks and get some money and some power?" declaring Bishop "abstifically a humbug."[109]

The scene takes place in an altar room and it involves "six men, dressed in cat robes," candles, a pea vine, incense, a doll that is assaulted and stabbed, and the ritual invocation of death. The men "cry out like great angry cats," before they strip naked, "stand nude and shining black," and then "dance fiercely":

(They all rub him violently for a moment with their hands until he trembles violently, then leaps away in terror as far as possible. Bishop begins to writhe and his Black skin begins to split at the top of his head.)

CAT-MEN: Slip 'em and slip 'em again!

BISHOP: *(The skin peels down to the neck.)* Cat men! Guard my skin! Cat men! Guard my skin from evil.

CAT-MEN: It shall be protected from pepper and salt! *(The Black skin peels on down slowly and Bishop stands dripping blood as he steps out of his skin and picks it up and stretches it before the altar. That done, he creeps downstage center and glares all about him.)*

BISHOP: *(In a thundering voice)* Where is my saddle cat? *(There is a great cat-call and the shadow of a huge bristling cat is seen on the back wall. Bishop makes to mount it. There is a great wail of cats. Darkness. Curtain.)*[110]

The cat-men are completely indistinct, moving and speaking in unison, and affirming associations of collective speech both with Blackness and with animality. It is a self-consciously exoticizing presentation.

Hurston clearly felt that dramatic performance afforded distinctive possibilities to the ethnographer that a merely written account could not achieve. At the beginning of the scene she notes: "Conjure scene can not be fully put on paper. Must be done in direction."[111] The play *Spunk* was never produced, so in her own terms the vision was never fully realized. However, some of the choric scenes closely resemble those which were performed separately in Hurston's various stagings of Negro folklore. *The Great Day* (1932), for example, was described by Alain Locke on the playbill as "a stage arrangement of part of a cycle of Negro folk-song, dance and pantomime collected and recorded by Miss Zora Hurston over three years of intimate living among the common folk in the primitive privacy of their own Negro way of life."[112] This pageant of a day at the railroad camp, full of collective speech and song, was initially intended to include a conjure ceremony called a "Pea-Vine Candle Dance," and one of the initiations Hurston undergoes in *Mules and Men* is called the "Pea Vine Candle Drill."[113] Both candles and pea vines feature in *Spunk*'s conjure scene. Anthea Kraut (who has done more than any other scholar to reconstruct the pageant) shows that Hurston excised the scene from the performance of *The Great Day*.[114] The scene was to have featured a character called Ant Judy " 'prostrate before the Death,' performing a chant in the voice of an inhabiting divinity while the female onlookers danced around the altar and echoed her incantations."[115] This is theatre with a documentary intention to present the results of Hurston's ethnographic work on the stage.

Pageants like *The Great Day* used a chorus to string together a variety of collective speech forms that Hurston saw as specifically Black, from the work songs of railroad workers to the rituals of the Black church and the good time music of the "jook joint" (informal establishments for drinking, gambling and dancing, now also commonly spelled "juke"). Black composers she approached with the project felt that white audiences would not be interested in such unpolished expressions, but (Hurston says) the performance was a success: "Because I know that music without motion is not natural with my people, I did not have the singers stand in a stiff group and reach for the high note. I told them to just imagine they were in Macedonia [Baptist Church] and go ahead. One critic said that he did not believe that the concert was rehearsed, it looked so natural. I had dramatized a working day on a railroad camp, from the shack-rouser waking up the camp at dawn until the primitive dance in the deep woods at night."[116]

Hurston felt that in more polished performances, collective speech could appear regimented: the somewhat loose performance style, with its unrehearsed feel, allows individual agency to the performer even in the context of group utterance. As Anthea Kraut argues, there was a widespread tendency to imagine the "folk" as a "homogeneous group who speak in a unified voice—a stark contrast to the hybridity, complexity, and cacophony that characterize "modern" culture." For Kraut, Hurston's staging of *The Great Day* was oriented against this static and homogeneous conception of folk culture. "While Hurston unquestionably sought to showcase the collectivity and collaboration that underwrote folk creativity," Kraut continues, "her revue simultaneously illustrated how individual innovation was prized within folk communities; her inclusion of solo performances in certain sections suggests as much."[117] The hoodoo ritual thus takes its place among a variety of other folk practices as part of a multifaceted dialogue between collective and individualizing forms of cultural expression.

As *The Great Day* shows, Hurston was inclined to link the essentially private rituals of hoodoo with larger and more inclusive occasions, in which collective utterance emerges as an important theme. While *Jonah's Gourd Vine* portrays hoodoo rites primarily as a vehicle for private animus and revenge, it also has a fire dance scene that seems to blur the distinction that Hurston emphasized in *Mules and Men* between the pleasure dance and African-derived folk religion. Following a day working in the cotton fields, the farmer Alf Pearson donates two pigs for a barbecue, and a big party breaks out involving laborers from neighboring plantations. The entertainment seems to start off as a square dance, with someone "calling figures"—but then it is interrupted by a reveler saying, "Us ain't no white folks! . . . Us don't want no fiddles, neither no guitars, neither no banjoes." We should hesitate to label what follows either as a religious ceremony or as a "pleasure dance":

> So they danced. They called for the instrument that they had brought to America in their skins—the drum—and they played upon it. With their hands they played upon the little dance drums of Africa. The drums of kid-skin. With their feet they stomped it, and the voice of Kata-Kumba, the great drum, lifted itself within them and they heard it. The great drum that is made by priests and sits in majesty in the juju house. The drum with the man skin that is dressed with human blood, that is beaten with a human shin- bone and speaks to gods as a man and to men as a God. Then they beat upon the drum and danced.[118]

Hurston's depiction of this party-ritual clearly participates in an anthropological debate which was important in the intellectual milieu of the Harlem Renaissance: to what extent could the cultural expressions of Black America trace their roots to African antecedents? Hurston addressed this directly in her ethnographic work: in *Tell My Horse* she describes "The Nine Night," a funeral rite which is the "most universal ceremony in Jamaica" and "an African survival" that is also full of singing and chanting:

> The shuckers do a magnificent muscle dance which they tell me is African. The drums and the movements of the dancers move so close together that the drums become people and the people become drums. . . . Truly the drum is inside their bodies. More rum, more fire.
>
> "Hand a' bowl, Knife a' throat
> Rope a' tie me, Hand a bowl"[119]

The description portrays this ritual as a specific creative product of Jamaican culture, and yet one that self-consciously performs its relationship to African religious life. Writing about Haiti, Hurston called voodoo "the old, old mysticism of the world in African terms" and—in her discussion of zombies—talks of "primitive practices that have been brought from Africa."[120]

Tell My Horse eschews explicitly theoretical discussion, but Hurston was very aware of the anthropological debates that such observations played into. She implicitly positioned herself as a "retentionist," emphasizing the African cultural inheritance among Black Americans, a position that would become associated with the name of her Barnard colleague and fellow Boas acolyte

Melville J. Herskovits and his book *The Myth of the Negro Past* (1941). David Scott has traced the later history of the debate between retentionists and "creationists," who emphasized the development of distinctively new Black cultures and institutions in the US. Both sides in this debate mobilize a variety of collective speech forms, though with different implications. For Scott, the debate is overdetermined by the ways in which both sides fixate on "the demonstration that African American cultures are, fundamentally, cultures of resistance."[121] Scott names a tendency within the discipline of anthropology (and perhaps within intellectual culture more widely) to frame those collective speech practices coded as Black in these terms: as if they were always politically engaged or protesting, and so belonged, exclusively, to chapter 2 in this book's schema.

Foreshadowing Scott's arguments, Hurston explicitly countered the idea that Black culture must be resistant by definition. As Lindsey Stewart demonstrates in *The Politics of Black Joy: Zora Neale Hurston and Neo-Abolitionism* (2021), Hurston consistently grappled with the overbearing expectation that African American culture must make an emotive appeal to the politically powerful for pity and recognition. Hurston counters this with an embrace of "Black joy." Stewart argues that the Black culture Hurston celebrates has a relationship to political power that should be characterized as "refusal" rather than "resistance." "Resistance locks us into a life-and-death struggle with our oppressor for recognition," she writes. "In contrast, refusal withholds recognition of the oppressor's power or authority to define our lives."[122] This refusal—echoing the "feminist refusal" of Euripides's bacchants—is an embrace and celebration of Black life *outside* Jim Crow political structures, not an attempt to change those structures.

This perspective is also reflected in Hurston's work on the Black church, which she sees as fundamentally continuous with hoodoo. Hurston's essay "Spirituals and Neo-Spirituals" observed the way each congregation would invent and creatively embellish its own distinctive set of ritual conventions. "These songs, even the printed ones, do not remain long in their original forms," she writes. "Every congregation that takes it up varies it considerably."[123] However, Hurston also emphasized that this assertion of liturgical independence should not be confused with the absence of set forms. "Beneath the seeming informality of religious worship there is a set formality." There are "definite forms," which are held, not in a book or by the preacher, but in the social expectations of the congregation: "The individual may hang as many new ornaments upon the traditional form as he likes, but the audience would be disagreeably surprised if the form were abandoned."[124] Not written down, except after the fact by the questing ethnographer—this is a liturgy embedded in the habits of the everyday.

One aspect of "set formality" that Hurston finds within the Baptist service is what she calls "bearing up." This describes the phenomenon whereby the congregation respond in unison to the words of the preacher, with formulas that are specific to the single congregation. Hurston writes:

> Chants and hums are not used indiscriminately as it would appear to a casual listener. They have a definite place and time. They are used to "bear up" the speaker. As Mama Jane of Second Zion Baptist Church, New Orleans, explained to me: "What point they come out on, you bear 'em up."
>
> For instance, if the preacher should say: "Jesus will lead us," the congregation would bear him up with: "I'm got my ha-hands in my Jesus' hands." If in prayer or sermon, the mention is made of nailing Christ to the cross: "Didn't Calvary tremble when they nailed Him down."
>
> There is no definite post-prayer chant. One may follow, however, because of intense emotion.[125]

As ever, Hurston deployed her anthropological findings in her literary and dramatic work. During her fieldwork she transcribed many sermons, including one by C. C. Lovelace, an emotionally intense meditation on the wounds of Jesus. Hurston later used this as the basis of a theatrical performance called *The Sermon in the Valley* and then put it into the mouth of John Pearson, the central protagonist of *Jonah's Gourd Vine*.[126] That novel stresses the importance of the collective vocalizations of the congregation in underpinning the sermon: "There had been a mighty response to the sermon all thru its length. The 'bearing up' had been almost continuous, but as Pearson's voice sank dramatically to the final Amen, Anderson lifted a chant that kept the church on fire for several seconds more."[127]

Bearing up resonates with, but is also clearly distinct from, the more sober call-and-response prayer patterns in the Book of Common Prayer, which I discuss in chapter 3, and where the words of both minister and congregation are set down in advance. In the traditions of the Black church in the US, the boundary between the sermon and the other parts of the ceremony are blurred, and in a certain sense the sermon *becomes* the collective prayer, building in cues such as "Jesus will lead us" to elicit the conventional response from the members of the congregation, confirming their approval and binding them together. Hurston is concerned to demonstrate that the complex set of formal rules governing preaching and prayer underpin a genuine counterpoint between individual creative self-expression and the generalized assent that brings the community together around the preacher's words.

This phenomenon of bearing up was explored in a more testing manner by James Baldwin, both in the personal reminiscences of his memoir *The Fire Next Time* (1963) and in the fictionalized portrait of his father, a preacher, in *Go Tell It on the Mountain* (1953). Baldwin, who became a preacher in the Pentecostal tradition as a very young man, is as compelling as Hurston about the emotional power of the services, though the mood is different: "The church was very exciting. It took a long time for me to disengage myself from the excitement, and on the blindest, most visceral level, I never really have, and never will. There is no music like the drama of the saints rejoicing, the sinners moaning, the tambourines racing, and all those voices coming together and crying holy unto the Lord. There is still, for me, no pathos quite like the pathos of those multi-coloured, worn, somehow triumphant and transfigured faces, speaking from the depths of a visible, tangible, continuing despair of the goodness of the Lord."[128]

The note of "despair" is, for Baldwin, a force behind "all those voices coming together." But the answer came in the form of an unshakable faith in the goodness of the Lord and in the embodied, earthly pleasures to be found in this fusion of music, dance, and prayer. The political stakes of this are addressed more explicitly in Baldwin's vivid account of what "bearing up" feels like from the perspective of the preacher:

> Nothing that has happened to me since equals the power and the glory that I sometimes felt when, in the middle of a sermon, I knew that I was somehow, by some miracle, really carrying, as they said, "the Word"—when the church and I were one. Their pain and their joy were mine, and mine was theirs—they surrendered their pain and joy to me, I surrendered mine to them—and their cries of "Amen!" and "Hallelujah!" and "Yes, Lord!" and "Praise His name!" and "Preach it, brother!" sustained and whipped on my solos until we all became equal, wringing wet, singing and dancing, in anguish and rejoicing, at the foot of the altar.

Baldwin can view this experience from the distancing secular perspective of someone has left the church, and he speaks candidly of the "shabbiness of my motives."[129] Bearing up has a phenomenal power that Baldwin recognizes, but that power feels potentially deceptive, allowing him to believe—however temporarily—that he is carrying "the Word," and to conceal, even from himself, his real motives.

As his faith begins to fray, Baldwin is increasingly tempted to urge the congregation to leave the warm embrace of the church to focus on more political forms of collective action: "When I faced a congregation, it began to take all the strength I had not to stammer, not to curse, not to tell them to throw away their Bibles and go home and organize, for example, a rent strike."[130] For Baldwin, in this later period, the forms of salvation and repair offered through the collective prayers of the church become a distraction from the imperative of political engagement. *The Fire Next Time* recommends a turn towards the polis, but it also conveys a profound sense of what must be left behind, emotionally, in that turn.

The spirituals that were sung by the congregations in Black churches have been central to debates about the politics of the collective voice in the US. The foundational argument was made by W. E. B. Du Bois in *The Souls of Black Folk* (1903), where he influentially presented the Negro spirituals as "sorrow songs," seeing in them an ongoing response to the violence of slavery and a call for racial justice. In her 1938 essay "Art and Such," Hurston lambasted Du Bois (without actually naming him), taking to task the kind of "Race Leader" who would "call spirituals 'Our Sorrow Songs' and other such tom-foolery in an effort to get into the spotlight if possible without ever having done anything to improve education, industry, invention, art and never having uttered a quotable line."[131] In "Spirituals and Neo-Spirituals," Hurston wrote, "The idea that the whole body of spirituals are 'sorrow songs' is ridiculous."[132] Du Bois had celebrated these spirituals as the "articulate message of the slave to the world." They were "the music of an unhappy people, of the children of disappointment; they tell of death and suffering and unvoiced longing toward a truer world."[133] Du Bois recalls a song ("Do ba-na co-ba, ge-ne me, ge-ne me!") which he sees as in some senses typical of the sorrow songs: "The child sang it to his children and they to their children's children, and so two hundred years it has travelled down to us and we sing it to our children, knowing as little as our fathers what its words may mean, but knowing well the meaning of its music."[134] As in Hurston's hoodoo initiation, the meaning of the words is unknown or lost. But Du Bois wants to say that all these songs, regardless of their semantic content, convey the sorrow of the Negro and "a faith in the ultimate justice of things."[135]

Hurston's objection to Du Bois's characterization of the spirituals as sorrow songs is brilliantly parsed by Stewart and linked to the two writers' contrasting views of voodoo or hoodoo (which Stewart calls "root work"). Stewart shows that Hurston sees the collective vocalizations of the Black church as essentially continuous with those of root work.[136] Du Bois, however, sees "voodooism" as a futile and ineffective rebellion, which needed to be moved past and brought into a dialectical synthesis with Christianity in order to generate the sorrow songs that were a more effective response to the conditions of slavery.[137] This impulse is "neo-abolitionist," Stewart claims, and she links it to Frederick Douglass's "alignment of Negro spirituals with the abolitionist message."[138] For Stewart, Du Bois tends to celebrate Black cultural expression only as a response to slavery, racism, and oppression, relegating root work to the status of a primitive and immature cultural stage. When Du Bois celebrates the spirituals' "articulate message . . . to the world," this is seen skeptically by Hurston as effectively a message to white people, asking for "justice." This is perhaps a reductive reading of Du Bois, but it explains Hurston's repeated and vehement rejection of his account of the "sorrow songs." In the terms of this book, Hurston characterizes Du Bois as attempting to turn the collective utterances of Black people towards the polis, narrowing the functional and emotional range of the spirituals such that they only express suffering and ask for pity, justice, and advancement.

Hurston argues that the songs Du Bois focuses on are not real spirituals at all, but "neo-spirituals." Neo-spirituals tended to be written down, polished up with complex harmonic arrangements, and rehearsed for performance outside of religious settings by glee clubs and the like, often for white audiences. In *The Souls of Black Folk* Du Bois celebrates the work of the Fisk Jubilee Singers, who in the late nineteenth century toured the Northern United States, where "the magic of their song kept thrilling hearts."[139] Hurston noted that the Fisk singers "have spread their interpretation all over America," but that they created a distorted picture of Black culture. In effect, the neo-spirituals, with their polished harmonies, presented a version of Black culture in which opportunities for individual self-expression and self-realization are subsumed by a form of collective vocalization that was in fact heavily scripted, requiring detailed preparation and premeditation, and to be performed by professional singers. This was the sound not of the Southern church, but of the "talented tenth," a term Du Bois used to think about the possibilities of Black advancement: "the Best of this race" whose task it was to "guide the Mass away from the contamination and death of the Worst."[140] The Fisk Jubilee Singers were acting in this way, as a highly trained elite—part of "an aristocracy of talent and character"—with a polished routine amenable to the tastes of white audiences in the Northern states.[141] Hurston considered "Race Leaders" in the Du Boisian mold as suspect, and she wanted to stress the value in the music, art, and culture of those he characterized as the "Mass" and the "Worst."

To distinguish the spirituals that she loved from the polished productions of the Fisk singers, Hurston emphasized that "Negro songs to be heard truly must be sung by a group, and a group bent on expression of feelings and not on sound effects." She was seeking to document a form of collective voicing that incorporated significant spontaneity: "The harmony of the true spiritual is not regular. The dissonances are important and not to be ironed out by the trained musician. The various parts break in at any old time. . . . The congregation is bound by no rules." She goes on: "The real Negro singer cares nothing about pitch. The first notes just burst out and the rest of the church join in—fired by the same inner urge. Every man trying to express himself through song. Every man for himself. Hence the harmony and disharmony, the shifting keys and broken time that make up the spiritual."[142]

Paul Gilroy saw Hurston's contrast between the "real Negro singer" and the Fisk singers as an inauthentic representation of Blackness, as a symptom of her "ethnic absolutism."[143] Mark Christian Thompson goes further in this direction by associating her with "Black fascism." Noting that Hurston rejected a "biological conception of race" that she associated with both Nazism and Garveyism, Thompson argues that her novel *Moses, Man of the Mountain* (1939) propounds a version of "black cultural nationalism" that was to be "achieved along lines similar to the creation of the fascist authoritarian state." The emphasis on culture rather than biology as the foundation of the ethno-state is compatible, for Thompson, with "generic European fascism," if not with Nazism itself.[144]

However, while her stance of refusal rules out accommodation with and assimilation in white institutions, Hurston constantly emphasizes the internal diversity of Black culture against what she sees as the homogenizing tendency of Du Bois's account of the sorrow songs. Where the neo-spirituals of the Fisk Jubilee Singers were tightly scripted performances with every voice bound into a harmonic structure and a neo-abolitionist message, the spirituals she celebrates are spontaneous collective outpourings which allow for "glorious individualistic flights." And the songs are more diverse in their contents than Du Bois's neo-abolitionist interpretation would allow: they are not to be heard primarily as political resistance, but "cover a wide range of subjects from a peeve at gossipers to Death and Judgement," she writes.[145] Hurston in this case wants us to pay more attention to the actual semantic content of the words sung, to capture their variety and emotional range, and so to counter the pervasive assumption that they are all defined by a plaintive expression of Black suffering. Reading Hurston's engagement with the folk culture of the US South as if it were part of a Black fascist, state-building project arguably downplays the genuinely fugitive impulses in her work. She answered Du Bois not with an alternative political program, but by challenging the assumption that the collective speech forms she collected, analyzed, reworked, and performed ought to be thought of in political terms.

This chapter began by showing that collective vocalizations that take up the position of refusal or exile are often caught up in a dialectic of racialization. Racist representations of collective speech by Black people can be seen as a reaction to the real threat of collective Black resistance, as embodied in the Haitian Revolution. For obvious reasons, Black culture does also respond to and reject such racism. But Hurston's work emphasizes repeatedly that the collective cultural expressions she sought to document ethnographically cannot be defined or determined by their relationship to white culture. She is a writer of fugitive sociality and Black joy, and her collective utterances occupy a space outside of politics—outside the polis—refusing to be co-opted into its logic. Stefano Harney and Fred Moten express this position in forthright terms: "We're more than politics, more than settled, more than democratic. We surround democracy's false image in order to unsettle it. Every time it tries to enclose us in a decision, we're undecided. Every time it tries to represent our will, we're unwilling. Every time it tries to take root, we're gone."[146] Harney and Moten's "We're more than politics" is a lucid restatement of Hurston's critique of Du Bois, and their embrace of fugitivity underlines the continuing power of this stance. Yet the speech forms I have surveyed in this chapter also suggest that there is some indeterminacy surrounding the distinction both Scott and Stewart make between refusal and various forms of engagement with the polis. The writers I now turn to in the following bridge, Jacques Roumain and Ousmane Sembène, recognize the value of refusal, but self-consciously walk this line, exploring ways in which the refusing collective can turn towards the polis.

BRIDGE

• • •

TOWARDS THE POLIS

REFUSAL, AS HONIG ARGUES, has an arc. In its purest, fugitive form, it is opposed to any demand for redistribution, political recognition, or advancement. Yet refusal can be mobilized in such a demand. Perhaps the most obvious example of this would be the strike, in which the refusal to work becomes a bargaining chip in a negotiation about working conditions. This bridge section focuses on two writers, Jacques Roumain and Ousmane Sembène, whose wide-ranging obsessions with collective speech charted its refusing power, as well as its potential to become politically active. The strike is an important form for both of them, and they see the picket line as an important location for a form of collective speech that is refusing, but that also seeks to turn that refusal in a political direction, just as the bacchants returned to the polis to issue their demands. Roumain and Sembène are therefore transitional figures within the overall schema of this book, showing the route from refusal and exile, to protest and engagement.

"Even the Tom-toms Will Have Learned / the Language of the International": Jacques Roumain

Chanted rituals, and ethnographic descriptions of them, were important to the revolutionary, anticolonial project of the Haitian writer Jacques Roumain. His posthumously published novel *Gouverneurs de la rosée* (1944)—translated as *Masters of the Dew* (1947) by Langston Hughes (whom Roumain had befriended studying at Columbia University in 1932) and Mercer Cook—mobilizes several overlapping genres of collective vocalization to investigate their political and social meanings. The story centers on a village community in Fonds Rouges, riven by drought and famine, in the aftermath of the US occupation of Haiti (1915–34). Following the Haitian revolution, the sugar industry collapsed, and Roumain's book documents a subsistence farming community struggling to grow enough food to survive. The hero of the story, Manuel, has returned to Haiti after fifteen years working on a sugar cane plantation in Cuba, where he got an induction into trade unionism and socialism. He is driven by a quest to find a new source of water, to build a canal, and so to irrigate the land and heal the divided community.

Vodou ritual practice, which Roumain had studied in his ethnographic work, bears a complicated relationship to the socialist politics that emerge in *Masters of the Dew* as a somewhat contrasting epicenter of social solidarity and collective speech. Manuel's mother Délira is particularly associated with vodou elements, and it is she who invites Dorméus the *houngan* (vodou priest) to lead a ceremony intended to end the drought, improve the harvest, and regenerate the community. These chanted rites do form a demand for a redistributive, material improvement in the condition of the Haitian peasantry, but they are also a refusal of politics. In the terms of Steven Connor's *A History of Asking* (2023), they are petitionary prayers, as opposed to political petitions, and as such one of their key functions is to invoke beings who operate beyond the human sphere of secular political institutions, but who are presumed to arbitrate over questions of resource distribution.[1]

Chanting in unison with his female aides (the *hounsi*), Dorméus invokes "papa Legba"—traditionally invoked at the beginning of all vodou rituals—and the narrator reports that "Legba, that old god of Guinea, was there," having possessed Fleurimond, one of the congregation.[2] Legba promises to lead the people out of the drought, and they respond with chanting:

> A unanimous chant arose, based on ancient rhythms, and the peasants began to dance their supplication, knees bent, arms outstretched:
>
> *Legba, show us how!*
> Alegba-sé, it's you and me!

Manuel, the novel's central character, is "conquered by the magic beat of the drums in the depths of his being" and is described "dancing and singing with the rest."[3] The language here already suggests that in Manuel there is a resistance to the ritual that needs to be overcome. Manuel needs to be "conquered" by the drums and to dance and sing "with the rest," where "the rest" forms an implied unity that Manuel is outside of, and can choose to join, or not.

As the ritual proceeds, this sense of unity begins to wear. Following the sacrifice of a cock, another of the peasants becomes possessed, this time by Papa Ogoun—a vodou god associated with metalworking and rum making. Ogoun addresses Manuel directly in song, singing:

> *We'll dig a canal, I say! Ago yé!*
> *The vein is open, the blood flows.*[4]

Délira whispers to Bienaimé (Manuel's father) that she does not like Papa Ogoun's song, even as the ritual intensifies:

> The banners waved, the dull rumble of the drum resounded, urging the chant on to a new outburst. The women's voices shot up very high, cracking the thick mass of song:
>
> *Légba-sé! Légba!*
> *Blood has been drawn!*
> *Blood! Abobo!*
>
> . . .
>
> Manuel let himself go in the upsurge of the dance, but a strange sadness crept into his soul. He caught his mother's eye and thought he saw tears shining there.[5]

The unifying solidarity of the ritual shows signs of cracking. Some of those participating do so with anxiety, questioning their conviction. The narrator concludes this extraordinary chapter by remarking: "Dancing and drinking anesthetized them—swept away their shipwrecked souls to drown in those regions of unreality and danger where the fierce forces of the African gods lay in wait."[6] Undoubtedly powerful and profoundly absorbing, the ritual is presented as dangerous, anaesthetizing, and so absorbing that it might lead, metaphorically, to drowning.

This ambivalent depiction of a vodou ritual puts it at an interesting angle to the work that Roumain and other Haitian intellectuals had been doing to study the nature of vodou and to foreground it as a site of cultural refusal of the legacies of French colonialism and of the US occupation. Jean Price-Mars, whose work on the voodoo chant "Eh! Bomba!" I discussed in chapter 1, was the leading figure in this group; he had conducted the first significant ethnography of Haitian vodou in his book *Ainsi parla l'oncle* (1928).[7] Price-Mars (who had written a glowing preface to Roumain's first novel, the 1931 *La Montagne ensourcelée*) was engaged in "launching a cultural nationalism" by "embracing Afro-Haitian popular religious culture."[8] For Price-Mars, the

Haitian Revolution had too readily "donned the old frock of western civilization," and, from 1804 until Price-Mars's present, "tried her utmost to realize what she believed to be her superior destiny in shaping her thought and sentiments, by drawing closer to her former mother country, by copying her, and by identifying with her." Price-Mars reacts against this "absurd and grandiose task" and turns to Haitian folklore as a repository of a folk identity that exists *outside* of colonial structures.[9] Vodou is, Price-Mars argues, a "religion," albeit a "very primitive religion," whose elements can all be traced to African antecedents.[10] Price-Mars invokes the revolutionary scene of the Bois Caiman ceremony in 1791—when (he says) Dutty Boukman intoned "Jetez portraits Dieu blanc" ("cast down the image of the god of the whites")—and positions Haitian vodou as a distinct belief system which conversion to Christianity can only superficially affect: "The new religious state of the slave was only a facade; . . . his fundamental beliefs were only slightly shaken by his official conversion and remained unchanged in the mysteries of his infrangible consciousness."[11]

This sense that the slaves possessed an underlying consciousness that was "infrangible" and whose roots could be located in African spiritual practices lent itself to the characterization of voodoo chanting in racial terms. Price-Mars is a significant figure in the intellectual prehistory of *négritude,* and his work inhabits a speculative, primitivist orientation, which seeks to define Blackness *outside* of the logic of "Western civilization."

> In regard to the black man, it seems to me there is reason to determine the role that music and dance perform in his spiritual life. . . . [T]heir influence over the organism assumes a clearly biological character for the Negro. . . . Music and Dance become an organic need for the black man. . . . They color all the modalities of Negro life, whether in a mourner or a grave-digger chanting in rhythm the lamentations in funeral processions in order to avert a spell, or be it in the crowds where joyful exaltation brings forth gay songs and the explosion of superabundant emotions in spinning rhythmic steps. . . . [I]t is not difficult to comprehend how the Negro religion makes use of the double cadre of Music and the Dance to express a moment of racial feeling.[12]

Price-Mars's argument may seem disconcerting in its deliberate embrace of what are normally thought of as racist tropes. Laura Marcus has explored racist discourses that connected Blackness to a hardwired biological propensity to rhythmic forms of vocal and bodily expression.[13] For example, the collector of African art Albert C. Barnes discusses (in Alain Locke's *New Negro* anthology) the association of the Negro with "the picturesque, the rhythmic, and the euphonious," and argues that these characterize his "daily habits of thought, speech and movement": the Negro is idealized, but fundamentally different.[14] However, Marcus is not inclined to see such moments purely in terms of a racist discourse about Black people. Instead, they formed part of a pattern of "evocations of a fundamental and universal rhythmicity" which was "in tune with concepts of human and natural/environmental interactions." If these were "not entirely divorced from racialized thought" then neither were they "wholly contaminated by it."[15] The strains of primitivism in Price-Mars's thought are also allied with a utopian impulse to "negate the social logic of globalizing capital" by straining to imagine a space outside it.[16]

Price-Mars led a group of Haitian intellectuals in the 1920s under the slogan of *indigénisme,* and as a part of that group, Jacques Roumain became one of the founders of *l'école indigène* and its organ *La Revue indigène* (1927–28). In the 1930s *indigénisme* gave way to *noirisme,* which can be seen as the Haitian brand of *négritude,* and which was promoted by the journal *Les Griots* (1938–40), a title that invokes a link to the oral storytelling tradition of West Africa. Roumain's work took shape in the context of a political and aesthetic project to recover and celebrate the ritual and religious cultures of Haiti, and he became the founder and first director of the Bureau d'Ethnologie in Haiti in 1941, overseeing its archaeological and ethnographic collections and writing prolifically on anthropological matters.[17] In researching his book *Le Sacrifice du tambour-assoto(r)* (1943), Roumain "assisted at ceremonies performed by his informant, the *houngan* Abraham" and recorded (both in Creole and in French translation) many vodou chants.[18] The book—which starts by asserting that "religion is intimately associated with song, dance and music"—is predominantly a detailed descriptive survey of the various vodou ceremonies Roumain witnessed, including invocations of Papa Legba that echo the scene from *Masters of the Dew.*[19] The chants themselves, as well as Roumain's commentary, invoke Guinea, Dahomey, and Nigeria, and gods that originated in West Africa, including the prominent vodou deities Ogoun and Legba. He draws on Herskovitz's work (and echoes Price-Mars) as he emphasizes vodou's connections with its African antecedents. This was a set of religious practices that Roumain would not only describe but also defend. He protested in a series of articles against the violent, Catholic-sponsored "antisuperstition campaign" in 1941 that had destroyed vodou altars and sanctuaries.[20]

Yet if Roumain saw in vodou a culture that needed to be respected, and a source of collective solidarity for an oppressed people, the horizon of his political hopes was not bounded either by religion or by ethno-nationalism. A Marxist who founded the Parti Communiste Haïtien in 1934, Roumain placed an emphasis on international proletarian solidarity. Celucien Joseph argues that Roumain's "non-theistic humanism" in the end trumps his interest in religion and ritual: "Only through effective human solidarity and collaboration can serious social transformation and real human emancipation take place."[21] As Roumain concluded in his critique of the antisuperstition drive, "What's needed in Haiti is not an anti-superstition campaign but an anti-poverty campaign."[22] This is an inflection point at which refusal starts to turn into resistance and—more pointedly—into a demand for redistribution.

Roumain's desire to shift the ground from a debate about belief and ethnic identity to one about poverty helps to interpret Manuel's ambivalence about the voodoo ritual in *Masters of the Dew.* Later in the novel Manuel explains: "No, I respect the customs of the old folks, but the blood of a rooster or a young goat can't make the seasons change, or alter the course of the clouds and fill them with water like bladders. The other night, at the Legba ceremonies, I danced and sang to my heart's content. I'm a Negro, no?"[23] Vodou ritual practice is respected here and even linked—with irony—to racial identity. But Manuel's is a secular anthropology which rejects any supernatural belief in the power of animal sacrifice or vodou chanting to effect a change in the weather. Ending the drought will require concerted political action—and so Roumain's novel looks to an alternative set of organizing principles for collective speech.

The narrative in *Masters of the Dew* is repeatedly interrupted by nostalgic memories of the older ways of working the land, which were based around the specifically Haitian institution of the *coumbite.* This names an informal grouping of agricultural workers freely cooperating on manual tasks to the accompaniment of drumming and singing. In Fonds Rouges, Simidor was the song leader who led the chants. Roumain describes the *coumbite* in action as follows:

> The moving line of peasants took up the new refrain in a single mass voice:
> *Stroke it in!*
> *Who's that, I yell,*
> *Inside that house?*
> *Some man yells back,*
> *Just me and a cute*
> *Little cousin of mine—*

And we don't need you!

They raised their long-handled hoes, crowned with sparks, and brought them down again with a terrific precision:

I'm in there now!
Bring it out! Oh!
What one bull can do,
Another can, too!
Bring it out! Oh!

There sprung up a rhythmic circulation between the beating heart of the drum and the movements of the men. The rhythm became a powerful flux penetrating deep into their arteries and nourishing their muscles with a new vigour.

Their chant filled the sun-flooded morning.[24]

The implied connection between agricultural work and sex was emphasized by Langston Hughes during the translation process (he replaced Mercer Cook's "Hoe the ground!" with "Stroke it in!").[25] The incantation flows from the bodily rhythms of the labor process, more than any ritual tradition with connections to a specific ethnic identity. It is not explicitly political or spiritual, but it does express a form of social solidarity, from a distinctively male perspective. In the context of the novel, this mode of working—which has disappeared since the land was parceled up into individual plots—is linked with peasant plenty, as the *coumbite* winds down in time for a bounteous lunch.

The memory of the *coumbite* provides a template for the socialism that Manuel believes is possible in Fonds Rouges. But this is supplemented by Manuel's memories of Cuba: a much more agriculturally productive country, but, unlike Haiti, a colony, and one where workers—including many Haitians who had left their impoverished country in search of opportunities—were ruthlessly exploited. Roumain's Cuban contemporary, the anthropologist and writer Fernando Ortiz, contrasted the production of sugar with that of tobacco in his classic work of anthropology, *Cuban Counterpoint* (1940). Ortiz bemoans the proletarianization of the Cuban worker on the sugar plantation, in contrast with the persistence of small-scale craft production of tobacco: "Sugar is produced to the orchestration of noisy machines; tobacco is worked up in silence or to the accompaniment of the spoken word. Sugar calls for choral harmony; tobacco for a solo melody. The sugar worker's tasks are active, heavy, deafening, and monotonous; the cigar worker sits down to his labours and can enjoy the pleasure and advantages of talking and listening."[26] Ortiz contrasts the dialogism of the tobacco factory with the monological environment of the sugar plantation—as we find in Richard Sennett's portrait of the highly skilled and cooperative environment of Stradivari's workshop, the craft process of tobacco production is held up as a model of unalienated labor, before the industrialization and proletarianization of modern work.[27]

Yet for a communist like Roumain, the "choral harmony" that accompanies sugar production is a valuable resource for solidarity. Manuel explains that the workers in Cuba had initially been divided along ethnic and racial lines, until they "realised we were all alike" and united in a strike. Manuel compares the strike to a clenched fist, stronger than any of its fingers: "Well that's what a strike is: a *no* uttered by a thousand voices speaking as one and falling on the desk of the boss with the force of a boulder. 'No, I tell you! No, and I mean no! No work, no harvest, not a blade of grass will be cut unless you pay us a fair price for our strength and the toil of our arms!'"[28] In contrast to both the vodou ritual and the *coumbite,* the form of collective utterance brought into being by the strike crosses national, ethnic, and racial lines in the name of proletarian solidarity. While this collectively uttered "no" is an example of an apparently intransigent refusal, the strike transforms refusal into engagement: the refusal becomes active in a negotiation, which aims to produce a political and economic change. Manuel's experience of proletarianization in Cuba as well as his immersion in the vodou culture of the Haitian peasantry, are both vital ingredients in his imagination of a retooled, modern form of the *coumbite*: "We'll call a General Assembly of the Masters of the Dew, a great big *coumbite* of farmers, and we'll clear out poverty and plant a new life," he says, in a moment of utopian speculation.[29] Vodou and work songs are transitional forms that gesture towards an internationalist genre of collective speech that—rather than emphasizing cultural specificity—asserts the unity of the international proletariat.

The tension between ethnic particularism and the possibilities of international proletarian solidarity is further explored in Roumain's posthumously published poetry collection *Bois d'ébène* (1945). The second poem, "Sales Nègres," spoken by a plural "we," powerfully tests the scope and the limits of the first-person plural as the basis of a group racial identity. Langston Hughes translated the poem in 1945 under the even more provocative title "Damned Nigger." When Hughes offered it to *Phylon,* the editors rejected it because they found it "a little too 'rough' for PHYLON and the southern area in which we have to live."[30] A more recent translation into English is perhaps a little less rough in rendering the title as "Filthy Negroes."[31] I quote from Hughes's powerful version:

Well,
it's like this
We others
The Negroes
The niggers
The damned niggers
We won't take any more
That's plain.
Finished
In Africa
And America
Being your Negroes
Your niggers
Your damned niggers.[32]

This poem raises interesting questions about the category of secondary collective speech, which I outlined in the introduction. Remember, I call moments when two or more people actually present are joined in simultaneous vocalization "primary" collective speech. Secondary collective speech happens when the choric utterance is indicated by a linguistic notation. Should first-person plural pronouns ("we," "us," "our") in a lyric poem count as such an indication? It is not completely unusual to encounter a lyric poem that speaks, as "Sales Nègres" does, consistently from the perspective of a plural "we." More commonly, we find one that is spoken mostly from the perspective of a lyric "I," but which nevertheless deploys one or more first-person plural pronouns. T. S. Eliot liked to do this in *Four Quartets*:

The only wisdom we can hope to acquire
Is the wisdom of humility: humility is endless.[33]

Presumably, in this case, the speaker of the poem is not literally joined by one or more other voices at the moment the "we" is uttered, or for the slightly more sustained period in which the speaker temporarily occupies the plural point of view of an undefined group. I have never heard *Four Quartets* read in that way. To do so would create an interesting effect by delimiting the speaking group and excluding nonspeakers from the utterance (thereby setting them free to acquire forms of wisdom other than "the wisdom of humility"). Eliot seems to be speaking singly, but—with a notable lack of humility—on behalf of the whole of humanity.

It is very common for single speakers to deploy plural pronouns to speak on behalf of some wider group, but this can seem dangerously presumptuous. Peter Womack has explored the political function of these pronouns, showing how politicians and activists have exploited ambiguities around who is included in a "we," "us" or "ours": "Saying 'we' has a performative character: it does not name a collective entity that is just extra-linguistically there in the world; rather, it *is* the act of forming such an entity, forging its necessary links and exclusions."[34] Womack's examples are not predominantly from poems, novels, or plays, and they focus on the coercive character of the way these pronouns are used in political discourse. However, Bonnie Costello argues that poets are often given greater freedom to use these pronouns: "We allow a great deal of license to the literary imagination, but in public speeches, journalism, or politics, for instance, this . . . invocation of an indeterminate 'we' can sound hollow, coercive, or presumptuous. Does the orator or writer presume to speak for me? Does 'we' have any real antecedent for an unbounded, diverse populace?"[35] Costello's own use of an indeterminate "we" in the first sentence quoted implies a tolerance for such usage that extends beyond creative writers to literary and cultural critics too. For myself, I tend to rebel against critics who claim the authority to speak on behalf of a wider group without saying who is included in, or excluded from it (though I find I sometimes do this myself, including in this book). Even when critics don't literally say "we," cultural criticism often inhabits a first-person plural perspective. As an experiment, try rephrasing the first sentence of the above quotation from Costello, without the "we." You will find that you can also invoke the plural authority of an indeterminate and unbounded group by using the passive voice: "The literary imagination is allowed a great deal of license . . ." and so on. Costello actually does this in the second half of the sentence, noting that the use of "we" "can sound" presumptuous, without attributing the perception to a particular person or group. Most uses of first-person plural pronouns, whether in poetry or not, are not collective speech acts in the full sense: they are usually moments when a single speaker speaks for or on behalf of a wider group.

The problem of the first-person plural pronoun points to what might be thought of as a latent collectivity in language itself. In the preceding analysis, and in this book as a whole, a phrase such as "from eight thousand throats rang out the royal salute of '*Koom*'" (from *King Solomon's Mines*) has been taken as a legitimate example of collective vocalization, as have the choruses in Hurston's play *Spunk*, which I encountered on the page, and which neither she nor I ever saw performed as part of that play (though—additional complication—she observed them being performed collectively in her fieldwork). Still, these are examples of *secondary* collective speech. Once one has admitted that this phenomenon exists, it soon becomes clear that there are many borderline cases where collective speech is not "really" present but is nevertheless, and to varying extents, implied.

One can easily find utterances where the spoken "we" (or "our" or "us") does name an embodied community speaking in unison. This is the case with some celebrated elements of the Anglican liturgy, including most prominently the Lord's Prayer ("Our father, who art in heaven"), which is intended for performance as primary collective speech. The Apostles' Creed is normally spoken by the whole congregation using first-person singular pronouns ("I believe in God, the Father Almighty") but in some churches "we" replaces "I" throughout. As I explore in chapter 2, communist poets in the 1930s, such as Edgell Rickword and Jack Lindsay, wrote political poems or "mass declamations" for reading at gatherings of the Popular Front. Most relevant to the present discussion of Jacques Roumain is the tradition of first-person plural protest songs, such as "We Shall Overcome," which became important in the civil rights movement. "Sales Nègres" does seem to think of itself partly in relation to this tradition and to take seriously the possibility of embodied collective utterance, in line with Roumain's assertion in an earlier essay that poetry is a "frontline weapon in the service of the people."[36]

The "we" in "Sales Nègres" contains an echo of Claude McKay's powerful sonnet, "If We Must Die," a key text of the Harlem Renaissance. As in McKay's poem, the "we" in "Sales Nègres" is not apparently indeterminate—it includes all Black people, and it excludes everybody else. In this respect it resonates with Richard Wright's *Twelve Million Black Voices: A Folk History of the Negro in the United States of America* (1941), which narrates Black history entirely from a first-person plural perspective: "We had our own civilization in Africa before we were captured and carried off to this land," writes Wright.[37] But a moment's thought reveals the porosity of the line these utterances draw around the speaking group. The white supremacist "one-drop rule," or "hypodescent," meant that "one could appear as emphatically and unambiguously white as models in a Nazi racial hygiene magazine and still not be so officially."[38] In Roumain's case, by locating the performative construction of the speakers' "we" in racial slurs—most viscerally, in Hughes's translation, the N-word—it highlights that the group is constructed and defined by racism, and not by a shared set of biological or cultural characteristics.

The subsequent arc of the poem's argument bends towards the utopian possibility of a world that is rid of racist categories, mobilizing international proletarian solidarity in that cause, while also according respect and power to the persistence of African culture in the diaspora and across the middle passage. Addressing the coming conflict by which Black liberation will be achieved, the poem's speakers say:

> until the heart of the hellish jungle
> vibrates with the quickening telegraphic
> stuttering
> of the tom-toms
> repeating tirelessly repeating
> that the Negroes
> will no longer take
> being your niggers
> your damned niggers.

Those tom-toms echo the vodou ceremonies in *Masters of the Dew* and in Roumain's ethnographic work. What is being imagined here is a collective ritual, embodied in the beating of the tom-tom, that refuses another form of collectivity, created by the imposition of racial categories. The speakers go on to imagine a dramatic expansion in the refusing group:

> . . . even the tom-toms will have learned
> the language of the international
> and we shall have chosen our day
> the day of the
> damned niggers
> of the damned Indians
> of the damned Hindus
> of the damned Indo-Chinese
> of the damned Malays
> of the damned Jews
> of the damned proletarians
> and here we are rising
> all the wretched of the earth
> all those at last in charge of justice
> marching against your barracks and your banks
> like a forest of funeral torches
> to put an end forever
> to this world
> of Negroes
> of niggers
> of damned niggers[39]

The utopian destination for Roumain is a dialectical fusion of the tribal and the international, the tom-toms learning the language of proletarian internationalism rather than being displaced by it. When Roumain evokes "the wretched of the earth," his French *damnés de la terre* is a direct quotation from "L'Internationale"—another poem, designed for collective utterance, which deploys the indeterminacy of the first-person plural to good effect: "Nous ne sommes rien soyons tout" ("We have been nothing, we will be all").[40] Drawing the European revolutionary tradition into its purview, Roumain's poem invites a form of Black Jacobinism, recalling C.L.R. James's depiction of Toussaint. "Sales Nègres" borrows from "L'Internationale" its suggestion that a massive expansion of the referential scope of the first-person plural pronoun forms a vital pretext for a social revolution. For Roumain this is explicitly extended to other exploited and racialized populations and (finally) to a proletariat that embraces all these groups. The object beyond this is "to put an end for ever / to this world / of Negroes": to do away with—to refuse—the racist categories that brought together the collective voice of the poem in the first place. The racial identity that makes the poem possible is thus figured as transitional to a politically charged, proletarian solidarity—and meanwhile, the resources of Black culture and its collective expressions (the beating of the tom-tom) is seen as essential to that transition.

Ousmane Sembène's Counterethnographies

Few have thought more powerfully about the competing varieties of collective speech than the Senegalese writer and filmmaker Ousmane Sembène. He was more skeptical of anthropology than either Hurston or Roumain, and outright hostile to what he termed "ethnology"—primarily thinking of ethnographic film—which he associated with colonial ways of seeing. In a discussion with Jean Rouch, whose films I touched on in chapter 1, Sembène challenged him on this point. Rouch argued that the value of ethnology lies in the encounter with foreignness: "Someone confronted with a culture that is foreign to him sees certain things that the people on the inside of this same culture do not see." Sembène responded: "You say seeing. But in the domain of cinema, it is not enough to see, one must analyze. I am interested in what is before and after that which we see. What I do not like about ethnography, I'm sorry to say, is that it is not enough to say that a man we see is walking; we must know where he comes from, where he is going." Sembène criticized the use of the ethnographic present, and the racializing tendency to represent social formations in terms of their synchronic structures rather than their diachronic development. Famously, Sembène reproached Rouch for seeing Africans "as insects."[41] Whereas Hurston and Roumain trained as anthropologists, and developed critical positions within that discipline, Sembène has been thought of as producing "counterethnography."[42] Jean Jonassaint defines Sembène's counterethnography as "a radical reversal, [wherein] it is not the dominant who appropriates the tools or knowledge of the dominated, but the dominated, the African, who makes the tools and knowledge of the French colonizers his own, in order to talk about himself, about his encounter with this France which becomes an object of investigation."[43] As Jonassaint also points out, ritual acts in Sembène's work rarely signal the passive observance of timeless traditional forms. Instead Sembène "makes dynamic, dialogical, dialectical use of traditions," so that rituals often seem instrumental in driving the plot to its denouement.[44]

Wanting to step outside of the relentless novelty of modernity, anthropologists sought primitive societies where things were done because "things have always been this way," and because this "was the command of the gods or the teaching of the ancestors."[45] The rituals and incantations that feature prominently in some of Sembène's most striking works are not seen as part of a static African culture whose very timelessness offers a site of resistance to French imperialism. Instead, ritual moments of collective vocalization appear as moments of rupture, challenges to vested interests, and drivers of historical change. In the terms of this book, they often express elements of fugitive sociality, but also at times move towards an engagement with the polis.

Sembène's masterpiece, *Les bouts de bois de Dieu* (1960), translated as *God's Bits of Wood* (1962), is a historical novel set during a rail strike on the Dakar-Niger line in 1947–48. The novel explores a number of overlapping genres of collective speech in highly suggestive ways. As with Roumain, the influence of Marxist ideas is palpable, and where in *Masters of the Dew* the strike was part of the protagonist's memory of his time in Cuba, here it is center stage. When the workers first come together to discuss the strike, a collective articulation echoes out around the city: "All through the hall clenched fists were raised, and voices cried out, 'Yes, we must strike! Strike!' Then, from the hall into the courtyard, and from the courtyard to the neighbouring streets there seemed to be only one voice, crying 'Strike!' Everyone wanted to present his evidence give his opinion, and the din became indescribable."[46] There is perhaps an echo here of Manuel's discussion of the strike "as a *no* uttered by a thousand voices" in *Masters of the Dew*, a novel that Sembène greatly admired.[47] As it was for Roumain, the possibility of international proletarian solidarity is clearly on Sembène's mind, and the novel produces a complex and layered view of Africa, refusing the simplistic binary of "tradition" versus "modernity" through which African fiction is often read.[48] The train line—a hugely symbolic piece of colonial infrastructure, nearly a thousand miles long—has brought the workers together in a new and previously unimaginable formation: the different indigenous groups along that line, with their various ethnic and linguistic cultures, are linked by a thousand miles of steel into a collectively speaking community that says, emphatically, "Strike!"

Where the utopian political horizon of *Masters of the Dew* is deeply rooted in peasant life and the memory of the *coumbite*, in *God's Bits of Wood* it is the machine that has the utopian potential to liberate workers from the effects of racism: "Their fellowship with the machine was deep and strong; stronger than the barriers which separated them from their employers, stronger even than the obstacle which until now had been insurmountable—the colour of their skin."[49] Yet this veneration of the machine should not be understood as a victory for a so-called Western conception of progress over African culture: the model of modernity versus tradition is too crude for this novel. One effect of the enforced idleness the strike imposes is that "ceremonies that went back to time immemorial were revived, and pageants that had been long forgotten." These revivals are deliberate, and they gain their social and political meaning from their context: "Something was being born inside them, as if the past and the future were coupling to breed a new kind of man, and it seemed to them that the wind was whispering a phrase they had often heard from Bakayoko: 'The kind of man we were is dead, and our only hope for a new life lies in the machine, which knows neither a language nor a race.' "[50] Sembène's orientation towards the future, and his rejection of static and anthropological conceptions of African culture, are intended quite polemically. As he was writing *God's Bits of Wood*, the *négritude* movement was a dominant force, especially in the decolonizing movements of the Francophone world. Sembène "distanc[ed] himself from what he saw as the cultural essentialism" of that movement.[51]

The politics of *négritude* had a particular significance in Senegal, where Léopold Senghor, one of the founders of *négritude*, had been a key figure in the anticolonial movement and served as president of the country from 1960 to 1980. Senghor represented the neo-colonial Black elite, and Sembène frequently lampooned him in his work, either explicitly or implicitly—the president's speech in *Xala* (1974) is "clearly a parody of Senghor's notion of 'African Socialism,'" and an affronted Senghor accordingly banned the film from being screened in Senegal.[52] Interviewed in 1965, Senghor described *négritude* as "the ensemble of civilizational values in the black world. Blacks have a certain way of dancing, singing, sculpting . . . laughing, crying. It's in all that, Negritude. More precisely, Negritude is characterized by certain values. In social and political customs, for example, by a certain form of democracy which is expressed in palaver. . . . But for us Negritude is essentially expressed in the field of art."[53] Senghor's conception of *négritude* thus develops a speculative anthropology of African-diasporic culture, with "rhythm" at its heart, expressed in collective singing and in dance. It echoes the arguments (discussed earlier) of Price-Mars, whom Senghor called "The Father of Negritude."[54] In Black culture, Senghor argued, "words are chants, an incantation, words used primarily for their values of rhythm and fabulation, for words are rhythmic imagery."[55] David Murphy argues that "the Negritude school of writers took on board the standard colonial depiction of the African as being a more primitive and sensual creature than the European, and used it to assert a distinctive African identity in the face of the coloniser's domination of African society"—it was, for Murphy and for Sembène, aligned with the racist assumptions of colonial anthropology.[56] Sembène also objected to the default Francophonie of *négritude*. At a time when the literacy rate in Senegal was around 20 percent, who were Senghor's French-language poems actually for? It is this that led Sembène to a deeper engagement with African languages (principally Wolof), and to making films which could potentially be watched and understood by more Africans than any written text at that time. Eventually, he described *négritude* as "the burning desire of some complex-ridden Negroes living in Europe to be accepted by Western culture."[57] He aligned it, in other words, with a quest to be *recognized* by colonial governmental institutions and their cultural counterparts. Sembène lofted a critique of what Fraser would describe as the "folk paradigm of recognition," in which "the remedy for injustice is cultural and symbolic change," including "upwardly revaluing disrespected identities and the cultural products of marginalised groups."[58]

Counter to the claims of Senghor, and to the overall project of *négritude*, there is for Sembène no collective speech form or style that is "Black." Indeed, he stated that "there are no races: yellow, black, white, none of them exists."[59] The collective articulations of his characters are therefore not rooted in some essentially African orality, but take their bearings from the specificity of the situation, while drawing on local linguistic and ritual forms. For Eileen Julien, this results in a "powerful anticolonialist fiction that moves beyond the opposition between two static moments or sets of values ('tradition' and 'modernity' or 'good' authentic ways and 'bad' alien ones)."[60] Choric utterance in Sembène draws on a deep reservoir of ritual practice, but it does so in order to highlight its emplacement and political efficacy in specific historical situations.

In *God's Bits of Wood,* as in Roumain's *Masters of the Dew,* the strike form shows how collective speech as refusal may turn towards the polis. The action of the book is distributed along nearly a thousand miles of train track, and it is a deliberately "decentered" work with no central protagonist, "casting the community, through multiple narratives, as the hero."[61] Simon Gikandi has well described Sembène's technique in this text: "The narrator has positioned himself on the wall, like a fly, and from this vantage point he can watch the people losing their individuality and metamorphosing into the mass character that plays such an important role in the novel."[62] This is not to say that there are not prominent individual characters in the novel but that they join, or enter into dialogue with, large and unified groups, underlined by the use of a variety of collective speech forms. As in many of Sembène's works, the women and their choric utterances prove particularly pivotal.

In one scene, many weeks into the strike, the union officials have a meeting in the union building in Thiès with Edouard, the personnel director who has been sent to negotiate on behalf of the rail company. As Ibrahim Bakayoko—a leader of the strike, idolized by the workers and their families—arrives at the union building, he has to make his way through "a crowd dominated by women and animated by the sound and movement of the children and the steady drumming of the tam-tams." Bakayoko is accosted by a friend in the crowd:

> But before Bakayoko could answer, the sound of voices raised in chorus interrupted him, and they both stood motionless, listening. Led by Penda and Dieynaba, the women had formed into a solid rank and were improvising words to a chant dedicated to their men:
>
> *The morning light is in the east;*
> *It is daybreak of a day of history.*
> *From Kolikoro to Dakar*
> *The smoke of the savanna dies.*
> *On the 10th of October, fateful day,*

We swore before the world
To support you to the end.
You have lit the torch of hope,
And victory is near.
The morning light is in the east;
It is daybreak of a day of history.[63]

The improvisatory character of the chant is essential to its meaning: this is a collective utterance that bubbles up spontaneously from the creative energies of the crowd, rather than something that is pre-scripted. The chant develops a ritual character as the refrain "The morning light is in the east . . ." is repeated many times during the women's march from Thiès to Dakar in support of the strike.[64] The relation of this chant, and of the strike, to traditional forms is complicated. The "tam-tams" recall musical and lyrical forms that may derive from a ritual culture that is centuries old, but the content of the chant insists that is anything but timeless: "It is daybreak of a day of history."

The opponents of the strike meanwhile persistently imply that the strike form is itself a European import. Sembène tended to view Islam as a regressive force in Africa, and here the imam says that the strikers are "just the instruments of a band of infidels who are using them for their own purposes. It is the Communists who are really directing this strike."[65] Invoking indigenous ritual practices, rather than Islamic ones, the mayor deputy says that "the strike is the work of a few black sheep, acting on the advice of foreigners, because such a way of acting is not in keeping with *our* habits or *our* customs."[66] Here, the anthropological invocation of a distinctively African or Wolof *ethnos* undermines the strike, which is motivated by socialist ideas that are dismissed as a European import. By contrast, the chant of the women of Thiès is imagined not as part of an essentially static archive of time-honored folk custom, but as a dynamic, improvisatory, and collective response to a specific historical situation.

This incantation becomes powerfully effective as the negotiation moves from the union building to the headquarters of the colonial Dakar-Niger rail company, and the crowd of women move with it. Edouard had obviously been powerless to settle the dispute, and the expanded negotiation brings in more senior executives of the company, who feel oppressed by the chanting outside: "The shouts and the singing, which seemed to have become a kind of hysterical chanting, invaded the room."[67] When Dejean opens the window to let in some air, "The singing and the beating of the drums hit him like a blast of wind," and he begs Bakayoko to make it stop.[68] Pierre (who finds himself present at the negotiation) is a young Frenchman, new to the colonies, and naively curious about their racial politics:

> Since he understood little of what they were talking about [i.e., in the negotiation], Pierre had gone back to the window and was watching the spectacle in the street. Some groups of men and women were dancing, and the young man remembered having been told at school in France that, for the Negroes, the slightest pretext was good enough as an occasion for singing and dancing. Thinking of the letter he would write to his family at home, he tried to catch some of the words to the song that came up to him from the crowd. He turned to the group of men standing around the green-covered table.
>
> "Do you understand what the women are singing? It may have something to do with the strike."
>
> "Don't be a fool," Isnard snapped. "It's just shouting and yelling, as usual. What do you think they know about the strike? They're just making noise because they like to make noise."[69]

Sembène's characters articulate quite directly the anthropological stereotype (which Pierre had been "told at school") that Black people are—as Senghor and Price-Mars had also claimed—more rhythmic and more prone to chanting than are the white French colonists. The point is not that the French colonists in *God's Bits of Wood* do an equal amount of collective chanting and drumming: they do not. In fact, Sembène commented in an interview that ritual had "practically disappeared" in Europe and that "when you lose your own rituals, you lose part of your soul."[70] Part of my purpose in this book is to show that certain rituals *do* persist as important features of modern life in Europe (alongside discussions about the decline of ritual, and programmatic attempts to revive old rituals, import them from other cultures, and invent new ones). In chapter 3, I discuss the ongoing importance of the collective speech practices of the Anglican liturgy in modern Britain. Sembène's observation is not racial essentialism but historically grounded counterethnography. It forms part of an overarching orientation which sees Africa as at "the centre of the world" and not at some periphery of modernity.[71]

In Sembène's film *Emitaï* (1971), the relationship between tribal traditions, colonial power, and political agency is explored through a remarkable constellation of collective speech forms. This historical film, set during the Second World War, was shot in French and Diola (a minority language in Senegal) on location in a remote village in the Casamance region, with an amateur cast: "The people in the movie are not actors, but people from the village," Sembène explained. His account of how he made the film is reminiscent of deep ethnographic fieldwork. He explains how "we would rehearse beginning fifteen minutes before the filming, but all the movements were free."[72]

The film concerns the capture and forcible conscription of Africans to serve in the French infantry (as so-called *tirailleurs*) during the Second World War, and the attempt of the French authorities to requisition the village's rice to feed their army. In *Emitaï* the women in the village hide the rice and refuse to hand it over, and the men are massacred because of this act of resistance. As in *God's Bits of Wood*, the protagonist of *Emitaï* is a collective rather than an individual. As Sembène explained: "This story happened to be a collective story. I wanted to show action of a well-disciplined ethnic group in which everyone saw himself only as an integral part of the whole."[73]

What we know of Sembène's working methodology suggests that the rituals that *Emitaï* commits to film are the result of a negotiation between Sembène and the villagers who still worshipped the gods in question. These gods are not brushed aside by Sembène, but neither are they protected from critique: whether or not gods and religious rituals might help to repel the whites is a divisive question debated by the film's characters. One of the village elders, Djimeko, suggests that recent events put the powers of the gods in question: "Where were the gods when the whites razed the village?" he demands. "When the whites took our sons for their war. . . . Where were our gods? . . . Where are they now?"[74] While others advocate making a sacrifice to the gods to prevent the requisition of the rice, Djimeko prefers a secular and military response: "A man lives or dies with a spear in his hand. Let he who feels himself to be a man follow me." This rallying call brings together an improvised armed unit (deprived, of course, of the young conscripts who are away fighting for France). They affirm their solidarity and common purpose with a collective chant and a battle cry.

This warlike singing is offered as an alternative to the ritualistic and religious response advocated by the other elders, but it also operates as a counterpoint to the military songs of the villagers who have been recruited into the French army. These *tirailleurs* are marched around the village early in the film, following their forcible conscription, singing "Maréchal, nous voilà," a hymn in praise of Marshal Pétain, the leader of the Nazi-collaborating Vichy puppet state. This song to some extent displaced "La Marseillaise" as the national anthem of France during the Vichy years—two rival collective utterances vying to speak for the nation.[75] The recruits sing:

> A sacred flame
> Rises from the native soil,
> And France, enraptured,
> Greets you, Marshal!
> Marshal, here we are!
> Before you, the saviour of France,
> We swear, we your guys,
> To serve and to follow in your footsteps.[76]

Sembène's use of this anthem of blood-and-soil nationalism raises questions about the claims of collective speech acts to embody an ethnic identity. The invocation of the "native soil," which clearly alludes to France itself, strikes a slightly bizarre note in the mouths of the Diola *tirailleurs* who have never been to France, and whose limited knowledge of the French language likely means they do not understand the song itself (in this early part of the film, French officers address the recruits via a translator). The use of the first-person plural here implies an ethnically homogeneous French nation that "rises from the native soil," in support of Pétain. However, the assimilationist policy of the French empire also commands colonial subjects to join the chorus and to express their identity as part of a national "we" that puts itself at the service of the "saviour of France."

Further irony is poured on this song later in the film, when posters of Maréchal Pétain have to be replaced with posters of General de Gaulle, to the embarrassment and consternation of the French officer in charge (de Gaulle became provisional governor of the French Republic in 1944 so there is a real event behind this, though in general the film playfully subverts historical accuracy).[77] A Diola corporal (recruited to the French army) objects viscerally to the sudden change and berates the sergeant: "This morning you were singing 'Maréchal, nous voila!' Now it'll be 'General, nous voila!'" This short-lived Vichy anthem claimed to root Pétain's rule in French soil, but (as the corporal's incredulous joke implies) it seems easy enough in practice to transplant in a political opponent. "Maréchal, nous voilà" represents a case where collective singing is an important technique of the disciplinary mission of empire (and as such it is an example of the hegemonic collective speech forms I discuss in chapter 3). But by exposing it as an internally contested and unstable utterance, and by positioning it within a matrix of other collective speech forms,

Sembène implies that its imperial ideology is less powerful than it may seem. What matters is force: the men with guns will decide what is sung.

To return to Djimeko's attempt to lead a military response to the grain requisition, it clearly succeeds in bringing together an improvised armed unit (deprived, of course, of the young conscripts who are away fighting for France). But their spears and arrows are no match for the French guns wielded by the *tirailleurs,* and Djimeko (along with others) is gravely wounded. The most fully realized religious ritual in *Emitaï* is staged in response to Djimeko's wounding, as a desperate plea to the gods to save the life of the man who deserted them. A chicken is sacrificed, and the elders raise a chant, performed in unison and again not translated. Sembène uses camera tricks to give the scene its supernatural quality. Jump cuts make the other elders disappear suddenly from their seats. Then—as masked gods appear to the dying Djimeko—there is a dreamlike sequence, shot with a heavy red filter, in which Djimeko revives and berates them: "Don't you see that the village is dying? What have you done for us?" he says. The gods can only say: "You no longer believe in us, you will die." And Djimeko replies: "So be it. I am a danger to you! Yes, these new times don't forgive. So, I must die. Alright, but you will die with me also." Djimeko dies, and (with another jump cut) the god disappears—perhaps now also dead, we are left to reflect. This sense of a dialogue with the gods, in which the film takes them as real but insists on making them accountable to their followers, cuts through the monologic chanted invocation which summoned them to the scene. And in general the force of Sembène's film is to move the gods from a ritual space (characterized by collective chanting) into a discursive one.

When Sembène completed the film, he returned to its location and screened it for the villagers who starred in it. For most of them, it was the first film they had seen, and "their reaction was that of children looking at themselves in a mirror for the first time." Sembène stated that "the old men . . . weren't happy with the presentation of the gods . . . the gods were still sacred and helped the old men maintain authority." For Sembène, the value of discursively questioning such authority trumps any automatic respect for the rituals of indigenous religions in themselves.

It is becoming increasingly difficult to affirm Sembène's own characterization of *Emitaï* as a depiction of "a well-disciplined ethnic group in which everyone saw himself only as an integral part of the whole."[78] Attending to the variety of collective speech forms in the film reveals a fractious and divided discursive landscape, where ritualized patterns of collective utterance are subject to almost constant challenge and put into dialogue with other collective speech forms. These challenges do not derive only (or even predominantly) from the French colonialists, who appear as an alien force: discursive debate is just as important as ritual practice in the village as Sembène depicts it, if not more so. Sembène's collective voices—even when they appear as the traditional utterance of an indigenous ethnic group—do not express a tribal cohesiveness but map tensions and divisions that are inescapably political.

The most powerful collective utterance in *Emitaï* comes when the women (who have hidden the rice and are refusing to hand it over) are gathered together by the French authorities in the center of the village. They are made to sit on the floor in the sun, some holding babies and small children. They will be forced to sit in the heat until they give up the rice. But the women start an insistent chant of refusal. I cannot translate the chant, which becomes almost overwhelming in its insistence. The sergeant—recruited by the French—yells "Keep quiet!" Eventually, the French massacre the men of the village. The force of Sembène's work is to metabolize collective-speech-as-culture (in the anthropological sense) into collective-speech-as-politics, revealing it as discourse, rather than identity. In that sense, with Roumain, Sembène forms a bridge to the second phase of my argument, in which the collective voice turns towards the polis and seeks to change it, to demand recognition, rights, and redistribution. Though steeped in African culture, Sembène does not ground the collective voice primarily in ethnic belonging. His work points to a necessary embrace of more agonistic forms of collective vocalization, in the process of turning towards the political realm.

The turn towards the polis does in Sembène's case also mean giving the collective voice a more discursive and agonistic accent then we would expect in fugitive utterances of exile and refusal. It wants something, and in a sense, it asks for it. But the collective utterances I have analyzed here are far from taking the polis on its own liberal terms. Neither are they content, in Arendtian terms, to leave the social at the door as they enter the space of politics. The approach to politics may often be discursive, but Sembène shows that it does not necessarily involve negotiating with the powers that be. His work mobilizes collective vocalizations that are thoroughly uncompromising, and that face the polis with a view to disruption, refusal, and resistance.

TWO

PROTEST/ENGAGEMENT

WHEN THE CHORUS HAS, or seeks, a voice *within* the polis, it nevertheless gains some of its power from the wild strains of refusal I have discussed in the previous chapter and the bridge. This is one of the things that is brought into view by thinking about collective vocalization positionally, and in terms of a conceptual passage into the polis from the woods outside, and then to the hegemonic heights of political power. This chapter is concerned with the second stage in that trajectory, when the chorus departs from a position of pure refusal and determines to act politically. In Bonnie Honig's argument, which is a touchstone for this book, the moment when the bacchants return to Thebes with a set of demands (at the end of Euripides's tragedy), is "fundamental to a feminist theory of refusal that aims to transform the city, not abandon it." For Honig it embodies a "normative, civic, and feminist obligation to risk the impurities of politics on behalf of transformation."[1] The intransigent refusal and the orgiastic violence of the bacchants is followed by a renegotiation of their position within the polis—and an attempt to change it.

As much as Nietzsche scorned the idea, this chapter shows how—for many writers, dramatists, and political philosophers—the collective voice provides an opportunity (or even a demand) to consider how "the people" might be represented on the stage, and in the political sphere. The Greek tragic tradition has proved an indispensable resource for thinking through this problem. Aeschylus's trilogy of tragedies *The Oresteia,* for example, positions the chorus in different relations to political power in each of its three plays. In *Agamemnon* the chorus consists of the old men of Argos, while in *The Libation Bearers* it is made up of female slaves. In the final part, *Eumenides,* the chorus are the furies themselves, apparently driven by a primal lust for revenge against Orestes. But even *Eumenides* tells the story of how the furies are, through the effective political maneuvering of Athene, effectively tamed and brought in line with the values of Argos. At the end of the play they can say (in Ted Hughes's version):

> And we bless all
> Who live in this city,
> Who love this rock,
> Who walk with the gods.
> All who fear us
> And welcome us, all
> Whose prayers are humble,
> We shall bless you.[2]

Aeschylus and Ted Hughes are both interested in how the chorus—even one constituted as a violent, socially destructive, and antipolitical force for revenge—might be brought within the polis, and even join a state-building project. Like the bacchants in Honig's reading, the furies at the end of the *Oresteia* set aside their refusal of the state, and take up a position within it.

The Chorus and the People: A Debate in Nineteenth-Century German Philosophy

The Nietzschean, Dionysiac reading of the chorus which animated the investigations of my first chapter was articulated against the background of an intellectual tradition which *did* see the chorus—albeit in various ways—as a "constitutional representation of the people."[3] The Greek chorus was an important theme for German philosophical idealism—in particular in the work of Schelling, the Schlegel brothers, and Hegel—and in turn, these German idealist debates became important for many subsequent understandings of the chorus.[4] "When we look at the chorus of Greek tragedy," Simon Goldhill writes, "we are always viewing through German-tinted spectacles."[5] Intellectual debates about the function of the chorus must then be historicized within the ferment of the age of revolutions, when "the people" seemed to enter the political stage in a new way. As Goldhill writes, "Through these political upheavals, there is a changing sense of what community, the crowd, the collective, the voice of the people, can mean, and this dynamic inevitably affects the conceptualization of the chorus."[6] Joshua Billings goes further still, arguing that from Aristotle until around 1800, discussions of the Greek chorus had essentially seen it as an individual character: only when the French Revolution unleashed its popular and democratic energies did philosophers begin to rethink the chorus as a genuinely collective entity.[7] These philosophical theorizations of the chorus constitute an important genre of secondary collective speech—the term I use for *representations* of the collective voice, as distinct from primary collective vocalization where two or more speakers are really present, synchronously saying the same words. This philosophical work is a genre which is preoccupied with the relation between "the people" and political life. Debates within the German idealist tradition were taken up by twentieth-century critics and philosophers, and they form a vital context for the story this chapter tells about the collective voice as the voice of the people.

The most influential statement of the chorus's function comes from Schlegel's *Lectures on Dramatic Art and Literature* (1809–11): "Whatever it might be and do in each particular piece, [the chorus] represented in general, first the common mind of the nation, and then the general sympathy of all mankind. In a word, the chorus is the ideal spectator."[8] The extent to which Schlegel's argument projects a modern conception of the "nation" onto Athenian tragedy (and the city-states such as Thebes and Argos in which it is set) has been highlighted by both Goldhill and Billings. It is a telling anachronism that has often been reflected in modern translations and performances. Steinbrüchel's Romantic-era translation of Sophocles's *Antigone,* for example, rendered the political language of the original in a starkly nationalist idiom. As Billings notes: "The chorus is listed in the dramatis personae as consisting of 'the senate of Thebes,' when the Greek describes them simply as a group of old men. . . . for χθονός (368: 'land, country') [Steinbrüchel] gives *Vaterland,* for ὑψίπολις (370: 'high in the city'), he translates *Patriot,* and ἄπολις (370: 'cityless') becomes 'kein Bürger mehr' ('no longer a citizen'). Where Sophocles' chorus speaks quite generally of belonging to a *polis,* Steinbrüchel's describes citizenship in the *Vaterland,* emphasizing patriotic duty."[9] Reflecting on the translation of ancient languages into modern, one often has to acknowledge the basic incongruity between premodern concepts and categories, and their modern equivalents. We use modern ideas—"the nation"—as a lens through which to view alien concepts such as the polis. My use of the idea of the polis in this book works the other way. Viewing the modern nation-state through the lens of the polis is a defamiliarizing anachronism that highlights what is distinctive about the nation-state as a mode of political organization. Steinbrüchel's alignment of the chorus with national consciousness seems jarring in some respects, but it also illustrates the extent to which nationalism had, in the nineteenth century, become naturalized as a normal way of thinking about the relationship between culture and political power.

This idea that the chorus speaks as a "voice of the people," where "the people" is understood in national terms, seems at odds with the positioning of many tragic choruses in the Greek canon: Euripides's bacchants or Aeschylus's furies appear violently oppositional, even if the plays are interested in how they might, in the course of the tragic action, be reincorporated into the polis. Schlegel's argument is obviously flawed as a generalization about the Greek chorus, but then so is Nietzsche's counterargument: I am interested in these claims not because I suspect any of them might be true, or even particularly illuminating for a reading of the plays, but because they are powerful examples of secondary collective vocalization that index important historical shifts in the ways that collective political action has been imagined. Schlegel's was an inaugurating statement in a critical and political tradition that many of the choruses discussed in this book still inhabit.

In Schiller's introduction to *The Bride of Messina* (1803) (the play in which he reintroduced the chorus on the German stage), he complained that while the chorus was a powerfully effective feature of Greek drama, in touch with collective life, its function in modern drama had been delegated to an individual character. He condemns the "dissolution of the chorus and the conflation of this sensitive and powerful organ with the characterless, boring, and ever recurring figure of a simple confidant."[10] Though the immediate target of Schiller's critique is recent French drama, he also implicitly rejects, first, the Aristotelian reading of the tragic chorus as a character and, second, a tendency to understand individual characters in modern drama as performing the chorus function from an individual rather than a collective standpoint. The fool in Shakespeare's *King Lear*—called an "admirable chorus" by L. C. Knights, and considered as such by many subsequent critics—is perhaps the classic example: the collective chorus is sublimated in the voice of an asocial and deracinated individual whose nuggets of wisdom are interspersed with mockery and irony.[11] Against the individualistic tendency of such drama, and in the wake of the French and American Revolutions, Schiller sought to bring a genuinely collective chorus back on stage.

Around the same time, Friedrich Hölderlin was working on new translations of Sophocles, whom he described as "the poet of revolution."[12] In the notoriously cryptic notes that accompany his translations of *King Oedipus* and *Antigone* (brilliantly explicated by Billings), Hölderlin set out a new theory of tragedy which "begins with an individual act so extreme that it causes a shift in the relation of man and god, which initiates a larger social transition."[13] Within this scheme, Hölderlin emphasizes the role of the chorus as the "antithesis" of the "dialogic form."[14] The politically important dialectical relationship in *Antigone* is not therefore to be located *within* the dialogue between Creon and Antigone. Rather, the opposition is between "the constant to and fro of the dialogue" on the one hand and "the chorus as its antithesis."[15] The cool detachment and apparent objectivity of Sophocles's chorus is a long way from Honig's more Dionysiac conception of the "revolutionary chorus." The very fact that the chorus can contain, and treat with a degree of even-handedness, the opposed viewpoints of Creon and Antigone signals for Hölderlin a shift of the entire discursive underpinning of Theban society, opening the way for Athenian democracy. Thus, the "impartiality with which the chorus observed the claims of Antigone and Creon became the reigning social principle, spelling the end of the ruler's absolute power." Sophoclean tragedy therefore works as the "representation of a comprehensive societal transformation, which is mediated by the chorus."[16] The revival of this most ancient of dramatic devices became the aesthetic means by which social change from below could be encapsulated in narrative form.

While many commentators have been baffled by Hölderlin's version of *Antigone*—Billings really seems to be the first to make lucid sense of it—Georg Wilhelm Friedrich Hegel (whose thought about the chorus is also parsed by Billings) did engage meaningfully with it, coming to quite different conclusions. Hegel associated the chorus with an ancient and essentially static polytheism: "It is the common people per se whose wisdom finds utterance in the *chorus of the elders,* and it is in the powerlessness of the chorus that the common people find their representatives, because they themselves constitute only the positive and passive material for the individuality of the government confronting them."[17] For Hegel, the chorus does represent the people, but as an essentially conservative force: its wisdom is purely customary. The chorus acted as a dead weight of inherited know-how that needed to be cleared out of the way to allow for the progressive unfolding of the more reflective and individual relationship to ethical life that was embodied in the dialogue of tragedy's principal characters.

A key inheritor of these debates, and a figure who had an enormous influence on Nietzsche's *Birth of Tragedy,* as well as on key twentieth-century discussions of the chorus, is Richard Wagner. Wagner's trio of Romantic operas, *The Flying Dutchman* (1843), *Tannhäuser* (1845), and *Lohengrin* (1850), all made extensive use of the chorus. The chorus in *Lohengrin,* for example, acts as the people of Brabant, in a way that seems a self-conscious contribution to the debates about the function of the chorus that had animated German idealist philosophy, as well as manifesting Wagner's fascination with ancient Greek tragedy. Act 1 stages a *Gottesgericht* (trial by combat), after Friedrich von Telramund has accused Elsa of murdering her brother Gottfried. The chorus is initially unwavering in its support for Telramund: when he asks "Who of you / dares fight against my honour?" the Brabantians reply, "None of us! We will only fight for you!" But when Lohengrin comes to the rescue of Elsa, arriving on a swan to be her champion, the hundred-strong chorus greets his arrival by singing "Ein Wunder ist gekommen" and "Gegrüßt du gottgesandter Held!" Lohengrin himself—who has been seen as a "populist figure" and a "manmade idol"—proves capable, through sheer charismatic magnetism, of bringing the swelling chorus of Brabantians under his sway.[18]

As in Hölderlin's reading of *Antigone*'s revolutionary chorus, the dramatic action of *Lohengrin* drives a historical *movement* of the people, who are (at the end of the piece when Lohengrin departs the scene) ready to accept Gottfried—miraculously reincarnated apparently at Lohengrin's request—as their leader. *Lohengrin* shows how the collective speech of "the people" can both reflect and underpin revolutionary change, and in doing so, it highlights the power of charismatic authority, which would develop populist and authoritarian meanings in the twentieth century. This fact has not been lost on the opera's directors: in David Alden's 2018 production at the Royal Opera House, costumes and flags gestured blatantly to the Third Reich; in Kornél Mundruczó's 2022 production at the Bayerische Staatsoper, the word "Führer"—with which the chorus hails Gottfried in Wagner's libretto—was replaced with "Beschützer" ("protector" or "guardian"). The first collapsed the nationalist aspirations of the 1848 revolutions into the genocidal horrors of Nazism, while the second crossed out the inescapably Hitlerian associations of the word "Führer," suppressing and thereby drawing attention to them.

Lohengrin is the last of the operas that Wagner composed in the German Romantic style, and it was composed in Dresden in 1846–48. Tim Blanning has linked the nationalism that is explored in the opera with Wagner's turn towards republicanism, which culminated in his involvement in the Dresden uprising in May 1849. Wagner played his part in the revolution and was accused of "being one of the leaders and, more specifically, of holding meetings at his home to plan the insurrection; of ordering the manufacture of hand-grenades; of manning an observation-post on the tower of the Church of the Cross (Kreuzkirche); and of raising support in the countryside around Dresden."[19] The libretto for *The Ring of the Nibelung* was drafted in 1848 (with the music composed over the following decades and its first full performance in 1876), and *The Ring* has often been thought of as the most revolutionary of Wagner's work.[20] However, as Blanning argues, *The Ring* was not "informed by a nationalist perspective" in the way that *Lohengrin* was.[21] In Wagner's post-*Lohengrin* operas, he continued to experiment with large choruses, as in *Die Meistersinger von Nürnberg* (1868) and *Parsifal* (1882), as well as with a more attenuated or displaced chorus function in *The Ring*. Wagner was also preoccupied with the device in his theoretical work.

Opera and Drama (1851), for example, is more skeptical of the idea of the chorus as the "voice of the people" than a first encounter with *Lohengrin* might lead one to believe. Wagner was particularly scathing about the operatic choruses deployed by his contemporaries (especially in the French opera and by his erstwhile champion Giacomo Meyerbeer). He saw these choruses as facile shadows of the people: "They did not want the people, but the mass; or, in other words, the material residue of the people, after their life-spirit had been extracted. The massive chorus of our modern opera is nothing else than the scene-machinery of the theatre, trained to march and sing: the dumb glitter of the coulisse [a flat piece of scenery], transformed into noisy motion." One should not ignore the fact that Wagner's rejection of these operas was profoundly entangled with his Francophobia and antisemitism. Racism tinged his need to distinguish his own art from these contemporaries, who he thought had converted the Greek chorus's living and dynamic figuration of "the people" into a "mass": a static and flat background that merely framed the meaningful words and actions on which the soloists held a monopoly. This operatic chorus is dumbly subservient, "a mass drilled to march, hither and thither, in accordance with the beat of the opera aria."[22] *Lohengrin*'s chorus is deliberately more than that: not only does it shift in position (from an identification with Telramund, to Lohengrin, to Gottfried) in ways that suggest the dynamic political evolution of the social world, it also splits itself up in various ways. The men and women sometimes sing separately and contrastingly, and at certain points the nobles seem to split away from the people, displaying residual loyalty to Telramund even when Lohengrin is in the ascendancy. These complex social dynamics of the chorus have a musical analogue. Thomas S. Grey points out that, in the scene in which Lohengrin first enters, "an eight-part chorus gradually coalesces out of fragmentary ejaculations of wonder and surprise, emerging into regular block-chordal homophony only when the hero's peculiar vessel reaches the shore."[23] The chorus in *Lohengrin* regularly sings in seven part harmony (SSATTBB), marking significant internal differentiation of voices within an overall harmonic pattern.[24] Grey suggests that this aligns with Wagner's call (in *Opera in Drama*) for "a new treatment of the chorus as a collection of individuals rather than as a homogeneous harmonic backdrop."[25]

Wagner seems to have grappled, then, with two choruses: first, the Greek tragic chorus which he venerated but that belonged irredeemably to the ancient world; and, second, the wooden contemporary operatic chorus that presented the people as an undifferentiated mass. This complex position accounts for Wagner's simultaneous and contradictory quests both to abolish the chorus and to raise it to new heights.[26] Some of his thinking seems to be directed toward a question something like, What would a modern *equivalent* of the Greek chorus look like? Shakespeare pointed the way: "The tragedy of Shakespeare stands incontestably above that of the Greeks," Wagner wrote, precisely because "it has succeeded in dispensing with the necessity of the chorus." Shakespeare had instead managed to embody "the people" on the stage "by means of sheer personal participation in the action on the part of subordinate characters."[27] In *The Ring*, Wagner went further, and sought to shift the chorus function to the orchestra, rather than any singers. His wife Cosima reported in her diary that Wagner described Siegfried's death march in these terms: "'I have composed a Greek chorus,' R. exclaims to me in the morning, 'but a chorus which will be sung, so to speak, by the orchestra.'"[28] In the design of the *Festspeilhaus* at Bayreuth, Wagner specified that the orchestra was to be hidden from the audience's sight, so that the chorus function, now etherealized in the music itself, would seem to emerge from a "mystic abyss."[29]

Wagner's work is a signal contribution to the tradition of thinking about the chorus that I have described. It brought together a reckoning with the idealist tradition of philosophy about the chorus, an engagement with revolutionary politics, and a conscious artistic experimentation with the possibilities of collective vocalization, which built on these engagements. His work provided models—both positive and negative—for the generations that would follow him.

Chorus and Assembly

These German debates form the vital pretext for the various ways in which the twentieth century imagined the chorus—or the collectively speaking group—as representative of the people. In the sphere of literary theory, the basic coordinates of the debate had been set, and leftist critics often used the arguments I have sketched above as a springboard, asking similar questions: Where had the chorus gone? Did it imagine "the people" as a static and unchanging bloc, or could it accommodate the possibilities of individual agency, social division, and political change? Could it be revived? If not, could there be a modern equivalent?

Perhaps the most important and influential twentieth-century inheritor of this debate was Georg Lukács. He argued in *The Historical Novel* (1937) that, despite the aesthetic failure of *The Bride of Messina*, "Schiller sensed, very rightly, that the presence of the chorus in Greek tragedy sprang spontaneously out of the social-historical conditions of Greek life, and that the key question for the modern dramatist was to portray all events in such a way, to raise all manifestations of life to such a level that they could sustain the presence of the chorus."[30] For Lukács, the various attempts to solve this problem only showed "how difficult it is to portray life publicly in modern drama."[31] Modern dramatists, including Shakespeare and Pushkin, had echoed elements of the chorus function by using crowd scenes, but there was a fundamental difference: "The classical chorus is omnipresent, while the crowd scenes are no more than isolated factors of the drama. The most important scenes between the protagonists often take place in the absence of these witnesses."[32] Because of its omnipresence as Lukács argued in *The Theory of the Novel* (1920), "the chorus was able to provide a background which closes the work in the same way as the marble atmospheric space between figures in a relief closes the frieze, yet the background of the chorus is also full of movement and can adapt itself to all the apparent fluctuations of a dramatic action not born of any abstract scheme, can absorb these into itself and, having enriched them with its own substance, can return them to the drama."[33] The powerful crowd scenes in *Coriolanus*, *Julius Caesar*, and so forth cannot claim to produce this effect, and Lukács would see this as symptomatic of a fundamentally distinct modern relationship between the individual hero (or ruler) and the people.

When the plebeians speak in unison in *Julius Caesar*, for example, this form of collective speech is distinct in type from the Greek chorus as Lukács saw it, and arguably recognizably modern. This can be illustrated in the famous scene when Brutus and Mark Antony compete in oratory to sway the people of Rome, Brutus arguing that killing Caesar was justified in the national interest, Antony that it was cold-blooded treason. After outlining his self-justification, Brutus tries to bring the plebeians onside with coercive rhetoric:

> BRUTUS: . . . Who here is so base that would be a bondman? If any, speak, for him have I offended. Who here is so rude that would not be a Roman? If any, speak, for him have I offended. Who here is so vile that will not love his country? If any, speak, for him have I offended. I pause for a reply.
>
> ALL THE PLEBEIANS: None, Brutus, none.[34]

To disagree with Brutus's arguments, and to break away from the collectively speaking mass, one would have to own up to being "rude," "vile," or "base." They are urged to speak only if they fall into one of these categories, and Brutus orchestrates when they can speak, too, emphasizing his decision to "pause for a reply." More than engaging in a debate, they are being asked to tick a verbal box. The plebeians initially ride the wave of this rhetoric, and when Brutus says, "I slew my best lover for the good of Rome. I have the same dagger for myself when it shall please my country to need my death," they say in unison, "Live, Brutus, live, live!"[35] After hearing Mark Antony's more gently persuasive "Friends, Romans, countrymen" speech, the plebeians pivot a full 180 degrees, proclaiming in unison "We'll mutiny" (i.e., against Brutus's rule).[36] The moment when Antony tells them that Caesar has bequeathed every man in Rome seventy-five drachmas seems to be particularly decisive in consolidating the crowd's new position.[37] When this crowd pivots, it is different from the gradual shift in the discursive ground that Hölderlin sees in the "revolutionary" chorus in *Antigone,* or the deliberately polyvocal evolution of the Brabantians' position in Wagner's *Lohengrin.* For Lukács, "speaker and chorus in Greek tragedy are of the same fundamental essence, they are completely homogeneous with one another."[38] *Julius Caesar,* by contrast, relies on a total separation between the elite—the people who make the persuasive speeches—and the mass of plebeians, which moves as an undifferentiated bloc, and speaks only to express approval or disapproval of those speeches.

Of course, on the horizon of Lukács's argument is the realist novel: in a conjuncture in which the theatrical chorus can no longer hold everything together, the expansive canvas of the historical novel is best suited to representing the social totality. The modern novel must find ways to embed the collective voice in sublimated, secondary ways. As with Lear's fool onstage, the chorus function in a novel may be carried by an individual character in the novel form: a "chorus character" or "spokesman."[39] But in a more radical formal innovation, the omniscient narrator may perform something like the "omnipresent" function Lukács describes. Lukács's later critiques of Beckett and Kafka were on account of their failure to achieve this, and their tendency to emphasize the alienated perspective of the deracinated individual. Subsequent Marxist reappraisals of modernist fiction have often answered Lukács by claiming to find the collective voice buried in the texts in a heavily mediated and even sublimated form.[40]

For many modern writers, the chorus represents everything that we are not, and as such, it is a corrective for the individualism of modern politics, society, and art. Raymond Williams, for example, felt that "the modern system . . . misinterprets the plays" by mistakenly assuming that "the mainspring of the action is . . . the isolation of [the] hero":

> uniquely, this is a choral tragedy. The specific and varying relations between chorus and actors are its true dramatic relations. . . . The known history is enacted by the three masked actors, who have separated out from the chorus but, as their sharing of roles and their formal relations with the chorus make clear, not separated out altogether. What the form then embodies is not an isolable metaphysical stance, rooted in individual experience, but a shared and indeed collective experience. . . . It is no accident that as this unique culture changed, the chorus was the crucial element of dramatic form which was weakened and eventually discarded. The structure of feeling which, in the great period, had developed and sustained it as the dramatised tension and resolution of collective and individual experience, weakened and was lost, and with it a unique meaning of tragedy.[41]

More than an artistic effect, the chorus was, for Williams, a significant social institution that mediated effectively between the individual and the collective in the "unique culture" of fifth-century Athens. "We," Williams writes, "think of tragedy as what happens to the hero." But "when we confine our attention to the hero, we are unconsciously confining ourselves to one kind of experience which in our own culture we tend to take as the whole." Where modern tragedies can "end with the destruction of the hero," in Greek tragedy this (inevitable) death is followed by a "new distribution of forces, physical or spiritual. . . .

This is ordinarily a religious affirmation, but in the words or presence of the chorus, which is then the ground of its social continuity."[42] Where modern tragedy is individualistic in figuring the demise of the hero as final, Greek drama offers to reabsorb the tensions of the play into a choral harmony that precedes them and outlives them. One can think of many plays (ancient and modern) that will not fit into Williams's narrative, but his account stands as a distinctive imaginative projection about an ancient form of collective speech that underpinned "collective experience" and "social continuity."

Williams places the chorus at the center of collective social experience, as a way of imagining a less individualistic way of life. The idea of the chorus as the people speaking in unison has been taken in more stridently nationalistic directions. In modern times, as Butler noted, and as I discussed in the introduction, "to imagine every member of the group called 'the people' coming together and speaking in unison" represents a "terrifying" nationalist fantasy.[43] But Butler's work on assembly asserts the possibility of smaller-scale choral manifestations, below the scale of the nation, that have a protesting and engaged relation to the polis.

The political meanings as well as the affective dimensions of taking part in such a protest are insightfully discussed by Eve Kosofsky Sedgwick in *Touching Feeling* (2002). Sedgwick describes a protest she attended in the summer of 1991, "organised by an Ad Hoc Coalition of Black Lesbians and Gays." The immediate pretext for the protest is that the local PBS station had refused to air Marlon Riggs's film of Black queerness, *Tongues United*—and the wider context was "a fight about blackness, queerness, and (implicitly) AIDS: properties of bodies, some of them our bodies, of bodies that it seemed important to say most people are very willing, and some people murderously eager, to see not exist." Like Butler, Sedgwick draws on speech act theory to theorize the performative function of assembly. While the protesters chant slogans—"'We're here, we're queer, and we won't pledge this year'; or better, 'Snap! Snap! Snap! What is this racist crap?'"—Sedgwick wants to show that, beyond their semantic content, the performative function of these collective speech acts is to claim and to manifest a stake within the polis: "Performatively, our object was not merely to demand representation, representation elsewhere, but ourselves to give, to be representation: somehow to smuggle onto the prohibitive airwaves some version of the apparently unrepresentably dangerous and endangered conjunction, queer and black."[44] Part of the meaning of the assembly—perhaps the most significant part—is to assert the presence of a group which had been silenced and excluded from any definition of the people. In both demanding representation and being an instance of representation, these speech acts operate in a doubled way. They respond self-consciously to "an internal shimmer that affects words like *act* or *perform*." As Steven Connor elaborates, "Acting means both doing something for real and pretending to do it, just as performing a duty means both really doing it and putting on a performance."[45] In looking at collective vocalizations that seek to take up a position within the polis, this chapter reckons with speech forms that combine representation and embodiment: they achieve their democratic effects by *being* the thing that they represent.

Mass Declamation: Jack Lindsay, Jane Harrison, and the Choric Voice

Choruses that act like one of Butler's assemblies—sometimes metonymically as the people as a whole, but in practice as a distinct grouping, claiming a form of popular legitimacy and demanding recognition and political change—can readily be found in the Greek dramatic tradition. Aristophanes's comedy *Lysistrata,* for example, has a split chorus, with the men and women of Thebes at odds with one another. The women are on a sex strike, refusing to sleep with their husbands until the men call off the seemingly interminable Peloponnesian War. As I argued in the first bridge, with reference to Roumain and Sembène, the strike is an act of refusal, but it is also transitional to political engagement, a way of making demands on bosses and political leaders, and negotiating with them. *Lysistrata* imagines the political sphere as an agonistic realm in which opposing groups and opposing interests come into conflict. This vision of politics is achieved partly by empowering a group traditionally excluded from political life—women—and giving them a collective voice.

The sense that collective speech played an important role in political dissent or protest was shared by Jack Lindsay, the Australian poet, classicist, translator, dramatist, and scholar, who arrived in England in 1926 with his new translation of *Lysistrata,* seeking to make his way on the literary scene, and establishing Franfolico Press in Bloomsbury Square. Becoming radicalized in the mid-1930s, Lindsay joined the Communist Party of Great Britain (CPGB), and became a leading intellectual in a group whose abiding interest was the Greek and Roman classics—a subject now too easily associated with class privilege, and with the education of Boris Johnson, but which was a major fascination of the mid-century British left.[46] Lindsay was the author of over 150 books on a remarkably wide range of subjects, and was a key intellectual figure in the British far left, with a significant strand of his work dedicated to the historical understanding and modern revival of collective speech.[47] As a translator of ancient Greek drama, he grappled with questions about the significance of the chorus and how it might be performed. As an intellectual with a historical and anthropological interest in the development of culture, in "fertility-ritual, . . . the passage-rites of initiation . . . tribal society itself," he was fixated on the relationship between art and ritual.[48] And in the British Popular Front in the 1930s, he mobilized these ideas in a new form of engaged political and dramatic poetry, which he called mass declamation. As the name implies, this was a poetry designed to be spoken by many voices. As Colin Chambers has put it, Lindsay saw this as "a way of bridging the gap that had arisen under capitalism between the spoken word and poetry and between art and the people."[49]

Early experiments in the form participated in the Popular Front's national turn, celebrated English radical traditions, and placed an "emphasis on the nation as the legitimate locus of revolutionary struggle."[50] But mass declamation had a significant internationalist dimension and came to life within the popular movement around the Spanish Civil War. Lindsay's friend the poet Randall Swingler wrote a mass declamation called *Spain,* which opened at the Unity Theatre on 13 November 1936. In a review of that production (on whose opening night "the chorus had to read from a script") Derek Khan noted: "The language has force and grace, the narrative flows rhythmically, and there can be no doubt of the emotion, with which the whole work is fused, taking its dramatic effect. It is not, in the literary sense, an ambitious construction, and perhaps for that very reason is successful—since ambitious lyricism often deprives a poet of theatrical sense."[51] Kahn's review suggests that mass declamation was not simply a performance strategy that could be applied to any poem. It was a new verbal art form whose most successful expressions were likely to appear crude, if they were viewed from the perspective of established literary taste. But that would be to view them from the wrong perspective. Mass declamation was at its most "effective" when it was most itself: politically strident, didactic, eschewing nuance, almost embarrassingly direct. It was a poetry tailored to an era and a conflict in which poets were enjoined to set aside the delicate poise of the aesthete, in order to "take sides."[52]

The Spanish Civil War also provided the occasion for the most successful, widely performed, and frequently discussed of the mass declamations, Lindsay's *On Guard for Spain* (1937). Written in defense of the Spanish Republic at the moment of crisis when Franco's fascists were gaining ground, *On Guard* was "first performed at a rally in Trafalgar Square in 1937 and subsequently on a great many occasions throughout Britain by the amateur Unity, Left Book Club and other political theatre groups."[53] The poem "rhetorically binds popular struggles in Britain to the anti-fascist struggle in Spain," as Elinor Taylor argues.[54] In the genuinely widespread agitation and political organization in response to the Spanish Civil War, mass declamation took its place as a strikingly new form of poetry that claimed to be a collective response to the excessive individualism of bourgeois poetry and capitalist society.

Lindsay's mass declamations seemed to be written (and in some cases they were published) without any indications about how they were to be performed. The version of *On Guard* printed in *The Left Review* was set simply as a poem, without stage directions or indications about who was speaking different parts, with the subheading "A Poem for Mass Recitation." This published text was used as the basis for performances around the country in which different lines (and longer passages) were allocated to individuals, to subgroups speaking in unison, or to the whole chorus. The typescript copy among the papers of the Bristol Unity Players' Club, which performed *On Guard* in 1938, shows the poem divided into many parts, creating an interplay between individual voices, small groups, and "All."[55] Sections of the poem were spoken by twelve distinct voices: a male narrator, a woman narrator, a Spanish woman, a Spanish man, and voices numbered 1 through 8. These parts sometimes spoke as "All," and sometimes in various combinations: male narrator and woman narrator together, "all men" and "all women," and various other pairings.

That contrast between the written, typed, or printed text of the poem and the live performance must have been palpable for Lindsay, too. During the 1930s, he was living an itinerant and impoverished life in Devon and Cornwall, far from the main performance locations of the mass declamations. Indeed, he wrote later: "On account of my remoteness I never saw a performance of any of the poems." Lindsay must have been sending his poems to the Left Book Club Theatre Guild for printing, to various Unity Theatre groups for performance, or to *The Left Review* for wider publication. Lindsay had diagnosed a fatal rift that had opened up between poet and audience, and to heal that rift, "devised the most active form of writing," as he put it, "the only one that went into direct action."[56] Yet he would never stand among that audience and experience his mass declamations first hand. The most deliberate and intentional form of primary collective vocalization discussed in this book—devised explicitly to overcome the individualism Lindsay saw in lyric poetry—left the desk of its creator as a silent, second-order representation of collective speech: collective vocalization by post.

To look at the production script rather than *The Left Review* version is to see the poem in quite a different light. The performance opened like this:

> Male Narrator: What you shall hear is the tale of the Spanish people.
> Woman Narrator: It is also your own life.
> M.N. & W.N.: On guard we cry!
> All: It is the pattern of the world today. . . .
> Spanish Woman: I speak for the Spanish people.
> Spanish Man: I speak for the Spanish people to the workers of the world.
> W.N.: Man and woman, come out of the numbered cells of
> harsh privation mockingly called your homes,
> M.N.: break through the deadening screen with your clenched fists,
> unrope the bells that jangle in the steeple of the sky,
> W.N.: make the least gap of silence in the wall of day (pause)
> All: And you will hear the guns in Spain.[57]

It is hard to say that the separate voices act as individuated characters, but having the line "I speak for the Spanish people" spoken by a "Spanish Woman" implies that some of these voices will bring distinctive subjective perspectives—they do not all know the same things, and they report on distinctive experiences. The narrators make it clear that the function of the declamation is to hear the "tale of the Spanish people" and the two Spanish voices promise to speak "for the Spanish people." But the narrators' framing also insists (to the English audience), "It is also your own life." The group assert in unison that the Spanish experience reveals an underlying "pattern of the world today"—the Spanish experience is meant to be a key, providing something more than a parallel with the British experience: "the voice of the people crying to the people," as Swingler's mass declamation put it.[58]

Built into the performance contexts and perhaps the form of mass declamation was the idea of an audience that was already receptive to the political message. The focus was not primarily on converting people with different views, but nor is this just preaching to the converted: "The most fruitful result of *On Guard,* and this may have a bearing on socialist theatre in general, was to galvanise those who were nominally members of a movement, nominally supporters of a cause, but who had to be drawn into concrete activity."[59] As

Lindsay put it himself, the mass declamations "could only appear effectively when there was a large number of people strongly sharing certain ideas which related to an urgent situation." He went on to ask: "Is one then preaching to the converted? I do not think that is a relevant point. One is playing one's part in compacting the unity of the mass-group, and the virtue of the work lies in the degree of validity in the emotions stirring that group and the force of the form which one achieves in the dynamic interplay between poet-spokesman and actively responding group."[60] Not converting sceptics but "compacting the unity of the mass-group"; like the protest Sedgwick described in *Touching Feeling*, there is an autotelic performative dimension to *On Guard*. Part of the function of the collective speech is to constitute the group, taking their shared political alignment as a precondition for the collective utterance rather than an effect of it.

Jack Lindsay's essay "A Plea for Mass Declamation," published in *Left Review* in 1937, has been seen as a "manifesto for the form," but readers could be forgiven for feeling that its central policy recommendations were vague.[61] As manifestos go, it is somewhat weighed down by the burden of its literary-historical argument, which aims to show in seven pages how poetry—from Homer to Byron via Petronius, the Troubadours and Elizabethan lyric—developed from a collective into an individual art. "Only when capitalism started to come into its own was there driven a wedge between poetry and the speaking voice," Lindsay claimed, which was also a "wedge driven between consumer and producer."[62] In a line of argument that notably prefigures those of post-war theorists of oral culture—from Claude Lévi-Strauss to Marshall McLuhan, Walter Ong and Elizabeth Eisenstein—Lindsay posits that the rise of print had helped to erode oral poetry:

> The invention of printing, of course, had much to do with the deflection of poetry from the living voice. But printing did not arise in a social void. It was part of the whole process of capitalism. As a spreader of knowledge, it had a concrete good-effect; as a part of the capitalist forces, it intensified the forms of abstraction arising from bourgeois individualism. To analyse the way that these two aspects of the printed book—its uniting and its dividing powers—operated, we would need to go into much detail. It is enough here to note how the book helped the severing of poetry from its communal basis.[63]

This story about how modern individualism is mirrored in its poetry—not only in the attitudes of poets, but in poetry's characteristic forms, and the social organization of its production, distribution and consumption—is the vital pretext for the emergence of mass declamation. "Here, then, I make my pleas for Declamation, Mass-recitation, as the initial and primary form of our new poetry," Lindsay went on. "For there we get the most direct contact with the new audience."[64] As Colin Chambers put it, mass declamation offered to its advocates "a way of bridging the gap that had arisen under capitalism between the spoken word and poetry and between art and the people."[65] It offered a means of "overcoming the barriers which had been erected between poetry and its audience."[66]

In this context, the term "mass" does not have the deadening implication it did for Wagner, as he applied it to contemporary operatic choruses, or for Cavarero in her distinction between the "voice of the masses" and the "voice of the plurality."[67] As Wagner sought to put on stage a chorus that represented a dynamically polyphonic collectively speaking "people" (in contrast to the "mass"), his operas also actively silenced the audience, who were discouraged (and still are) from applauding arias or any other spectacular vocal feat, as they did (and still do) in the Italian opera. Wagner's audience must hold their cheers for the end of each act. This was implied by the shift from an opera of "numbers," a drama punctuated by songs, to Wagner's conception of a "through composed" piece of continuous musical drama. By contrast, like many of his 1930s contemporaries, Lindsay embraced the term "mass," shouldering its usually negative associations in the hope of blurring the borders between the collective vocalizations of the chorus and those of a potentially more active audience. Wagner's idealized representation of the people on stage becomes a more informal, embodied assembly.

Lindsay's "manifesto," and indeed mass declamation itself, is only really comprehensible within his intellectual milieu, where arguments about the collective origins of poetry circulated widely. Lindsay and Swingler were important figures in an interwar Popular Front culture whose contours have been described by scholars such as John Connor, Andy Croft, Ben Harker, Elinor Taylor, and Glyn Salton-Cox, and whose intellectual project resonated throughout the war, into the post-war years and, after 1956, filtered into the cultural politics of the New Left.[68] The diagnosis that poetry had lost touch with its collective origins and consequently with "the people" was widely shared by communist intellectuals such as Alan Bush, Christopher Caudwell, A. L. Lloyd, Edgell Rickword, and George Thomson (as well as Lindsay and Swingler). It was promoted in books like Caudwell's *Illusion and Reality: A*

Study of the Sources of Poetry (1937) and Thomson's *Marxism and Poetry* (1945), as well as periodicals like *Left Review* (1934–38), *Poetry and the People* (1938–40), and *Our Time* (1941–1949), all of which were edited at times by Swingler, and which included various contributions from the figures I have named and their wider circle.[69]

Central to their cultural mission was a desire to reconnect poetry with song. Alongside short cultural manifestoes, reviews, political commentaries and so forth, *Poetry and the People* published poems for group singing, mostly sent in by proletarian readers. A "Song for a Choir of Agricultural Workers to Sing at Covent Garden" reworked a popular hymn to give it a radical message:

> We plough the seeds and scatter the good seed for a job,
> And we receive in wages a lousy thirty bob.
> The men who run the markets reap profits from the seeds,
> And we get thirty shillings to satisfy our needs.

The song—which, if it was ever performed in the proposed location, would have seemed quite confrontational—channeled its anger at exploitation into an imagined agrarian revolt, concluding:

> All good things around us that from our labours grow
> Will harvest no more profits for them that do not sow.[70]

The attempt to generate a proletarian solidarity through collective vocalization was shared with Mass Declamation, only here it was grounded in a reinvigorated folk music, set in a conventional meter and sung to the tune of the well-known hymn "We plough the fields."

That such concerted attempts to revive an oral poetry of communal declamation and singing should be underpinned by print culture was an irony that echoed the dynamics of the late-Victorian boom in socialist song. As Elizabeth Miller showed in that context, the attempt to stimulate a radical and collective oral culture had the supposedly individualizing medium of print at its core: it was "not so much a rejection of print media in favor of oral media but an attempt to merge print and orality, to create a path from print to live public," she writes.[71] These printed traces—like Jack Lindsay's mailed-in mass declamation scripts—are exactly what I mean by secondary collective vocalization. These are printed, literary productions that seek to escape the page, to activate poetry's latent collectivity.

While some of those involved in the second folk revival were predominantly interested in a precapitalist agrarianism that was deeply English,

Lindsay's version of the argument for recollectivizing poetry was steeped in classical learning. He had been particularly influenced by the work of the classicist and anthropologist Jane Harrison—and via this route, the British left grappled with the legacy of evolutionist anthropology (which saw "primitive" cultures from every corner of the globe as representatives of a universal earlier stage of cultural development, and which was critiqued by Franz Boas and later by functionalist anthropologists). In his 1962 book *A Short History of Culture from Prehistory to the Renascence*, Lindsay argues that the reaction against evolutionist anthropology had gone too far. Writing of James Frazer, he argues that "his sin was not that he was an evolutionist, but that his conception of cultural evolution was so mechanically rationalist." He characterizes the reaction against Frazer and evolutionism in general as the "functionalist disintegration of the of the cultural scene," and claims that this had made a genuine *history* of culture impossible, by ruling out cross-cultural correlations and generalizations in advance: "The emphasis on each culture as a self-contained functional whole led to such impossible positions as the denial of any general meaning to the idea of Marriage and an attempt to posit a separate origin for marriage inside each society."[72] Lindsay approved of the functionalist emphasis on detailed empirical fieldwork, but found its antipathy for making comparisons and generalizations stifling. On the other hand, he warned elsewhere against "supplanting one abstract system with another, as we find happening with the Structuralism of Lévi-Strauss and his disciples."[73] In Lindsay's historical investigations, he aimed to give empirical justification to the widespread feeling that "culture" in general had developed from collective and ceremonial origins into something individualistic.

Lindsay's assertion that the chorus was the primal form out of which subsequent poetry and drama developed owes a clear debt to Jane Harrison's work, which he acknowledged "had a permanent effect on my thinking."[74] He adapted her idea that the dithyramb—a form of choral hymn, usually to Dionysus, "sung to the flute by a choir of fifty men and boys in a ring round the altar"—was the bedrock on which tragedy was built. Out of the dithyramb eventually a tragic hero emerged and engaged in dialogue with the chorus, and over time "the single masked actor turned into two, then three."[75] While Harrison's account was less directly motivated by a political commitment to collectivism, nevertheless, as one of the intellectual contexts for the emergence of mass declamation, it adds significant layers of meaning to Lindsay's project. Harrison significantly developed both the German idealist tradition and Nietzsche's critique of it in her account of the "queer anomaly of the chorus."[76] Nietzsche's insistence that the chorus derived from a primitive ritual emphasized *continuities,* suggesting that tribal chanting effectively persisted in tragic art. Sharing Nietzsche's belief that art developed out of collective ritual, Harrison was more interested in what *changes* in that development. As she later put it, she had been seeking to show "that Art is not the handmaid of Religion, but that Art in some sense springs out of Religion, and that between them is a connecting link, a bridge, and that bridge is Ritual. On that bridge, emotionally, I halt."[77] Harrison here summarizes the intellectual project of her *Ancient Art and Ritual*—a particularly significant work for Lindsay, as he noted in an introduction that he provided for a new edition. Lindsay did not see Harrison's book as a nostalgic bid to reverse the "secularizing" process by which collective ritual is reshaped into art.[78] Rather, purporting to reveal art's ritual origins, it tells a story about the way conscious art and spectatorship enable a critical reflection on culture (in the anthropological sense).

Harrison draws heavily on examples from Frazer in order to make broad generalizations about "primitive peoples" and their spring rites.[79] Rituals like these, celebrating fertility and asking for a good harvest, seem to Harrison to be pervasive features shared by many if not all agrarian societies. A person taking part in such a ritual act is engaged in the *dromenon*—"the thing done." Harrison argues that the *drama* developed out of these primitive rituals. Focusing her argument on ancient Greece, Harrison returns us to "the primitive Greek orchestra or dancing-place," usually a circular area surrounding a maypole:

> On this dancing-place the whole body of worshippers would gather, just as now-a-days the whole community will assemble on a village green. There is no division at first between actors and spectators; all are actors, all are doing the thing done, dancing the dance danced. Thus at initiation ceremonies the whole tribe assemble, the only spectators are the uninitiated, the women and the children. No one at this early stage thinks of building a theatre, a spectator place. It is in the common act, the common or collective emotion, that ritual starts.
>
> How, then, did this situation, in which there was no distinction between actor and spectator, develop into what we now understand as drama?

Harrison's argument, unlike those of her nineteenth-century German antecedents, is grounded in a historical account of the development of the theatre as space. She says that we need to understand "the actual *orchestra,* the space on which the chorus danced, and the relation of that space to the rest of the theatre, to the stage and the place where the spectators sat," in order to understand how art arose out of ritual in this paradigmatic case. Her key example is the Theatre of Epidaurus, where the "orchestra . . . is surrounded by a splendid *theatron,* or spectator place, with seats rising tier above tier."[80] Harrison supplies an illustration (fig. 3).

Harrison posits a historical sequence in which the orchestra—with its collectively sung ritual in which everyone participates—precedes the innovation of the *theatron,* and therefore the emergence of the spectator. It could be viewed as a version of the separation between poet and audience that Lindsay and his circle would come to associate with capitalist individualism and alienation, a schism which Mass Declamation was intended to heal, by reactivating the spectator as a speaker of poetry.

Harrison sees the emergence of the spectator—the fundamental shift that underpins the transition from ritual to art—as enabling a new and more reflective relationship to the choral dance: "The spectators are a new and differ-

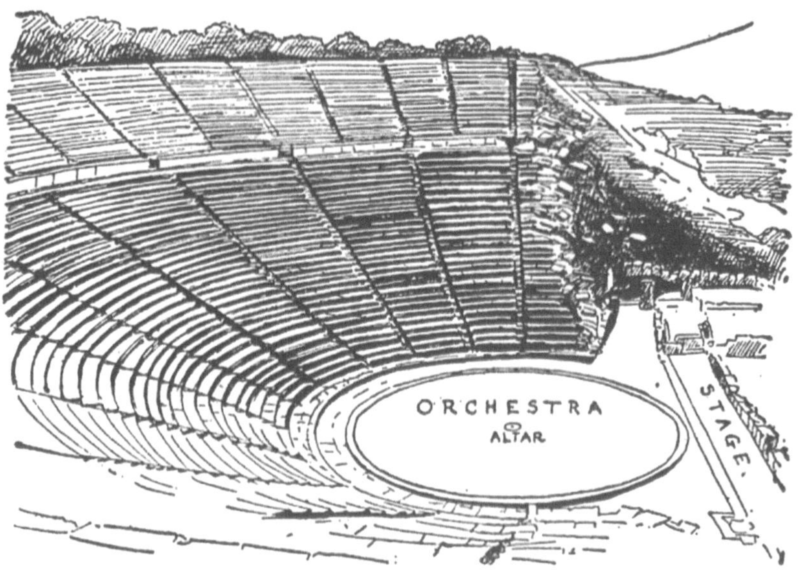

FIGURE 3: Illustration indicating the relationship between orchestra and theatron at the Theatre of Epidaurus. From Jane Harrison, *Ancient Art and Ritual* (1913).

ent element, the dance is not only danced, but is watched from a distance, it is a spectacle; whereas in old days all or nearly all were worshippers acting, now many, indeed most, are spectators, watching, feeling, thinking, not doing. It is in this new attitude of the spectator that we touch on the difference between ritual and art; the *dromenon*, the thing actually done by yourself has become a *drama*, a thing also done, but abstracted from your doing."[81] By emphasizing an "abstracted" spectatorship, in which spectators are "watching, feeling, thinking, not doing," Harrison suggested a model that was out of keeping with some later left-wing understandings of Greek theatre. C. L. R. James, for example, stressed the democratic nature of spectatorship in the festival of Dionysus: "The Greek populace behaved at these dramatic competitions as a modern crowd behaves at some football or baseball game. They were violent partisans. They stamped and shouted and showed their likes and dislikes in those and similar ways."[82] For all the difference of emphasis, James and Harrison picture the ancient audience on a bridge, poised between full participation in the collective vocalizations in the orchestra and a more abstracted spectatorship. Choral speech, which can enjoin its hearers to join in but also alienate them from the spoken discourse, is a device that thrives on this bridge.

If we take mass declamation as a practice that emerges from these discussions, then its intended democratic effect stems from the way it problematizes the audience's relation to the dramatic action. In outdoor performance, as Bim Mason has written, "the borders . . . between audience and performer and between the performance itself and the larger social event" become "less defined."[83] In this sense, Mason argues, "immediacy" is one of the key affordances of outdoor theatre—the effect of de-hierarchizing the relationship between audience and performers is to suppress consciousness of the "mediation" that opens the space for critical reflection.[84] In her recent critique of the aesthetic of immediacy, which she takes to be a pernicious aspect of the contemporary cultural landscape, Anna Kornbluh argues, "In the history of philosophy, in work from Aristotle, Hegel, Marx, Lukács, Adorno, Raymond Williams, Stuart Hall, and others, 'mediation' evokes the social process of making representation, connections, and meaning—which often reveals that the merely evident or intransitively existent does not already make sense. Immediacy style short-circuits and preempts this social process, swelling with self-identical thisness."[85] To clarify their relationship to this immediacy, we need to understand how mass declamations function simultaneously as political demonstration and drama. As political demonstrations, they make a virtue of presence and immediacy, modeling those forms of collective utterance that Sedgwick and Butler argued were speech acts in Austin's sense. The phrase "I do," (or "I will") uttered in the context of the marriage ceremony, does not *represent* a marriage or report that one has happened: it enacts the marriage, and it is the marriage.[86] Mass declamations share with performative utterances an element of "self-identical thisness"—they are doing the thing done, the *dromenon.* As both Butler and Sedgwick argue, political protests deploy or imply an inaugurating speech act, whose primary illocutionary intention is to establish the speaking group as democratically active within the polis: "We, the people." Other speech act theorists, such as Chrisman and Hubbs, have gone further in classifying protests as "complex speech act[s]," where the perlocutionary effects are to "(i) convey opposition to some object and (ii) prescribe redress related to that opposition."[87] Mass declamations seem to fit this model. Doing things with words and not only representing things with words, they seek to enact a pivot from secondary to primary collective voicing. Taken as political protests they *are* embodied social actions; they are *not* mediated representations of social actions.

But viewed as drama, the performative quality of mass declamation is undermined. Austin pointed out that making performative utterances in the course of a theatrical presentation tends to cancel their expected perlocutionary effects: actors who perform the marriage ceremony as part of a play may say "I do," but the context means that they are not thereby married: "a performative utterance will . . . be *in a peculiar way* hollow or void if said by an actor on the stage, or if introduced in a poem, or spoken in soliloquy," Austin writes.[88] The dramatic and representative aspect generates a form of critical and reflective distance from the protest itself, but it is far from the whole story. Kornbluh's critique of immediacy seems ill-equipped to capture the particular qualities of this form of politically committed art that is *both a* representation *and* the thing it represents. Mass declamation, hesitating on the bridge between *dromenon* and *drama,* puts the reflective and critical spectatorship whose emergence Harrison describes into a dialogue with an immediacy that is both performative (in Austin's sense) and politically urgent.

These qualities can be seen in the performance of *On Guard for Spain* by the Bristol Unity Players in Winterbourne in 1938, of which some wonderful photographs exist. The performance is outdoors, but not in a purpose-built amphitheater. It is possible that the actors are standing near the ha-ha that encircles the Parish Church in in Frenchay Common. The ha-ha itself would

FIGURE 4: Production still from *On Guard for Spain*, Winterbourne, 25 June 1938. From Papers of the Bristol Unity Players Club, Warwick University Archives, Warwick Digital Collections, https://wdc.contentdm.oclc.org/digital/collection/scw/id/14416/rec/3.

have been built to prevent the villagers' cattle, freely grazing the common, to encroach on church lands, but here it marks, in an informal and way and on a smaller scale, the distinction between *orchestra* and *theatron* that Harrison observed in the Theatre of Epidaurus. If the relation between performers and spectators had been de-hierarchized, then this is still recognizably outdoor "theatre," which Jan Cohen-Cruz classifies as a subset of radical street performance, "which typically keeps actors and spectators in their respective places through presentational conventions supporting a pre set script."[89] But the barriers have been lowered in several ways: the performers are amateurs, the spectators pay no fee, they stand together on common land. While in the first (indoor) performance of *On Guard* at the Unity Theatre's London premises on Britannia Street, the actors read from pages torn out of *The Left Review*, the Bristol Unity Players must have memorized their lines. Audience members may well have been familiar with the script, but it seems unlikely that they joined in (except perhaps to chant "No pasarán" along with the cast, as frequently happened at the end of performances of *On Guard*).[90] The conventions of naturalist theatre had been set aside, and the audience was addressed on common ground—but this was not pure "immediacy," and the reflective space of spectatorship still existed, perhaps even in a more self-conscious way.

Given Lindsay's extensive scholarly interests, and the self-reflexivity of the form, it is not surprising that his mass declamations often reflected on the history of poetry. In *Five Thousand Years of Poetry* (1939), the story of poetry's development into an individualistic modern idiom from its more collective origins was told. A remarkable "declamation in prose and verse," the piece also sought to reactivate poetry's latent collectivity by including choral recitations of poems of the preceding five millennia, from ancient Egypt to William Morris. This is a politicized literary criticism animated in performance. The typescript by Jack Lindsay is written in one voice, but the copy in the archive of the Unity Theatre has then been annotated for performance by an unknown hand, so that parts are allocated to "announcer," "1 woman," "1 man," "all women," "all men," "all," and so on—in some cases it is difficult to determine who is speaking.[91] As in *On Guard for Spain,* the company had significant autonomy to decide on the interaction of individual and collective voices.

In general the prose sections are spoken by the announcer, who effectively contextualizes and introduces mass recitations and dramatizations of the poetry. The opening salvo sets out the overall aims of the declamation:

> We are here to speak of the reality of poetry, more than five thousand years of poetry.
>
> We are here to claim the heritage of poetry.
>
> We speak as the people, the masses of toil, from whom all the values of life have derived. . . .
>
> We are here today to trace the voice of the masses through the centuries of poetry and to show what that voice has uttered.[92]

The poems declaimed by the chorus help to make the case that poetry has always been on the side of the people, and against bosses and political leaders. A tendentiously culled selection of radical sound bites from the history of literature—from Juvenal to Shakespeare and from Milton to Shelley—were performed, often using unison speech. These were interspersed with a great deal of anonymous—and perhaps collectively authored—folk lyrics, such that the overall effect of the piece was (as Harker put it) to "de-familiarise literary poetry by drawing attention to oral antecedents."[93]

Like the literary poetry included in *Five Thousand Years of Poetry*, the folk lyrics are shared between individual speakers and groups reciting in unison. This declamation reembeds literary poetry in a collective oral folk tradition that the chorus claims as its own. The act of laying claim becomes a refrain which the announcer uses to introduce readings: "Shakespeare is ours," "Milton is ours,"

> Burns is ours, hailing revolution in his song The Tree of Liberty
> Blake is ours, vowed to build the Jerusalem of freedom in
> England's green and pleasant land
> Shelley is ours . . .
> Byron is ours . . .
> Keats is ours[94]

These poets—in a notably Romantic tradition, with an individualistic bent—are reappropriated to a collective, democratic, and popular culture.

In an essay "May Day Tradition" from around the same time, Lindsay argued that "modern poetry emerged from the May rites of Provence" and that the "spring rite . . . provides the central image of all culture." Lindsay contrasts his radical approach to such traditions with those of "reactionaries" who fetishize "the 'élite' end-points in which each cultural outburst, rising from the masses to percolate through a class-society, exhausts itself." Where writers like T. S. Eliot used this elite conception of culture to "defend class hierarchy" Lindsay's saw culture embedded in the daily lives of working people, as a series of "attempts to merge dialectically with nature through work."[95] Poetry, in Lindsay's account, is born of the rhythms of manual agricultural labor and the seasonal rituals that accompany it. As he puts it in *Five Thousand Years of Poetry:* "Rhythm is the concentration of labour-process: men gathering into co-ordinated activity, the construction of significant speech, the dance and the song that utter the inner meaning of labour-process, its uniting of men." This reads as a politicized reformulation of Harrison's argument about ritual as the original basis of all art. Lindsay's declamation suggests that poetry's origins lie in the rhythms of collective labor, and that this makes it effective as a political tool. Poetry "has always spoken for brotherhood, against money-values," Lindsay writes, but it is not as the romantic tradition assumed, opposed to work: on the contrary it is its natural accompaniment.[96] "The unity of culture lies in the continuity of man's productive energy, his courageous attempts to merge dialectically with nature through work," Lindsay wrote.[97]

In *Five Thousand Years of Poetry*, Ernest Jones's work is presented as a moment when the tradition becomes self-conscious about its collective basis and its collectivist politics, bringing spring ritual and revolutionary action into a more direct relationship. The announcer says:

> The hope of peace and plenty no longer retreats into a distant mirage and a cry of reconciling pain.
> Now it is a revolutionary action.
> The spring-rite and the harvest-rite have been actualised in the Soviet Union.
> We too can actualise them, and in doing so we fulfill poetry.
> Poetry can be whole at last, for man can be whole.
> The dream is action now.
> Poetry is a revolutionary weapon.[98]

For Lindsay, the collective voice was latent all along in the individualistic poetry of the capitalist era. Mass declamation offered a mechanism for bringing this to the surface, reconnecting poetry with the collective rhythms both of ritual and of work. By rediscovering poetry's collective origins and its deep entanglement with productive labor, and by reactivating these through mass recitation, Lindsay hoped to sharpen its political edge. This revolutionary energy develops autochthonically from the culture and the labor of the people, and as such, it does not seem to be directed from outside the polis. Its grounding in the material labor process, moreover, seems to lend it hegemonic potential.

Work Songs

The seasonal rites that interested Jane Harrison and Jack Lindsay were already a second-order reflection on the labor process: they represented, through collective rituals, the pleasurable successes of the hunt, or promoted "fertility in plants, animals and men."[99] But by stressing the rhythms of labor itself as a source of poetic rhythm, Lindsay pointed to another crucial collective speech form with a distinct set of political meanings: the work song. In doing so, Lindsay invoked a rich seam of thinking about the work song that was animating many intellectuals in the ambit of the Communist Party of Great Britain, alongside Jacques Roumain, who saw the Haitian *coumbite* as a template for a new society (as discussed in this book's first bridge). As well as engaging in historical and folkloric efforts to recover an important oral from obscurity, these intellectuals attempted to rewrite, stage, and reanimate the work song, in an era when—as Raymond Williams would argue—poetic creativity was often seen as the very antithesis to the deadening and alienated routines of industrialism.[100] An emphasis on collective work songs as poetry's ideal type was a way of harnessing its political power, as well as a critique of modernist literary experiment, which these thinkers tended to associate with individualism. This section first explores the theorization of work songs as the collective origin of poetry on the interwar British left. It then looks at attempts to revive work songs and so to resurrect the collective voice as a politicized art form (turning towards the polis), first among the same group, and then crossing the Atlantic to return to Zora Neale Hurston and Langston Hughes.

A key figure in this rich seam of Marxist thinking about work songs was Christopher Caudwell, one the Communist Party of Great Britain's outstanding thinkers on literary and cultural questions, who died at only twenty-nine, fighting for the Spanish Republic. His *Illusion and Reality: A Study of the Sources of Poetry* (1937), informed by his reading of Jane Harrison, seeks to describe how poetry emerged, in prehistoric times, both as an accompaniment to work and as a "heightening of language on formal occasions."[101] Caudwell argues that poetry is at its origin a collective speech form: "Poetry is characteristically song, and song is characteristically something which, because of its rhythm, is sung in *unison,* is capable of being the expression of a collective emotion. This is one of the secrets of 'heightened' language."[102] These expressions of embodied collectivity served an essentially economic function in tribal communities: "Thus poetry, combined with dance, ritual, and music, becomes the great switchboard of the instinctive energy of the tribe, directing it into trains of collective actions whose immediate causes or gratifications are not in the visual field and which are not automatically decided by instinct." In this view, poetry began life as a collective force for the organization of work, and as the essential underpinning of prehistoric labor. Caudwell argued that poetry itself was "necessary to prepare the ground for harvest," and more generally "necessary to harness man's instincts to the mill of labour, to collect his emotions and direct them into the useful, the economic channel."[103] Such an instrumental account of literature's origins and functions runs counter to some of the received wisdom of literary studies, even reversing what later become the dominant Marxist positions. When Adorno celebrated the modern art that seemed (whatever its overt politics) to stand apart from the marketplace, and from the drudgery of wage labor, he emphasized art's capacity to gesture to a utopia *outside of* the purely economic relationships to which capitalism had reduced social life.[104] Caudwell's work points to a different utopian horizon, which would reintegrate poetry with productive labor: the work song as both the origin of poetry, and its ideal type.

Caudwell's arguments were taken further by the classicist George Thomson, whose book *Marxism and Poetry* argued that the work song was the origin not only of poetry but also of language itself. "In its initial stages the labour of production was collective. Many hands worked together," Thomson wrote. This created "a new mode of communication." He continued: "The cries of animals are severely limited in scope. In man they become articulate. They were elaborated and systematised as a means of co-ordinating the movements of the labouring group. And so in inventing tools man invented speech . . . speech emerged as part of the actual technique of production."[105] For Thomson, the individual speech that we use in dialogic conversation was a secondary phenomenon that developed out of the unison of the monologic collective work song that preceded it. This genealogy becomes a way of explaining the lasting distinction between poetic diction and "common speech": "And so we find in all languages two modes of speech—common speech, the normal, everyday means of communication between individuals, and poetical speech, a medium more intense, appropriate to collective acts of ritual, fantastic, rhythmical, magical."[106] Poetry derives from collective rituals, which in turn derive from the earliest work songs, themselves evolving from the rhythmical grunts of hard physical work undertaken in concert. Even when poetry became a predominantly individual medium, Thomson argues, the shadow of its collective origins persisted in the "fantastic, rhythmical, magical" character of its language. Thomson explicitly regrets the development of the novel, in which "poetical diction has been replaced by common speech."[107] He rejects the literary-critical suspicion of poetic diction, initiated in Wordsworth and Coleridge's preface to the *Lyrical Ballads* and subsequently institutionalized as a guiding principle of literary taste. Perhaps the overblown clichés which literary critics scoffed at were really better thought of as oral formulas, like Homer's rosy-fingered dawn, serving as a vital link to poetry's collective origins.

In order to corroborate this story, Thomson draws on his own experiences in Ireland (which still had a significant oral culture of folk song) and also refers to many anthropological sources about so-called primitive culture. Like many of the anthropologists he cites, Thomson's picture of primitive culture is idealized as a potential corrective to the individualism of modern capitalist culture: "Labour songs abound at all stages of culture all over the world—except where they have been silenced by the hum of machinery. And they have a special importance for our purpose, because in them, with some significant modifications, the original relationship between language and labour has been preserved."[108] Thomson's suggestion that industrial machinery has drowned out the work song supplies a technological explanation for the apparent decline of the work song in the developed world, at the same time that it persisted elsewhere. The office work that has come to the fore in postindustrial societies (and more recently the trend towards remote working), is even less conducive to collective vocalization. So Thomson looked to anthropological sources. Drawing on H. A. Junod's *Life of a South African Tribe* (1912–13), for example, Thomson cites a work song sung by a Thonga boy while breaking stones:

> They treat us badly, *ehé!*
> They are hard on us, *ehé!*
> They drink their coffee, *ehé!*
> And give us none, *ehé!*

As Thomson glosses the song: "The repeated *ehé* is the labour cry, marking the hammer strokes. This is the constant. It is prefaced each time with a few articulate words improvised to express the worker's subjective attitude to his task. The song has grown out of the cry, just as the cry has grown out of the work itself."[109] Anthropological observations—no doubt in ways that involved racial assumptions about the collectivity of "primitive" culture, as I described in chapter 1—furnish Thomson with an archive of contemporary evidence that a closer relationship between poetry and collective labor is possible.

Like some other significant collective speech forms examined in this book, the work song is often treated a little nostalgically, as a symbol of a form of collective expression and togetherness that has declined in modern times. Thomson contrasts the origins of poetry as a "social act" with a modern poetry that has been "individualised to such a degree that it has lost touch with its source of life" and "withered at the root."[110] Ted Gioia's book *Work Songs* (2006) is the most sustained recent scholarly treatment of the topic, and it is unapologetically of the same tendency. The work song is, Gioia acknowledges, "no longer a vital form of musical expression."[111] But his book makes the case for a revival of the form, as part of what he calls a "broad vision of art integrated into the everyday lives of people."[112] Work songs "often served a utilitarian purpose," Gioia notes, but they also had an "aesthetic component . . . of surprising intensity."[113] While Gioia sees work songs as a global phenomenon, he also claims that "the African diaspora served as the greatest source and repository of songs of agricultural labor."[114] Black culture, no doubt because of the shaping experience of slavery, the plantation, and the chain gang, represents a vibrant and living tradition of work songs for Gioia—and the British communist intellectuals I have been discussing thought so, too. Many of the work songs discussed by Gioia, Thompson, and Caudwell could be thought of as purely fugitive expressions that celebrate the power of work—and of the worker—independent of the polis, and in that sense, they could profitably be discussed in chapter 1. However, the specific tradition I am focusing on here is interested in how work songs might be activated politically: poetry as a "revolutionary weapon," as Lindsay put it in *Five Thousand Years of Poetry*. Because work songs originate in the rhythms and processes of labor, it can seem that they are automatically licensed to speak for the working people. This license makes them an ideal medium for politically engaged collective speech: the voice of the (laboring) people.

As communists sought to revive the work song, they frequently looked to the Black culture of the United States. A. L. Lloyd, a central figure in the communist-led Second Folk Revival, wrote in 1945 that "the English folk song as it is now is a museum piece," while in America "things are different" and "folk-music is, indeed, alive and flourishing."[115] The pageants that the composer Alan Bush organized, often in collaboration with Swingler, invariably assembled large choirs to embody popular collectivity on the stage. The Festival of Music for the People, for example, took place over several weeks in London, in the spring of 1939. As part of the festival, a pageant called Music and the People took place at the Royal Albert Hall, boasting "Five Hundred Singers" (made up of labor and cooperative choirs from the various districts of London, as well as the Rhondda Unity Male Voice Chorus) and "One Hundred Dancers" (from the progressive children's organization the Woodcraft Folk and from the Unity Theatre Dance Group).

Music and the People consisted of ten episodes, each of which dramatized different phases in the history of "the people." Who counted here was interesting—certainly there was a strong focus (familiar to the culture of the Popular Front) on recovering Britain's radical traditions, and there were scenes commemorating the Peasants' Revolt, the English Revolution, and William Morris. But the pageant was international, too, invoking the French

Revolution, and bringing in Paul Robeson, accompanied by "John Payne and his Negro Choir," to represent the struggles—and the music—of the enslaved people of the African diaspora in the American South. The peasantry was to the fore in each of the episodes, its apparently more communal way of life being reflected in its folk music: the "Carmagnole" gained precedence over the "Marseillaise" as "the real song of the people in revolution . . . the tune of which was an ancient peasant dance."[116]

Work songs formed a vital part of the texture of the "music of the people," framed by Bush and Swingler in an internationalist spirit that was nevertheless receptive to the particularity of the individual traditions that made it up. Bush himself was a reader of Caudwell and later of Thomson and he cited both in his own published writing about music's origins. Writing in the WMA's organ, *Keynote*, and citing Caudwell, Bush argued: "There can be no doubt that the original function of music was to organise movement and thus expedite labour performed communally. This applies equally to the actual tasks of lugging or heaving heavy weights, rowing, spinning, etc., or to the tribal mimetic dances, which magically enacted the processes of hunting or agriculture—aiding their concrete achievement *in the belief* of those taking part, but in reality educating and organizing the participants and thus improving their technique by practice."[117] The first episode of the pageant, representing "Feudal England," saw "Ploughmen and Reapers enter, singing songs that have lived in the peasant tradition of England for centuries," and concluded with "an age-old spinning song from the Hebrides."[118] The accompanying dance is supposedly based on "primitive fertility rituals," sounding the note of primitivism that often accompanies the revival of work songs.

However, in a way, the presentation of Robeson and the chorus of slaves he leads is more strikingly modern. Their performance was described in the program in the following terms:

> Those peoples are remembered here who suffered long years in the chains of slavery, and still suffer appalling conditions of exploitation and the persecutions of racial prejudice. The Negro people, in work, in captivity, in longing and in striving for freedom, have developed as rich and vigorous a musical culture as any people in the world. They enter singing a Chain-gang song, then a Cotton-picking song, and some songs of freedom, led by one of the foremost champions of freedom and international brotherhood
>
> PAUL ROBESON[119]

In the work songs that came from enslaved Black people on the cotton fields and plantations, the pageant did not celebrate an idealized precapitalist society, but sought to tap the creative and collective energies of resistance and community that sprung up in this definitively modern setting. At the beginning of the pageant, the Speaker emphasized the utopian orientation of song: "Music . . . is not a drug or a world of fantasy to which men can escape from the real problems of their life. Rather it is part of the pattern of the life they wish for, and a guide and inspiration to their efforts to attain it."[120] While the inclusion of Robeson and the plantation songs in the pageant was framed by racializing discourses, there was also an interest in seeing these in relation to work songs and other folk expressions from all corners of the globe. If in a sense the portrayal of peasant labor in medieval England was willfully primitivist, the plantation song responds to a distinctively modern form of labor, to the conditions of chattel slavery, and to the post-emancipation working conditions of Black agricultural laborers in the US. The performance also creates a link between the interwar British left's fascination with work songs and the thinking about that form that was underway in the African diaspora, in the US and beyond.

An epicenter for thinking about work songs and their relationship to the African diaspora was in the Harlem Renaissance, and in the work of Zora Neale Hurston in particular. Like her work on voodoo and hoodoo, which I explored in chapter 1, Hurston's interest in work songs crosses over between her anthropological and her literary work. Hurston collected work songs during her ethnographic research in Georgia and Florida, and when she was joined by a young Alan Lomax from 1935, he brought with him a recording machine and together they recorded work songs and other folk music.

One of the most significant songs to be recorded by Hurston is "John Henry," which tells the story of a freeman and railroad worker who, when faced with the arrival of the steam drill that threatens to render his work obsolete, challenges the steam drill to a contest. Armed only with his nine-pound hammer, Henry defeats the steam drill, only then to die from his exertions. Hurston calls it "the king of railroad track-laying songs," though "like all the other work songs," she says, it is also "sung in the jooks and other social places."[121] It is clear from the recordings made by Hurston and Lomax that "John Henry" was often sung for entertainment, outside of work—and Hurston reports in *Mules and Men* that she sang it, standing on a table at a dance, "to prove that I was their kind."[122] In this context, the work songs Hurston collected formed part of a Black folk culture defined by fugitive "Black Joy," and a refusal of the polis. We need to return to that world briefly here, in order to understand the significance of a later move to turn "John Henry" to political account, by Hurston's friend Langston Hughes.

Work songs tend to be defined as those that accompany work, and form part of its embodied practice: on this basis they ought to be distinguishable from songs performed outside work, that may comment on labor conditions and critique them. A. L. Lloyd made this distinction, seeing the blues ballad as an individualistic development of the more collective tradition of the work song. He described the "Negro tenant farmer in post-bellum America, who came out of slavery with a repertory of communal work-songs and spirituals, and gradually in his novel solitary state, with its joys and anxieties, created for himself his own solo songs of personal emotion, cast in new, more evolved forms—such as the Blues—because his expanding lyrical horizon demanded it, because he wanted to assert his new-felt individuality."[123] One of the reasons that "John Henry" is so compelling is because of the way it hesitates on the bridge between collective ritual and individual art. Recordings by Lead Belly, Woody Guthrie, Bruce Springsteen, Van Morrison, Johnny Cash, Big Bill Broonzy, Lonnie Donnegan, and Billy Bragg (to list only a few of them) are energized by the apparent emergence of the song from the collective labor of the railroad camp. It was, and to an extent remains, both a hammer song and a blues ballad.

Moreover, "John Henry" is not a single song but a rich mythological tradition, excavated in the pioneering work of Hurston's contemporaries Guy B. Johnson and Louis Chappell.[124] Johnson echoed Lloyd in arguing that "John Henry" was likely a collective work song first, which then gave rise to ballads. He claimed that "wherever Negroes drive steel or do any sort of work that requires regular muscle movements," they will sing, usually "mentioning John Henry in one way or another."[125] Hurston noted that "John Henry" is "suited to the spiking rhythm," and in some cases she goes into more detail about how certain work songs were embedded in the actual collective processes of labor. "Can't You Line It?" (sometimes called "Shove It Over!") is one of a number of "lining songs" she collected which accompanied the process of laying railway tracks: "This song is common to the railroad camps. It is suited to the 'lining' rhythm. That is, it fits the straining of the men at the lining bars as the rail is placed in position to be spiked down."[126] The song involves an alternation between the individual voice of a designated "singing liner" and the working group singing in unison:

When I get to Illinois
I'm going to spread the news about the Florida boys.
Chorus: (All men straining at rail in concert.)
Shove it over! Hey, hey, can't you line it?
(Shaking rail.) Ah, shack-a-lack-a-lack-a-lack-a-lack-a-lack-a-lack.
(Grunt as they move rail.) Can't you move it? Hey, hey, can't you
try.[127]

There is a wonderful recording of Hurston singing this song, made in 1939 when she was employed by the Federal Writers' Project to document the oral culture of the South. Hurston makes "Can't You Line It?" a solo performance, but her explanation emphasizes its collective origin: "When they say shack-a-lack-a-lack-a-lack they're getting ready to pull back and when they say huh they shove the rail."[128] As with the hoodoo ceremonies she collected in the course of her ethnographic research, Hurston also delighted in reworking these work songs in literary and dramatic works. Hurston's 1932 "Program of Negro Folklore," *The Great Day*, "featured a company of dancers singing work songs while simulating the labour of 'lining' and 'spiking' railroad tracks."[129] "Can't You Line It?" and "John Henry" were performed alongside other songs.[130] Hurston's project was not one of preservation, whereby the traces of a dying culture could be stored for future generations: she was interested in how these folkloric materials formed part of a living culture, happily "reinventing the folklore of the communities with which she identified."[131]

It was Hurston's friend Langston Hughes who pressed the work songs she had recorded—"John Henry" most particularly—into the service of a more explicitly political agenda. His radio ballad "The Man Who Went to War" was broadcast by the BBC in 1944 featuring an all-Black cast, and Alan Lomax (who had recorded work songs with Hurston in the South) served as musical director.[132] The play centers on a young Black soldier called Johnny, who travels to Europe to join the war effort, and the family he leaves behind. The action shuttles back and forth between soldiers at war in Europe and scenes from the US home front which depart strikingly from the real experience. Johnny's family suffers frequent air raids and is eventually bombed out: Hughes imaginatively transposes the British experience of the Blitz onto the cityscape of urban America. Songs from the Black folk tradition become a vital resource for the people living through this Blitz, and some of these are reworked with an explicitly antifascist message. The play was introduced by Paul Robeson, who informed listeners that "your thirteen million Negro allies in the United States" are also "a part of this great global war against fascism." The setting, Robeson continued, could be "anywhere that the war has been fought": it obviously is not intended to be a realistic portrayal of the experience of Black people in America. As Robeson says: "We are giving you a picture of what you yourself have lived through, Britain—only the words and the songs are our own, for these are the words and the songs that Negroes sing. Like your own, they are the songs of one more freedom loving people."[133] Hughes's play projects an antifascist and international identification between peoples that are understood to possess distinctive ethnic identities, grounded in their collective speech forms. Robeson, has recently been described as a representative of "cosmopolitan patriotism," and as such, he was perhaps the ideal carrier for such a message.[134]

The work song enters the fray in a scene that depicts Johnny's wife and his father, back at home, at work in a munitions factory. Josh White, a kind of wandering bard, sings a new version of "John Henry," intending to increase the rate of production. Neither Hughes nor Hurston were naïve about work songs: they knew that bosses used them to squeeze more productivity out of their workers. They were both interested in work songs as a collective speech form that dramatizes the tension between the self-expression of Black workers, and the interests of white bosses in the Jim Crow South. Hurston's play *Spunk* (1935), discussed in detail in chapter 1, started with a lining rhythm called "Let's Shake It!" (which Hurston would record for the Federal Writers' Project in 1939). When that finishes, the white boss instructs the singing liner: "Line another one before you spike. Come on bullies!" and the group starts singing "Can't You Line It?" with a stage direction indicating that they "grin and work furiously."[135] At the end of the song the boss says, "All right boys, that gets it. Hammers!" The song has brought this phase of work to completion, and they can now move on to spiking the rails (an activity which has its own set of songs patterned to accompany the rhythm of hammering the rails in place). The song provides meaning and pleasure to those who sing it, but it also structures the work in ways that the boss can use.

In *The Man Who Went to War*, the bard Josh White introduces the song by saying, "You make those machines turn faster than they ever turned before, while I tell you about a working man." Hughes's version includes some familiar phrases:

> John Henry, say, John Henry,
> How come your hands so hard.

How come you lay so many rails
Looks like you never get tired![136]

But new words have been riveted to the familiar frame to reposition it in a Second World War context:

Now that my country's fighting
And we have gone to war,
I'm determined to get this production out
Cause that's what we workers are for!
Yeah, man! That's what we workers are for.[137]

The significant contrast with the railroad camp in *Spunk* is that the work of this munitions factory is presented as being directed towards the national war effort rather than capitalist accumulation on the part of the white bosses. And this war effort is understood in the play as a concerted fight against fascism:

Everybody join with me
And everybody lend a hand
Cause we've got to push them fascists back
And make the Nazis understand.

Machines, start double-timing!
Workers, double-timing, too!
Cause the soldiers out on the fighting front
Are double-timing for you.[138]

The machines accelerate to the quickening rhythm until they drown out the song and fade into the sounds of the battlefield for the next scene. This song clearly participates in the John Henry tradition's celebration of an almost supernaturally hard worker. But the relation with the machine is more symbiotic that competitive, and John Henry's death is not even mentioned. Indeed, there is none of the sense of a critique of labor conditions, or the hierarchies and power relations that underpin them, that is often manifested in the John Henry tradition. This is war propaganda, and it imagines bosses, workers, machines, and state all pulling in the same antifascist direction, with work songs playing a key role in binding the proletariat to the project.

Hughes's earlier work had often used choral voices to portray a fundamental opposition between white and Black America. His agitprop play *Scottsboro, Limited,* for example, responded to the infamous Scottsboro case of 1931, in which nine Black youths were convicted of rape and eight sentenced to death, against the evidence. Hughes's play, written that year and published in *New*

Masses, though not performed until 1932 in Los Angeles, places a baying racist mob in the audience, whose members shout for a conviction, and whose perspective the "boys" initially internalize:

> JUDGE: *(Descending from the bench, to audience)* Don't worry folks, the law will take its course. They'll burn, and soon at that. (*He and the girls exit, talking and smiling)*
> MOB VOICES: *(Applauding and shouting)* Make it soon. Kill the niggers. Let 'em die.
> BOYS: *(Echoing the Voices)* Make it soon. Let us die. Make it soon. Soon. Soon.
> 6TH BOY: *(Breaking away from the dumb circle)* No, no, no! What do they want to kill us for?[139]

In the Scottsboro case, it was the Communist Party of the USA (CPUSA) that swept in to defend the accused, not the more liberal NAACP (it has been argued that the Scottsboro case played a key role in drawing Hughes towards communism).[140] In answer to the racist mob, another collectively speaking group, called the "Red Voices," speak up from the audience in defense of the accused:

> MOB VOICES: You oughta be through—Oughta be through. In this white man's land There's no place for you.
> MURMUR OF RED VOICES: *(In audience)* We'll fight for you, boys. We'll fight for you. The Reds will fight for you.

When the Red Voices take the stage for the finale and join with the boys, they form an insistently multi-racial grouping that stresses unity across racial divides:

> BOYS: Comrades!
> RED VOICES: Comrades! (They clasp hands and line up in a row of alternating Blacks and whites.)
> BOYS: Joining hands to build the right.
> RED VOICES: White and Black!
> BOYS: Black and white!
> 8TH BOY: To live, not die!
> ALL: To fight! To fight!

Rhythm and rhyme coalesce to suggest an almost ritualized sense of unity, and the word "together"—which Hughes would later deploy with a similar resonance in "We'll hammer it out together"—is a repeated mantra. But solidarity across racial lines, in this play, is the program of an insurgent communist grouping, which can hardly be thought of as characteristic of the nation. Indeed, the soaring rhetoric of American nationhood is only invoked bitterly:

> 5TH BOY: *(Earnestly)* So the people can see
> What it means to be
> A poor Black workman
> In this land of the free.
>
> 2ND BOY: *(Harshly)* Where every star in the flag
> Is stained with a lie![141]

The idea of America as the "land of the free" invokes the words of "The Star-Spangled Banner," which had become the official national anthem of the United States in the same month that those accused at Scottsboro were arrested.[142] But it is deeply ironic in this context. When the play ends with a rendition of "L'Internationale," with "the red flag raised above the heads of the Black and white workers together," it could hardly be clearer that, at this stage in Hughes's work, the collective voice of Black emancipation will not fit in a national frame.[143]

As implied in *The Man Who Went to War,* for Hughes, a national horizon for Black liberation became both possible and necessary during the war, and John Henry was a potentially unifying figure. The fullest expression of this idea comes in a radio ballad called *John Henry Hammers It Out,* a collaboration with Lomax for NBC's "Labor for Victory" series, broadcast in June 1943. Paul Robeson played John Henry (as he had on Broadway in Roark Bradford's play three years earlier), the playscript was by Peter Lyon, and Hughes wrote the lyrics to the new song "We'll Hammer It Out Together," that runs through the play and was performed in full at the end of the broadcast. The play begins with a rendition of "John Henry" by a quartet, but Lucy—John Henry's wife—interrupts them just when they sing, "And he laid down his hammer and he died": "That's what they say. They say John Henry died. . . . But I know different. . . . Fact is, he was just tuckered out, driving all that steel, and he went away by himself and lay down to take a nap."[144] This nap is supposed to have lasted thirty years, and when Lucy wakes John Henry up, America is embroiled in a European war against fascism. "There's lots of work you got to do with your big old forty-pound hammer," she tells him—and while his initial impulse is to enlist in the army, "to help shoot these bad folks," Lucy insists, "You're a better worker than you are a fighter," and John Henry resolves to take a job in a munitions factory.[145]

But this is the Jim Crow South, and the boss tells him, "No colored men hired here." John Henry then makes a patriotic case (recall *The Man Who Went to War*) for the importance of Black workers to the US war effort: "Mister, I do have to work. And not just for a living. This is my country, and I got to help it win, as much as you do and more than you do. . . . Mister, I got the strength of twelve million strong Black arms, and that strength has got to be put to work to win this war!"[146] This is a powerful articulation of the collective strength of Black America: it makes Black people—moving in unison, embodied in John Henry himself who acts as their avatar—indispensable to America's power. In these radio plays, Southern folk myth, with its deep roots in Black culture, comes into stereoscopic alignment with an imaginative projection of the American nation.

And in this play, the trade union movement plays a transitional role in harnessing "the strength of twelve million strong Black arms" for the US war effort. John Henry eventually finds work in a munitions factory, sweeping the floor at first, with the help of a union man, who promises to get him a better job. The strength of the union, he explains, "comes from the whites and the Negroes working together."[147]

The battle against racism, and against the Klan, becomes an essential element of the program of national unity set out in the play. And as John Henry insists that he is "big enough and strong enough to lick the stuffings out of Jim Crow," he starts to sing sections of the new work song Hughes wrote for the performance, his solo voice alternating with a quartet:

> We'll hammer it out together,
> White folks and black folks side by side.
> We'll turn our strength into tanks and planes
> For the troops on the other side.[148]

The whole song, which was sung solo by Kenneth Spencer at the end of the play, makes Black liberation an essential element of the international fight against fascism:

> The fascists try to stop us
> Teaching divide and rule.
> But the fascist and the Ku Klux Klan
> Must think that I'm a fool.[149]

Ultimately, "Foes within and foes without" will be defeated when the Black workers and white workers join to "hammer it out together," as the song's refrain puts it. In a substantial shift from the split chorus of *Scottsboro, Limited,* Hughes imagines a national coalition, singing "John Henry" together.

At the end of the play, as he introduces the final performance of the song, Robeson comes out of character and addresses the audience in his own voice. He argues that "Jim Crow has got to go—that every form of discrimination against an American on the basis of color, race, creed or national origin . . . has got to go." This is "not only because discrimination is an evil thing. The reason is far more practical than that. The reason is that it must go, if we are to win this war. And with it must go the poll tax, discriminating against the Negro and poor white people alike. The anti-Negro riots all over the country—they are Axis-inspired. They are treasonable. They must be stopped. The Negro people are aware of the role the progressive American trade union movement is playing in helping us stamp out Jim Crow."[150] John Henry offers the possibility of a collective vocalization that can draw Black and white workers together, unifying them against the fascist threat.

It is a measure of how much Hughes's ideas had shifted that in these radio plays, he and his collaborators are able to imagine an alignment between the Black folk culture of the South and the American nation itself. This was an extension of the Popular Front mentality, which led Hughes and some of his comrades (as Anthony Dawahare argues) to "somewhat uncritically embrace American nationalism."[151] *Labor for Victory* insists that it is now the Klan which is unpatriotic, presented as carping from the sidelines, rather than expressing a white supremacy that is typical of the US state that sentenced those boys to death in Scottsboro. Hughes's imaginative projection, provoked into being by the threat of fascism at home and abroad, is a world in which "John Henry" becomes the national anthem of the US.

Could the idea of the US nation flex enough to adopt an anthem that accommodated its oppressed, exploited, and excluded groups? The original Black national anthem, claimed as such by the NAACP in 1919, was James Weldon Johnson's "Lift Every Voice and Sing." This is a celebration of the power of collective singing, but its reception has consistently provoked questions about who is included in its first-person plural pronouns. Despite the patriotism of the lyrics—"May we forever stand, / True to our God, / True to our native land"—the song was seen by some during the Popular Front period as a "sign of black infidelity to the nation-state," and an expression of Black nationalism.[152] The possibility of an inclusive national anthem preoccupied Judith Butler and Gayatri Spivak in their conversation in *Who Sings the Nation-State?* (2007), which dwells on the singing of "The Star-Spangled Banner" in Spanish by undocumented "illegal" residents during protests in California in 2006. Butler wonders whether by singing the anthem in Spanish (and in defiance of President George W. Bush, who had declared that the anthem could only legitimately be sung in English), the singers may "help undo nationalism," and raise the possibility of a "non-nationalist or counter-nationalist mode of belonging."[153] Hughes's experiments with "John Henry" can be seen through the lens of such debates. They are a speculative way of imagining the collective voice of Black folk culture moving from a position of insurgency to one of hegemony. They speculate about the future possibility that this voice could become aligned or even identified with the nation-state.

I need to underline here just how fundamentally different this is from an understanding of Black folk culture in terms of fugitivity, exile, and refusal. John Henry inhabits that space, too: that is where Hurston found him, a creature of the Undercommons (as Harney and Moten call it). The use Hughes makes of John Henry in *The Man Who Went to War* and *Labor for Victory* transplants him into a radically different position, seeking recognition and even hegemony within a nation-state that has been imaginatively reconceptualized as inclusive, multiethnic, and antifascist. Such a vision is completely at odds with the form of fugitivity theorized by Fred Moten. This involves a "mode of blackness that I [Moten] would claim precisely as a result of a radical, principled rejection of national identity as such."[154] Here is a fault line, separating irreconcilable understandings of what Black cultural expression can do.

To reiterate, my purpose in this book is to map the different positions of the collective voice, rather than advocating for one position or another. To some—to Moten, perhaps—it may be profoundly dismaying to see the collective voice drawn from the railroad camp and the jook joint, and deployed in the service of a nation-building project (and by Langston Hughes, no less). Perhaps something important is lost when John Henry is put to work for the USA. But Hughes had perceived something fundamental about how the collective voice works: even the most resistant, refusing expressions contain hegemonic potential. And in turn, nation-states place a great value on those forms of collective utterance that serve to glorify their power. It is with this hegemonic collective voice that the rest of this book is concerned.

BRIDGE

BECOMING HEGEMONIC

LISTEN: THE COLLECTIVE VOICE can move from a position of insurgent protest towards the hegemonic status of a national anthem. The national anthem is a collective speech form which imagines itself sung by a whole nation in unison. It brings individuals together to articulate both a shared identity and a sense of belonging within a given political unit. As Cavarero puts it, "National anthems . . . have precisely the function of producing and giving vocal substance to the unity of the nation, a specific form of unity in which the individual voices mix and blend together."[1] Benedict Anderson proposed the term "unisonance" while linking this phenomenon to his own theory of nationalism as "imagined community": "Singing the Marseillaise, Waltzing Matilda, and Indonesia Raya provide occasions for unisonality, for the echoed physical realization of the imagined community. (So does listening to [and maybe silently chiming in with] the recitation of ceremonial poetry, such as sections of the Book of Common Prayer). How selfless this unisonance feels! If we are aware of others singing these songs precisely when and as we are, we have no idea who they may be, or even where, out of earshot, they may be singing. Nothing connects us all but imagined sound."[2] Unlike Cavarero, Anderson opens the space for on overlaying of secondary collective vocalization. Hegemonic collective utterance frequently relies on projections about others who may be imagined to be singing along while not actually audible.

All this means that when groups advocate for (or against) the adoption of a given anthem, and when states officially adopt one, when people sing it or refuse to sing it, change the words or translate them into a different language, they participate in a debate about the presumed cultural substance of the nation. Many national anthems, revolutionary ones in particular, follow a historical trajectory that shows what it means for a collective utterance to make the transition from a position of insurgent protest to one of hegemony.

This is nowhere truer than in the case of "L'Internationale," which I have already discussed in several contexts, and whose institutionalization as the national anthem of the Soviet Union embodies the sort of positional shift that this bridge section is interested in, from protest to hegemony. The text was composed by Eugène Pottier and first published in 1887 in his collection *Chants révolutionnaires,* where it is dated to "Paris, juin 1871," situating its composition on the barricades during the Paris Commune.[3] In 1888 Pierre Degeyter, director of the workers' choir Lyre des Travailleurs, added the famous tune, and a song sheet was published in a print run of six thousand copies. In 1896, the song was reportedly sung by twenty thousand people in Lille, at the 14th National Congress of the Parti ouvrier français.[4] The hymn became a popular anthem in the international workers' movement, and was translated into Russian by Arkadii Iakovlevich in 1902, where it "quickly became a tool of agitation in Russia." It was included in songbooks published by all the different factions of Russian socialism leading up to 1917.[5] In this period it competed with the Marseillaise as the favored anthem of revolutionary Russia. The hardline Bolshevik faction increasingly tended to prefer "L'Internationale," and to associate "La Marseillaise" with bourgeois revolution.

This tension between the two songs played out in a mass spectacle of 1920 directed by Nikolai Evreinov, called *The Storming of the Winter Palace.* Evreinov's spectacle re-created that event with many thousands of participants. It portrayed the Provisional Government (led by Kerensky) singing "La Marseillaise" "out of tune," on a white stage. From the red stage, "L'Internationale" "sounds out as if from underground" and then "hundreds of voices, shouting 'Lenin! Lenin! Lenin!'" After the battle, in Evreinov's own evocative description, "a rocket bursts, and the square falls silent to fill with a new sound, the powerful sound of 'The Internationale,' sung by a choir of forty thousand!" At which point "the Red army parade commences." It was a huge endeavor which Evreinov claimed "was written by a collective author, produced by a collective director, and performed by a collective actor."[6] This vast piece of political theatre used collective voicing as a means to break down the barriers between performers and audience, but it also showcased the military strength of the Red Army. One spectator remarked: "They fired less in 1917 than today."[7]

In the nineteenth century, "La Marseillaise" was "not simply or even primarily a French song," as Kate Bowan and Paul Pickering have shown. Around the world, it had "become synonymous with liberty and, for a century at least, was taken up by almost every imaginable freedom cause."[8] The force of Evreinov's *The Storming of the Winter Palace* is to suggest that, by 1920, "La Marseillaise" had lost its radical power by becoming institutionalized in the liberal state (after being banned by Napoléon, and again by Napoléon III, it was readopted as the French national anthem in 1879). Ironically, Evreinov's mass spectacle participated in the process by which "L'Internationale" consolidated its position as the anthem of a Soviet state that was destined to become increasingly nationalistic and militaristic under Stalin. A hymn that had started its life on the barricades during the Paris Commune was becoming a symbol of state power.

As I pointed out in my earlier discussion of Jacques Roumain, "L'Internationale" has a built-in aspiration to expand the referential scope of its first-person plural pronouns, and of the speaking group: "Nous ne sommes rien, soyons tout," the song suggests. "We were nothing, we will be all." This expansion of the referential scope of the "we," from nothing to everything, has a variety of intermediate stages, when the speaking group is a specific section of the human race, but not all of it. Most notably—as the anthem of the Communist International—it suggests a class basis for inclusion in the speaking group: "Ouvriers, paysans, nous sommes / Le grand parti des travailleurs" (Laborers, peasants, we are / The big party of the working people), and in fact the "tout" which the group is destined to become will retain an element of this identity as "L'oisif ira loger ailleurs" (the idle man will live elsewhere) and "les corbeaux, les vaoutors" (ravens and vultures) will disappear. The song's internal impulse is to expand of the collective voice to encompass the entire "genre humain" (human race). However, in practice, this expansion tended to get stalled at the level of the nation—ironically enough, given its title.

Mass singing, of "L'Internationale" but also of other socialist and patriotic songs, became a significant pastime in the Soviet Union. If Butler says (rightly) that it is impossible to imagine a situation when the whole people of one nation would actually sing the same words at the same time, then these deliberate attempts to expand the number of speaking voices seem to gesture towards that horizon. Lebedev-Kumach's 1935 mass song "The Song of the Motherland" is a famous example, proclaiming in its fourth verse:

> Nobody in the world knows better than we
> How to laugh and love.
> But we'll sternly knit our brows

> If an enemy should wish to smash us—
> We love our Motherland as if she were a bride,
> And cherish her as if she were an affectionate mother.[9]

There is no doubt that the speaking "we" is defined nationally, as the citizens of the Soviet Union, here destined not to follow the expansive utopian arc of the speakers of "L'Internationale" (from "rien" to "tout"), but to stop at the borders of the Soviet motherland, preparing to face down enemies beyond those borders and force out dissenters within. It mirrors Stalin's slogan "Socialism in One Country," which signaled a shift away from "international revolution" and towards "national modernization."[10] For Gerald Stanton Smith, "The function of this song and those like it is to promulgate and propagandize a set of myths and dogmas from the orthodox ideology, just as religious hymnology does."[11] Talk of promulgation and propaganda tends to emphasize the state's use of patriotic songs as a means of social control, but perhaps what is interesting here (as in the analogy with religious hymnology) is the way in which the "voice of the people" as a genuine outpouring of expressive sentiment and spiritual belief can come into alignment with a state-sponsored, nationalistic ideology, or church doctrine. The easy opposition between "top-down" (bad) and "bottom-up" (good) forms of collective speech is not much use here: one has to try to understand how a given collective utterance can be both.

There is no doubt, for example, that the enthusiastic uptake of Soviet "mass song" by sections of the British left was imagined as an extension of the project to rediscover, protect, and foster a tradition of radical folk song. The Workers' Music Association—a "central institution" in the communist-led Second Folk Revival—published an Anglicized version of the anthem of the Soviet Air Force in 1939 as "Soviet Airmen's Song," a "Mass (unison) song from the U.S.S.R.," with words adapted by Randall Swingler.[12] The *Left Songbook,* edited by Alan Bush and Swingler in 1938, included "The International" and "The Marseillaise" (the Soviet and French national anthems) alongside a variety of radical songs. The introduction praised music's "faculty of binding together in a single emotion all those who are united by a common interest and a common purpose." It was the socialist movement—"that movement which aims to make an equal community the basis of social life"—that was now capable of "utilising the power of music to the full."[13]

Such attempts to harness the power of populist nationalism for socialist ends arguably reached their apogee at wartime. *Salute to the Red Army,* an "agitprop pageant" performed at the Royal Albert Hall in 1943, during the wartime alliance between Britain and the Soviet Union, ended up bringing "The International" and "God Save the King" into an unlikely alignment. It was directed by Basil Dean, starring John Gielgud and Laurence Olivier, among others. As Claire Warden describes in her illuminating analysis of the piece, "the performance concluded with a Red Army soldier appearing in front of a vast Hammer and Sickle flag and, in a slightly jarring musical juxtaposition, the singing of the 'Internationale' and then the British 'National Anthem,' reminiscent of the WTM [Workers' Theatre Movement] agitprop events which often included the former if not the latter."[14] "God Save the King" is not in competition with "L'Internationale" in Dean's piece, as "La Marseillaise" was in Evreinov's *Storming of the Winter Palace.* The juxtaposition appears "jarring" from a post–Cold War perspective, but the Anglo-Soviet Pact temporarily made British patriotism and reverence for the Soviet ally two sides of the same coin. Pro-Soviet propaganda (including songs) was being pumped out on BBC radio during the war, and its in-house journal *The Listener* spoke of "fellowship and brotherhood in the common cause."[15] The gap that separated the national anthem of Britain from "L'Internationale" was narrowing—because a temporary framework had been created in which the left (or at least a significant part of it) could identify its own interests with those of the nation-state. The antistate protest song, born on the barricades during the Paris Commune, had become a symbol of state power and military might, performed in the Albert Hall, and funded by the Ministry of Information. Ironically enough, that same year, Stalin decided that he "had had enough of the French-penned Internationale"—a little too . . . international for the increasingly nationalistic Soviet Union—and he set up a national competition to write a new anthem.[16] On 14 December 1943 the Politburo approved "Anthem of the Bolshevik Party" (with words by Sergei Mikhalkov and G. El'-Registan and music by A. V. Aleksandrov) as the official state anthem. Leaving behind the appeal of "L'Internationale" to "the wretched of the earth," the new hymn celebrated "the mighty motherland of free people."

George Orwell reflected on these questions in *Animal Farm: A Fairy Story* (1945) by giving a variety of hymns and chants to the animals which interrogate the relationship between collective utterance and popular sovereignty. The anthem of animalism, "Beasts of England," is a knowing reference to radical socialist songs like Edward Carpenter's "England, Arise!" as well as Percy Shelley's "The Masque of Anarchy." "Beasts of England" is a rebel song of resistance and embattled solidarity, which looks forward to a "Golden future time" when "Tyrant Man shall be overthrown."[17] But like "L'Internationale," it changes its relationship to institutionalized power when it becomes established as the national anthem of a new workers' state. It is sung at official political occasions, as if to underline that Animal Farm has achieved the utopian promise of a "Golden future time."

Yet the words of "Beasts of England" continue to evoke a sense of hope for a better future, and so it becomes a means to articulate popular resistance against the pigs' tyrannical rule over Animal Farm. After a show trial in which several animals are brutally killed, Clover—a cart horse—begins singing the song as a "substitute for the words she was unable to find." The other animals take up the tune "slowly and mournfully, in a way they had never sung it before." The collective voice itself takes on a melancholy but also distinctly sardonic tone. The next day, "Beasts of England" is banned and replaced, in all its ritual roles, with a simple pledge of loyalty to the state: "Animal Farm! Animal Farm! / Never through me shall thou come to harm!"[18] Radical songs have the potential to become state anthems, but there is always the possibility that even rulers who strongly identify with those songs will come to find them inconvenient, or that new resistance movements will gravitate to them. Elements of their original radicalism can seem to be retained, despite their newly hegemonic position.

For the sociologist Ernest Gellner, the emergence of nationalism as an ideology can be understood as an effect of the transition from an agrarian to an industrial society. Gellner's theory can help us to understand what happens to collective speech practices that seem to be embedded in a specific *ethnos*—the Jane Harrison world of seasonal rituals, rain dances, and work songs—in the transition to industrial society, and in the context of the rise of the nation-state as modernity's basic political unit. Gellner points out that in preindustrial, agrarian societies, state power is wielded by a literate elite, which is "rigidly separate from the great majority of agricultural producers, or peasants." This elite may be "sub-divided into a number of more specialized layers," but the most fundamental separation of all is between these ruling classes and the rest, "another world" of peasant communities, "laterally separated" from one another and largely self-contained.[19] Gellner expresses this mapping of preindustrial society in a diagram (fig. 5). Figure 5 presents those peasant communities as laterally separated from each other, constituting relatively independent ethnolinguistic units, coexisting within the boundaries of the state. Each of these groups will have its own oral culture, often expressed in collective

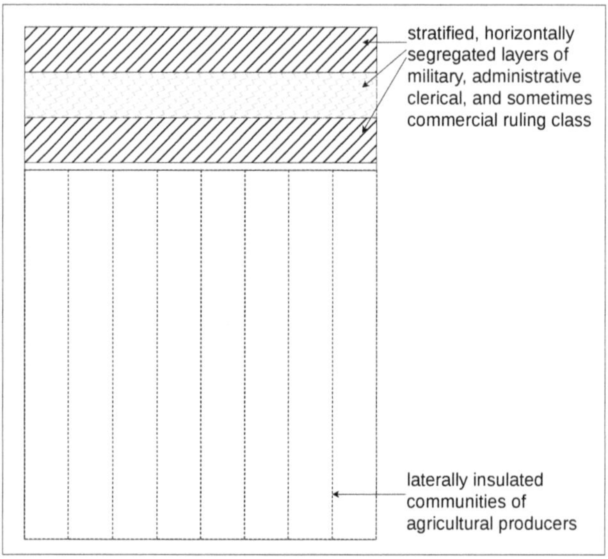

FIGURE 5: General Form of the Social Structure of Agrarian Societies. From Ernest Gellner, *Nations and Nationalism* (1983).

speech rituals: May dances, harvest festivals, fertility rites, work songs, and so on. Of course many of these cultural expressions may in reality be shared between multiple groups: Gellner explicitly rejects essentialist accounts of the ethnic purity of these groups, emphasizing the diversity of "cultures, often subtly grouped, shading into each other, overlapping, intertwined," and coexisting in the agrarian state.[20]

Sitting above this vertically segregated peasantry are the military, religious, mercantile, and political elites: the horizontally stratified hierarchy that operates at the level of the state, and that consciously distances itself, culturally, ritually, and linguistically, from the peasant producers. The literate strata also have a significant ritual culture, which can be called liturgy. Gellner points out that this is anything but a shared language of the people: "The tendency of liturgical languages to become distinct from the vernacular is very strong: it is as if literacy alone did not create enough of a barrier between cleric and layman, as if the chasm between them had to be developed, by making the language not merely recorded in an inaccessible script, but also incomprehensible when articulated."[21] Liturgical rituals, in an agrarian society, double down on the idea of an absolute separation between the literate minority and the majority of agricultural workers. Gellner refers most obviously to the liturgy of the Catholic Church, which was spoken in Latin, often inaudibly as well as incomprehensibly ("muttered in low tones, and in a language unknown to the people," as Alan Jacobs writes).[22] This ruling class is "much more interested in differentiating itself from those below than in diffusing its own culture to them," and moreover its culture—the Latin Mass, say—is "more than national," being the shared property of the ruling classes of multiple states.[23] The idea of a *national* culture is profoundly at odds with the way in which agrarian societies are structured in Gellner's view: at this stage, "to try to impose on all levels of society a universalised clerisy and a homogenised culture would be an idle dream."[24]

It is the transition to industrial society—Gellner worked in a Weberian tradition and prefers this term to "capitalism"—that gives life to the nationalist dream. In industrial society, national educational systems, promoting universal literacy and cultural homogeneity, supplement and to some extent replace "localized acculturation," supplying a "standardized medium, a common conceptual currency" which allows a diverse and dispersed population to imagine themselves as a cultural unit.[25] Gellner describes a process of cultural "entropy" by which state-backed educational and cultural projects work to eradicate internal cultural divisions, which now appear as an embarrassing residue of a more hierarchical form of social organization. Allegiance to the national culture—of which anthems are an eloquent symbol—now theoretically supersedes all other forms of ethnic belonging.

Gellner's argument supplies an interesting frame for understanding the social functions and historical development of a variety of collective speech practices. In his model of an agrarian society, such practices may be thought of as occurring on two sharply differentiated levels: the liturgical and the vernacular (which he sometimes calls "high" and "low" culture). In modern, industrial societies, there is a deliberate effort to synthesize the vernacular and the liturgical levels, to form a new and de-hierarchized, shared national culture. This is underpinned by literacy and "high" culture, but it is also manifested in new forms of national populism, which imagine the majority of people within a given political unit sharing a common culture that underpins the legitimacy of the state.

The collective speech forms that I have been inspecting in this book are partly defined by the ways they negotiate a Gellnerian transition between an internally variegated and hierarchical agrarian state, and the entropic, literate, national culture of an industrial society. Gellner does not attempt a diagram of a national, industrial society. Perhaps, by paying attention to the positionality of collective speech forms, as I have been doing, we can start to see that—while homogeneity may be the implied goal of nationalist politics—a simple circle representing a homogeneous national monoculture would not begin to illustrate the complexity of what is in reality going on. Such a diagram would somehow have to take account of the persistent cultural residues of agrarian society *within* the modern nation—often embodied in collective speech acts—whose desire and ability to hold out against the homogenizing and entropic effects of national education systems, media cultures, and so on Gellner perhaps understates. Along with this goes a certain persistence of the cultural hierarchies of agrarian society. Gellner's unidirectional "modernization" model also underrates the significance of the emergence of new and resistant subcultures, countercultures, and "emergent" cultures, which have been extensively theorized in the tradition of British cultural studies: "resistance through rituals."[26]

The preceding chapters are full of examples of collective speech acts that emerged *within* industrial modernity, among subnational groupings that are the loci of ethno-cultural belonging. In terms of my conceptual mapping of collective speech, the collective rites discussed in my first chapter and by Haggard, C. L. R. James, Senghor, or Hurston have different relationships to a presumed premodern, vernacular ritual culture. Hurston and James emphasized the syncretism and modernity of the rites they describe, where Haggard and Senghor saw them as expressions of a timeless, ontological Blackness. In both cases, they were taken to embody a refusal to be integrated into the "internally random and fluid totality" that is (white) national culture. They can therefore be seen as "entropy-resistant," in Gellner's terms, having "a marked tendency *not* to become . . . evenly dispersed throughout the entire society."[27] Channeling comparable acts of refusal into specific social, economic, and political demands (as in the collective utterances of striking workers), writers like Ousmane Sembène and Jacques Roumain imagined forms of collective utterance that were rooted in a culturally distinct *ethnos,* but implicitly directed towards the polis. Langston Hughes's work in the John Henry tradition (discussed in the previous chapter) took another step in that direction. Hughes took a work song, born in the railroad camp, and apparently belonging to the fugitive Black folk culture of the Jim Crow South, and wondered whether it might articulate (in the face of fascism at home and abroad) a unifying national myth. Could "John Henry" follow the route of "L'Internationale"?

The examples I have been discussing differ in important respects: while "L'Internationale" might be taken to be definitive of a particular socialist culture, it would not normally be taken as expressive of ethnic belonging, as "John Henry" sometimes is. And, while Hughes was thinking about the need for national unity at wartime, there is no indication that he was in fact interested in homogenizing US culture in the way that Gellner sees as essential to nationalism. In contrast, "Beasts of England" reflects Orwell's belief—articulated in *The Lion and the Unicorn* (1941)—that the aims of a socialist revolution should be fulfilled as part of "the task of bringing the real England to the surface."[28] Socialism already exists incipiently in the culture of what Orwell thought of as the ordinary, decent, English working class—the challenge is to make that the official culture of the state. Orwell's is, by Gellner's definition, a nationalist project. Gellner's scheme is a helpful tool for understanding why hegemonic collective speech—and its relationship to various preindustrial folk cultural expressions—becomes particularly important in industrial society. But if it provides a suggestive template, indicating what the fantasy of nationalism might look like, it also helps us to see that many collective speech forms will not fit into this, and in some cases deliberately resist such a fantasy.

Wole Soyinka: Collective Speech and the Postcolonial Nation

In the decades after 1945, the long arc of decolonization brought into being many new nationalisms, and with them many new national anthems. Wole Soyinka has explored the question of how ritual forms are incorporated into the cultural self-image of the postcolonial state across much of his work. His play *Kongi's Harvest* (1965) is perhaps the text in which he approaches this problem most directly, exploring how an authoritarian postcolonial state seeks to appropriate the ritual practices of an ethnic group, as a way to add cultural legitimacy to the pure exercise of power. Kongi is the autocratic president of Isma, often thought to be modelled on postcolonial leaders such as Kwame Nkrumah (Ghana) and Hastings Banda (Malawi) (though Soyinka downplayed these direct parallels emphasizing that the target of the satire was not Kongi himself, but "Kongism").[29] Meanwhile, Oba Danlola is at the center of an alternative power base, as the traditional and spiritual head of the people. The play dramatizes the preparation for the annual harvest ritual, at the center of which is a traditional ceremony in which the Oba tastes the first yam: the New Yam Festival.[30] Kongi—with the help of his scheming organizing secretary—is seeking to stage a set piece moment in which Danlola presents him with the new yam to taste. Kongi's often-stated objective is "harmony"—that is, a culturally homogeneous nation-state—and to achieve it, the Isma state will "replace the old superstitious festival by a state ceremony governed by the principle of Enlightened Ritualism" (as one of Kongi's henchmen puts it).[31] As in many of Soyinka's plays the action is punctuated with drumming, chanting, and singing, often in Yoruba. *Kongi's Harvest* stages a conflict over the ownership of these collective ritual forms, as the authoritarian, nationalist state seeks to absorb them, and thereby to assert its cultural legitimacy.

Kongi's symbolic updating of the harvest ritual is at best only a partial success. Danlola has been persuaded by Daodu (his son and heir) and Segi (a prostitute and Kongi's former lover) to yield to Kongi's demands and to present the new yam to Kongi at the festival. While it is hinted that this is part of a plan, neither Danlola nor the audience know that Daodu and Segi are plotting to assassinate Kongi. Just as Danlola is offering the yam to Kongi, Segi's father tries to kill Kongi, but instead is himself shot dead. Overcoming his initial fear, Kongi becomes triumphant and declares the opening of the feast with a speech that joins the fate of Isma to his own personal dominance, and ends in a collective call-and-response chant:

> KONGI: . . . The Spirit of Harvest has smitten the enemies of Kongi. The justice of the earth has prevailed over traitors and conspirators. There is divine blessing on the second Five-Year Development Plan. The spirit of resurgence is cleansed in the blood of the nation's enemies, my enemies, the enemies of our collective spirit, the Spirit of Planting, the Spirit of Harvest, the Spirit of Inevitable History and Victory, all of which I am. Kongi is every Ismite, and Ismite . . . [*shoots out a clenched fist*]
>
> BRIGADE: Is Might. . . .
>
> *[they beat on their drums and clash cymbals deafeningly]*
>
> KONGI: Ismite . . .
>
> BRIGADE: Is Might.[32]

While this call-and-response chanting has a ritualistic flavor, it is a simplistic celebration of state power that bears no relation to the traditional ritual cultures represented by Oba Danlola. Reversing that separation between actor and spectator described by Jane Harrison, the celebration descends into "*a genuine Harvest orgy of food and drink that permits no spectators, only celebrants.*"[33] A terrible parody of the traditional festival is enacted when Kongi is presented with a salver that contains, not the new yam, but the dismembered head of his would-be assassin.[34] Taken as a whole, the spectacle succeeds in underlining the state's power, but rather than glorifying it by associating it with the traditional rite, it exposes its reliance on violent compulsion.

This final scene—referred to in the stage directions explicitly as a "bacchanal"—seems a conscious reference to the ending of Euripides's *Bacchae,* a play which Soyinka would adapt for the London stage in 1973. In Euripides's play, Pentheus's bloody and dismembered head is brought onstage by Agave, who wields it as a trophy from the hunt. As Cadmus encourages her to reexamine the scene, Agave gradually realizes that she is cradling the head of her son and king Pentheus, and that it was him that she killed in her Dionysiac frenzy. At the end of the play Agave is exiled from Thebes, leaving Cadmus shaken but in charge.[35] This is a vital scene for the argument that Bonnie Honig sets out about the *Bacchae* in *A Feminist Politics of Refusal.* Honig claims, remember, that the bacchants' return to the polis enacts a substantial change, and a renegotiation of the women's position within the polis: it is a revolutionary regicide, as well as a tragic filicide. But Honig, of course, has to acknowledge the fact of Agave's exile, and her focus is on the agon between Cadmus and Agave as an "agon of fabulation." Honig asks us to recognize that the play's ending keeps two interpretations in view. "Agave wants to celebrate what Cadmus will want to condemn, to mythologize what Cadmus will pathologize, and to emplot as jubilee what Cadmus sees only as mournful tragedy."[36] This agon is a contest in which Cadmus's insistence on the tragic interpretation seeks to obscure the transformative politics of the former, which is grounded in the feminist sisterhood of bacchants. For Honig, the function of Cadmus's speech is effectively to "maternalize Agave," pulling her out of the chorus of maenads and reinserting her into a patriarchal hierarchy: "The leader of a chorus of free women is dead. She has been put back in her place."[37] As in *Kongi's Harvest,* the politics of the play turn on how the shocking presence of a bloodied and disembodied head onstage is interpreted.

Honig does not refer to Soyinka's *The Bacchae of Euripides: A Communion Rite* (1973), though it is a version that in many ways supports and supplements her reading of the play. Soyinka deliberately foregrounds the that the regicide was intentional, even if it (tragically) entailed Agave killing her son. Soyinka has sometimes been seen politically as on the liberal end of the anticolonial intelligentsia, but argued that "theater is perhaps the most revolutionary art known to man," in part because of "the sensual and the moral interaction, of the audience and the protagonist forces on the stage."[38] Throughout his theatrical work, Soyinka deploys choruses and choral speech in ways that self-consciously reflect on the democratic representation of "the people," the mediation between actors and spectators, and the centrality of ritual to both theatre and politics.[39]

What Soyinka does with the chorus in *The Bacchae of Euripides* is quite extraordinary. Alongside the Euripidean group of bacchants, he introduces a second chorus of slaves—bringing into the light the institution of slavery on which Theban society depended, as did the Athenian democracy in which Euripides first staged his *Bacchae*. Soyinka's slave chorus was also suggestive of the modern history of the racialized enslavement of Black Africans: he advised that the slave leader, at least, should be "fully negroid."[40] The slave chorus adds a significant political dimension to the play. As soon as the Dionysiac rites begin, the slave leader (who often leads the slave chorus in call-and-response chants) recognizes the Bacchic celebrants as potential allies—"fellow strangers to this land," he calls them, "fellow aliens."[41] If the slaves could join with Dionysus and his maenads, he speculates early in the play, there is potential to sweep away Pentheus's regime entirely:

> Nature has joined forces with us.
> Let them reckon now, not with mere men, not with
> The scapegoat bogey of a slave uprising
> But with a new remorseless order, forces
> Unpredictable as molten fire in mountain wombs.[42]

While Pentheus himself contrasts the apparent "chaos" of the Bacchic rites with his own attempts to "re-impose order,"[43] the slave leader's suggestion is that an alliance between the rebellious slave chorus and the chorus of bacchants is more than a disruptive force, and more than a "refusal" of the polis: it will itself wield the power of the state and bring a "new remorseless order." The chorus imagines itself moving from a position of rebellion to one of hegemony.

The fusion of the play's two choruses is fully consummated towards the end of the play, when Dionysus has set his trap for Pentheus, whose body will soon be torn limb from limb by his mother Agave and the other maenads. The voices of these two choruses join together in scene Soyinka describes in a stage direction: "Part of the Chorus of Slaves set up a dog-howl, a wail of death. Instantly a section separate themselves, move throughout the next speeches until they are joined with the Bacchantes. They form, for this last part, a solid fanatic front with the followers of Dionysos. The progress across should not be a dance, but a terse series of dramatic motions which takes its motif from the following invocation, the decisive gesture of throwing their lot with the Bacchae, the casting off of the long vassalage in the House of Pentheus."[44] The speeches that follow—spoken in canon rather than in unison, alternating between slaves and bacchants, but collectively owned by the group—give a strong political meaning to the killing of Pentheus. One slave says:

> Now we shall see the balance restored
> O Justice! O Spirit of Equity, Restitution
> Be manifest! A sharp clear sword
> With blood on its edge—drive
> To the gullet of Pentheus.[45]

While it is true that, at a similar point in Euripides's play, the chorus of bacchants do speak of administering "Justice," all the emphasis is on a religious understanding of the action: Pentheus must be punished because he disrespected the gods by suppressing the worship of Dionysus.[46] By bringing the slaves who are exploited and oppressed on Pentheus's estate into an alliance with the maenads, Soyinka's play makes a political reading of the play unavoidable while also changing the implied politics. Honig's reading emphasized the specifically feminist character of the bacchants' refusal, but Soyinka brings those bacchants into an alliance with male slaves who are bidding for revolutionary emancipation.

The significant changes that Soyinka makes to the ending of the play give a specific character to this political reading. Soyinka brings Tiresias back onstage to make this extraordinary speech (without an antecedent in Euripides):

> Perhaps . . . perhaps our life-sustaining earth
> Demands . . . a little more . . . sometimes, a more
> Than token offering for her own needful renewal.
> And who, more then we should know it? For all too many
> The soil of Thebes has proved a most unfeeling
> Host, harsh, unyielding, as if the dragon's teeth
> That gave it birth still farms its subsoil.
> They feel this, same as I, even through calloused soles.
> O Kadmos, it was a cause beyond madness, this
> Scattering of his flesh to the seven winds[47]

Tiresias's suggestion that there was a "cause beyond madness" driving the bacchants' murderous spree lends support to Honig's reading of the play, and loosens Kadmos's grip on the emplotment of the story as tragic filicide. As Mpalive-Hangson Msiska has argued, "In Euripides' play this is supposed to dramatize the barbarity of Bacchic worship; however, in Soyinka's text it is an extreme but understandable gesture of a radical dismemberment not of a son, but a monster of a tyrant."[48] Tiresias's speech also draws attention to the oppression of those for whom Thebes's soil has proved "hash, unyielding": the chorus of slaves on Pentheus's estate. Making this harsh treatment a material factor in the cause of the Dionysiac violence gives it a directly political meaning that Cadmus seeks to foreclose in Euripides's version.

But what happens next is an even starker reversal of the ancient original. Euripides showed Agave being banished from the city, as Cadmus becomes king and returns the polis to the patriarchal order. True, Cadmus had (unlike Pentheus) been willing to acknowledge Dionysos and to accord him his rites, so the change of king opens the possibility of a reformed polis that accords the Bacchic rites their place. But Soyinka's ending suggests a much more fundamental change. There is no banishment. Instead, "the theme music of Dionysos begins, welling up and filling the stage with the god's presence." Pentheus's disembodied head begins to glow red, and then, "from every orifice of the impaled head spring red jets," which Kadmos first assumes are of blood. Tiresias, however, tastes the liquid and says, "No. It's wine." Soyinka's closing stage direction is "Slowly, dream-like, they all move towards the fountain, cup their hands and drink. Agave raises herself at last to observe them, then tilts her head backwards to let a jet flush full in her face and flush her mouth. The light contracts to a final glow around the heads of Pentheus and Agave."[49] In this ending, the Dionysiac ritual has entirely enveloped the polis. The old patriarchal order is no longer in evidence: everybody has joined the chorus of bacchants. Where Honig imagined the bacchants' refusal on an arc that led to a renegotiation of their position within the polis, Soyinka's ending seems to imagine them taking over, and moving into a hegemonic position.

The visual rhyme between *The Bacchae of Euripides* and *Kongi's Harvest*—two plays that stage a bacchanal around a disembodied head—seems suggestive enough to help me build a bridge between chapters 2 and 3 in this book: from protest and political engagement to hegemony and liturgy. *Kongi's Harvest* can be read as an attempt to imagine what Dionysiac government would look like, and it does not stint in exploring the potential for authoritarianism in such a configuration. When the Carpenters' Brigade marches onstage to prepare the scene for the ceremony of the new yam, they are "uniformed, heavy mallets swinging from their waists." They are singing their own anthem, a kind of work song, that channels the working people's productive energies in the direction of a violently enforced national harmony:

> Men of peace and honour
> Are the Carpenters' Brigade
> But primed for fight or action
> To defend our motherland
> We spread the creed of Kongism
> To every son and daughter
> And heads too slow to learn it
> Will feel our mallets' weight.[50]

We have already seen in other contexts how work songs, which seem to be generated spontaneously from the rhythms of labor, can be corralled into democratic projects as an embodiment of "the voice of the people." Langston Hughes's variations on the John Henry tradition are a case in point—and as we saw, they eventually point, however uncomfortably, towards a *national* framing of the collective voice, putting productive labor at the service of the state. Soyinka's Carpenters' Brigade take this further:

> We sweat in honest labour
> From sunrise unto dawn
> For the dignity of labour
> And the progress of our land.

While the national unity promoted by Hughes's work songs was an optimistic projection about a possible future in which the USA could resolve its racial conflicts, the carpenters' anthem celebrates Isma as a completed utopia, while threatening violence to any dissenters. Soyinka's satire is not particularly subtle: at the end of the song, his stage direction has the carpenters "march downstage with stiff mallet-wielding arms pistoning up in the Nazi salute."[51]

Many writers, including Orwell and Soyinka, who envision a politically active function for the collective voice, are also fearful that its simplifying tendencies, and its impetus towards unison and unanimity, have the potential to turn revolutionary movements into repressive and even totalitarian states. In his post-9/11 Reith Lectures—published as *Climate of Fear* (2004)—Soyinka developed this intuition to a more generalized warning about the dangers of "rhetorical hysteria" and "the nurturing environment of the mantra."[52] Contemplating those forms of contemporary radicalism—from Marxist-Leninism, to Islamism, to postcolonial nationalism—that have inspired their most fanatical adherents to acts of terrorism and violence, he proposes a strong link between religious and political forms of fanaticism, asking, "Just what is it that turns the mantra of a beatific chant of faith, such as 'Allah akbar' into a summons to an orgy of death?" His third lecture, entitled "Rhetoric that Binds and Blinds," concludes with this thought: "The fault, of course, is not in religion but in the fanatic of every religion. Fanaticism remains the greatest carrier of the spores of fear, and the rhetoric of religion, with the hysteria it so readily generates, is fast becoming the readiest killing device of recent times. Even after half a century, films that touch upon the era of Nazi glorification, with their orchestrated chant of *Sieg heil,* continue to send a chill of apprehension down the spines of all with a historical memory. Scenes of mass religious frenzy increasingly resurrect these nightmares."[53] Of course, Soyinka recognizes the existence of more benign forms of religion, and hopes for "the dissociation of the chant of millions to the greatness of God from the gross ultra-nationalist politics lodged in the chant of *Sieg heil.*"[54] By imagining the collective voice weaving religion and politics in a toxic way that lends itself to fascism, Soyinka foreshadows some of the concerns of my next and final chapter, which turns to liturgical forms of collective vocalization, which support and are supported by ecclesiastical or state authority.

THREE

LITURGY/HEGEMONY

TO IMAGINE THE COLLECTIVE voice as a source of popular resistance, or in a democratic campaign for recognition, sometimes involves looking forward to a future in which the battle is won, and where political antagonisms have been satisfactorily resolved. The warmth and fellow feeling of the assembly, proclaiming "we, the people" in unison and in protest, can become a template for a polity whose boundaries are aligned with a shared, common culture—most obviously in the American Revolution, which culminated in the drafting of a constitution that begins with that exact phrase. In modern nationalism, collective utterance may become both a spiritual expression of ethnic belonging, and a pledge of political fealty to a state. By looking at the collective voice in toto, and thinking of it as a single object, one can see that the distance between vocalizations of popular sovereignty that have a protesting relationship with the polis (in chapter 2), and ones that are aligned with the polis (in chapter 3), is not—or at least not always—so very large.

Gramscian accounts of the interaction between politics and culture are useful here because they see the process of securing proletarian hegemony on the left—that is, securing intellectual and moral leadership within a broad alliance that brings together workers, peasants, and subaltern groups—as analogous with, and transitional to, the maintenance of a hegemonic state.[1] Gramsci foregrounds the "cultural aspect" of this process, arguing:

> An historical act can only be performed by "collective man," and this presupposes the attainment of a "cultural-social" unity through which a multiplicity of dispersed wills, with heterogeneous aims, are welded together

> with a single aim, on the basis of an equal and common conception of the world, both general and particular, operating in transitory bursts (in emotional ways) or permanently (where the intellectual base is so well rooted, assimilated and experienced that it becomes passion). Since this is the way things happen, great importance is assumed by the general question of language, that is, the question of collectively attaining a single cultural "climate."[2]

Collective speech acts of various kinds—including socialist songs, pledges of fealty to the cause, and so on—can be thought of as a part of a wider cultural climate that justifies and helps to maintain political power. The forms of collective vocalization that I discuss in this chapter seem to literalize that process by which "a multiplicity of dispersed wills, with heterogeneous aims, are welded together with a single aim."

To work effectively as a hegemonic form, collective utterances cannot simply be imposed by force. They need to feel like they express a sense of belonging in a community, or feed a deep, shared spiritual need. Modern, industrial societies, organized into nation-states, often foster collective speech acts that work like Eric Hobsbawm's "invented traditions": "a set of practices, normally governed by overtly or tacitly accepted rules and of a ritual or symbolic nature, which seek to inculcate certain values and norms of behaviour by repetition."[3] Sociologists (following Durkheim) often claimed that religious rituals play a significant role in generating social cohesion, helping to guarantee political stability.[4] Secularizing societies, like that of postrevolutionary France, therefore sought to develop forms of "civil religion," with their accompanying collective speech rituals.[5] In contrast, and at the same time, religious beliefs, rituals, and institutions have continued to play an important role in legitimizing and glorifying state power.

It is this phenomenon that animates Giorgio Agamben's *The Kingdom and the Glory* (2007, trans. 2011). Setting out to explore the relation "between power as government and effective management, and power as ceremonial and liturgical regality," Agamben asks, "Why does power need glory?"[6] Collective vocalization plays a small but symbolically significant role in the argument he unfolds around "acclamation." The word "amen," collectively uttered by Jews and Christians in response to, and at the end of, prayer, is described by Agamben as "the acclamation par excellence."[7] Originally a Hebrew term that "belongs to the semantic sphere of stability and fidelity," Agamben traces the history of its "nontranslation into Greek and Latin," and the subsequent "desemanticization" of a word whose "effect and function are more important than its meaning."[8] In chapter 1, we encountered apparently nonsemantic or untranslatable collective vocalizations—in Zora Neale Hurston's hoodoo initiation, or in the "Eh! Bomba!" chant associated with the Haitian Revolution—that expressed a fugitive sociality: a refusal of the polis and its semantic codes. "Amen" is functionally nonsemantic, and being uttered collectively, it could in some contexts express a fugitive sociality (e.g., in the Black church, discussed in chapter 1). But in many contexts—like the ones I focus on in this chapter—it acts in the opposite direction, binding religious observers to the power of the church, the nation, and the state. Agamben argues that collective acclamations—he names "halleluiah," "bravo," "Heil Hitler," and "Duce duce" as well as "amen"—serves to glorify political power.[9] They are therefore crucially important for an understanding of how power works in general since—in Agamben's view at least—power *needs* glory. This chapter focuses on forms of collective speech whose function is to secure and assert hegemonic power, rather than refusing or challenging it.

Just as the previous chapters focused on voodoo and the Greek chorus, this chapter uses the Anglican liturgy as its central example, tracing its political resonance as a key form of collective speech, through a number of texts and writers. These twentieth-century ideas about hegemonic collective speech were shaped by the earlier history of the Reformation, where fundamental political realignments were explicitly channeled through a ferocious debate about collective speech rituals.[10] The schism in the Western church still reverberated in twentieth-century literature and intellectual culture. This chapter investigates liturgical collective speech in works by T. S. Eliot, Benjamin Britten, Montagu Slater, Ngũgĩ wa Thiong'o, and Katharine Burdekin, to show how twentieth-century intellectual culture continued to process the English Reformation's realignment of church and state, glory and power.

Such literary work emerged from an intellectual context in which modern ills were frequently attributed to the legacy of the Reformation. In particular, thinkers from Max Weber to Walter Ong, and from Alasdair MacIntyre to Ian Watt and Elizabeth Eisenstein, characterized the Protestant Reformation as a powerfully individualizing force. According to these influential thinkers, the Reformation was an epistemic shift with profound social, political, and intellectual consequences, underpinned by the rise of print culture, increasing literacy, the privatization of silent reading, the development of a more secular, humanistic education, a loosening of the traditional bonds of feudal society, and the onset of capitalism. For scholars such as these, the Reformation was a decisive break from the collective and communal structures of medieval Catholicism, in the direction of a solipsistic and deracinated individualism.[11]

However, more recently, scholars have challenged this view, in ways that are suggestive for this chapter's consideration of the collective voice. For thinkers such as Brian Cummings, Alan Jacobs, and Ramie Targoff, the Reformation is best understood not as the invention of private individualism, but on the contrary as a concerted attempt to "subsume private devotion within the public liturgy of the church" and—through the agency of the newly established national church, acting as an arm of the state—to bring the individual conscience under political control.[12] This is most evident in the controversies that surrounded the Book of Common Prayer: the book that introduced a standardized Christian liturgy in vernacular English—including prescribing collective set prayers—for the first time. The daily pattern of services and rituals encoded in the Book of Common Prayer were established as the only legal form of worship from the first Act of Uniformity in 1549, and the book remained at the center of the official religious life of Britain and its empire for centuries, with two important hiatuses: first, when the Catholic Mary ruled from 1553 to 1588, and second, during the Puritan protectorate from 1645 to 1660.[13]

Because of its legal status as the "*only* legal liturgy in England," it became a "carrier of national identity." As Cummings affirms, "the book is thus by definition not only religious but political."[14] For Thomas Cranmer, the evangelical author of the first Book of Common Prayer, that book played the vital role of forming a political and religious community under Anglicanism. As Jacobs writes, "it was necessary *for the English church,* a theologico-political entity, that worship be embodied by one book, in one language, that mandated one use."[15] For a time, the penalties for refusing to take part in those same rituals included death. But it is also true that for many people over the long history of the Book of Common Prayer, its rituals provided solace, community, and spiritual fulfilment. It is an eloquent illustration of Gramsci's definition of the state as "dictatorship + hegemony," where brute compulsion is accompanied, to an extent concealed, and perhaps even partially superseded, by hegemonic cultural forms and institutions—associated with patterns of collective speech—that promote a sense of belonging, inclusion, and shared identity.[16]

To understand how the politics of the English Reformation resonate in twentieth-century literature, it is also important to acknowledge the ongoing importance of seventeenth-century *resistance* to this alignment of state power with hegemonic collective vocalization. Puritans objected to the whole principle of reciting prayers in unison. John Milton's *Eikonoklastes* (1649), for example, abominated "the servile yoak of liturgy." The attempt, Milton argued, "to imprison and confine by force, into a pinfold of set words, those two most unimprisonable things, our prayers, and that divine spirit of utterance that moves them, is a tyranny."[17] This idea that the spoken unison of set prayers is inherently tyrannical points to a strong individualist streak among the Puritans who won a brief political victory in the English Civil War (even if their forms of worship did also involve other forms of embodied collectivity). Scholars like Watt and MacIntyre erred when they took Puritanism as a development that distilled the essence of the Reformation, which they then interpreted as a fundamentally individualistic movement. Part of the force of the revisionist account of the Reformation set out by Cummings, Jacobs, and Targoff is to relegate the individualistic impulses of Puritan prayer from their epoch-defining status. Instead, Puritanism can be seen as the ideology of an insurgent and often embattled minority as they resisted a hegemonic Anglicanism. It was briefly in the ascendancy during the Cromwellian protectorate, when the Book of Common Prayer was temporarily abolished. But a central project of reformed Anglicanism was to align the praying conscience with political power, via the promulgation of set prayers for collective utterance.

T. S. Eliot: Chorus as Liturgy

The new understanding of the political functions of the Anglican liturgy in the Reformation that I have just described can also help to illuminate the politics of twentieth-century debates about collective speech. T. S. Eliot famously described himself (after his conversion in 1927) as "Anglo-Catholic in religion," and invested a great deal in the potential of Christianity to *counter* what he saw as the excessive individualism of capitalist industrial society, which he attributed, like Watt and MacIntyre, to the Reformation. This was reflected in his devotional practice: he had a predilection for Latin rites and even included these in his pageant *The Rock* (1934). In his own worship Eliot used *The English Missal,* a 1912 translation of the Roman Missal, rendered in sixteenth-century language that often drew on Cranmer's Prayer Book, which had become prevalent in Anglo-Catholic devotional practices.[18] Yet, in his literary work and his activities within the sphere of liturgical reform, he showed himself deeply committed to the key texts of the English Reformation: the King James Bible, the Book of Common Prayer, and in particular (incorporated in both) the poetry of Myles Coverdale's 1535 English translation of the Psalms. Influential Anglo-Catholics such as Gregory Dix saw this an impossible fusion, holding that (in Jamie Callison's words) "the Anglican liturgy was as Protestant as it came, representing a break with . . . Christian heritage."[19] At once an Anglo-Catholic and a vigorous defender of the Book of Common Prayer, Eliot spent his religious life trying to ride two bicycles at the same time.

Eliot felt that the foundational Anglican texts of the Reformation prescribed collective utterances in a shared vernacular as a way of binding the nation together under the hegemony of the Church. With conscious anachronism, Eliot mobilized the language of the Book of Common Prayer in *Murder in the Cathedral* (1935), in order to "emphasise Catholic continuity rather than Protestant rupture," as Barry Spurr points out. In the twelfth century of Eliot's play, centuries before the schism in the Western church or the emergence of a vernacular liturgy of any kind, "Thomas Becket himself uses Thomas Cranmer's words."[20] This telling anachronism suggests that Eliot saw the Book of Common Prayer as a stabilizing point in English culture that could effectively be projected back into the pre-Reformation period, being essentially equivalent to the liturgical practices of medieval Catholicism.[21] Spurr arguably underplays just how idiosyncratic a gesture this was: as Callison argues, twentieth-century Anglo-Catholics tended to see the Book of Common Prayer as an essentially Protestant deviation from Catholic worship.

Still, Spurr is right to point out that the history of the Book of Common Prayer after the Reformation saw it become increasingly associated with High Church tendencies. Following the restoration of the monarchy in 1660, another Act of Uniformity in 1662 reinstated an updated version of the Book of Common Prayer as the official liturgy of the church. Jacobs points out, with reference to this later history, that "the image of one nation bound together by one use and one book, sometimes put forth by lovers of the Prayer Book, is a consoling fiction."[22] But Jacobs also notes that the Prayer Book was disproportionately influential because it was so embedded in the daily habits of England's ruling elites. The rituals it set out were particularly important for the upper middle class: in public schools and, right up to the early twentieth century, in the colleges of Oxford and Cambridge, it was compulsory to attend morning prayer every day and to participate in the liturgy as set down in the Prayer Book of 1662.[23] These are the hegemonic collective utterances of the British establishment, and they echoed throughout its empire.

Eliot thought deeply about the social and cultural role of this liturgy, and, at least from the moment of his conversion in 1927, these thoughts infused his poetry, drama and cultural criticism. His "Dialogue on Poetic Drama"—presented as a wide-ranging conversation between seven interlocutors who express differing views on these topics—one of the speakers ("E") makes a strong link between drama and liturgy, and expresses a programmatic desire to bring them back together: "I say . . . that drama springs from religious liturgy, and that it cannot afford to depart very far from religious liturgy. . . . When drama has ranged as far as it has in our own day, is not the only solution to return to religious liturgy?"[24] This argument Christianizes Jane Harrison's claims about the origins of drama in pagan rituals, as well as gesturing to the specific history of medieval religious drama in Britain.[25] In *Sweeney Agonistes* (as I touched on in chapter 1), Eliot had brought onstage a primitive chorus, recognizable from Jane Harrison and from Nietzsche, framing it in racist terms. After his conversion, Eliot imagined that drama and religious ritual—which had drifted apart with the emergence of reflective spectatorship—could be put back together again.

Eliot's first attempt to achieve this came in *The Rock*, a pageant play commissioned to raise funds for the Forty-Five Churches Fund, which aimed to build new churches to serve London's northward suburban expansion. As Jed Esty has written, this offered Eliot "a chance to connect more directly to the public by using a popular and traditional English form."[26] The main action of the play has a contemporary setting, dramatizing the building of a church, but this is interspersed with tableaux from English religious history. The Puritan strains that came to the fore in the English Revolution are explicitly identified, in *The Rock*, as a threat to the unity of the church. In a crowd scene set in the revolutionary ferment of 1640, a Puritan preacher speaks up to condemn "their stinted service"—that embodied in the Book of Common Prayer—as "a Popish beadroll of full of vain repetitions as if seven paternosters did please the Lord better than six."[27] The critique of set prayers was familiar to Eliot from his reading of Milton, Bunyan, and other Puritan writers. The preacher echoes that critique as he compares the "tossing to and fro of psalms and sentences" to "tennis play whereto God is called a judge who can do best and be most gallant in his worship." Coming onto the stage carrying piles of "altar-books"—the Book of Common Prayer—a crowd of Puritans "deface and cut them, and, bringing more fuel, make a bonfire," in a direct attack on liturgical ritual. In 1934, the spectacle of a group of zealots burning books had an obvious resonance with contemporary events in Nazi Germany.[28]

As is often the case in *The Rock*, the point is made not only through a satirical portrayal within the dramatic tableau, but also through the direct statements of the chorus in an ode which immediately follows it. The Puritans have already been made to look like Nazis—but next, the chorus accuses them of puffed-up vanity: "they walk in the street proudnecked, like thoroughbreds ready for races." The same ode also objects to the whole mood of the preacher's address, demanding, "Who is this that has said: the House of God is a House of Sorrow?" The chorus pleads that the Puritan emphasis on private penitence can and ought to be transformed into a more joyful public worship:

> Let us mourn in a private chamber, learning the way of penitence,
> And then let us learn the joyful communion of saints.

This is implicitly linked to the building of the church, and, within it, the practice of its liturgy:

> Out of the sea of sound the life of music,
> Out of the slimy mud of words, out of the sleet and hail of verbal
>   imprecisions,
> Approximate thoughts and feelings, words that have taken the
>   place of thoughts and feelings,
> There spring the perfect order of speech, and the beauty of
>   incantation.
>
> LORD, shall we not bring these gifts to Your service?[29]

The chorus both embodies a revitalized ritualism and argues for it. Those improvised prayers that the penitent sinner utters in private may be necessary, but they are part of a "slimy mud of words," inevitably approximate and imprecise. Only liturgical language—the shared property of a whole religious community, repeated over centuries—can attain "the perfect order of speech, and the beauty of incantation." These are the gifts that the congregation—brought together in churches and guided by the inherited wisdom and the beauties of the altar book—can offer to God.

The chorus plays a central role in *The Rock,* but its relationship to the dramatic action of the tableaux is often in question. Is this collectively speaking group a representation of the audience onstage, of "the people" themselves, or of Eliot as author (of what was in practice a collaborative work)? In an opening stage direction in the published script, the chorus is said to be composed of "seven male and ten female figures" who will "speak as the voice of the Church of God." This collective voice is *not* of the people as a whole, and indeed represents an embattled Christian minority in modern society, marginalized by the "cultural disintegration" that Eliot diagnosed in his 1948 jeremiad, *Notes Towards the Definition of Culture.*[30] The chorus opens the play by complaining that the church has lost its centrality in English life:

> . . . the Church does not seem to be wanted
> In country or in suburb; and the town
> Only for important weddings.[31]

The chorus is the church, bemoaning its own marginalization, but it is also Eliot himself. Eliot later argued in his essay "The Three Voices of Poetry" that poetry can speak in only three voices: "the poet talking to himself—or to nobody," "the poet addressing an audience," or "the poet when he attempts to create a dramatic character speaking in verse."[32] Reflecting on the chorus in *The Rock,* he decides that "it was the second voice, that of myself addressing—indeed haranguing—an audience, that was most distinctly audible."[33]

This explanation, written around twenty years after the event, is a post hoc rationalization that does not fully explain how the chorus functions in *The Rock.* It is true that having one's own words spoken by a seventeen-person chorus is one way of simply amplifying them, and that this could create the effect of a harangue. After seeing the 1936 Group Theatre production of Auden and Isherwood's *The Dog Beneath the Skin* (1935), Eliot was irritated by what he saw as the preachiness of its chorus.[34] Anonymous choruses, Eliot implied, risk becoming the didactic carriers of the playwright's own views, with the multiplication of speakers in unison tending to create a monologic drone. Eliot felt that he had resolved this to some extent in *Murder in the Cathedral* by writing "not for an anonymous chorus, but for a chorus of women of Canterbury."[35] This is a move from the second to the third voice of poetry in Eliot's schema—that is, from "the poet addressing an audience" to the creation of "a dramatic character speaking in verse." Eliot may have absorbed from Wagner the sense that the chorus can thrive in modern drama only when it functions as a group of characters within the fictional lifeworld of the play's dramatic action (as I discussed in chapter 2).

In *The Rock,* the chorus wants to imagine the possibility that it—as the voice of the church—could provide a unifying liturgy to bring a divided and fractured cultural scene together. The Puritan burning of the "altar-book" suggests one origin for the fragmentation diagnosed by the play. But Eliot also takes aim at modern political movements, which offer concerted political action—also embodied dramatically in collective speech—as a remedy for modern alienation. The chorus is confronted at one point by groups of young, ideologically militant redshirts (communists) and blackshirts (fascists). As the redshirts come onto the stage, the chorus turns expectantly to them, asking, "Bring you some succour for our failing strength?" The redshirts speak "in unison, with military gestures":

millions and millions of workers
all working
all loving
in the cities
on the steppes
production has risen by twenty point six per cent
we can laugh at God!
our workers
all working
our turbines
all turning
our sparrows
all chirping
all denounce you, deceivers of the people!’[36]

This militaristic unison solidifies around a soulless, materialistic creed, where an increase in industrial productivity makes God a laughing stock. Nodding to the Marxist critique of religion as the opium of the people, the redshirts also echo the sentiments of the agitator, who encourages those workers engaged in building the church to "lay down your tools and refuse to work on a buildin' which is only for the purpose o' dopin' the workers."[37] Marxism is portrayed as a divisive force whose atheism ultimately undermines the only hope of social cohesion: the church.

Concluding that the redshirts offer no hope of cultural and spiritual renewal, the chorus says, "Alas! There is no help here," then turns hopefully to the fascist blackshirts who enter "in military formation." Also speaking in unison, they profess to be "*law-keeping fellows who make their own laws*," ask insistently for money, and spout antisemitic slurs, refusing to "*descend to palaver with anthropoid Jews*."[38] Reflecting on both communism and fascism (which are made to seem equivalent in the scene, as in Eliot's cultural criticism from the period) the chorus says:

There seems no hope from those who march in step,
We have no help from those with new evangels.

The "new evangels"—here meaning the new holy books of these political religions—seem to produce a rote conformity that is familiar from other derogatory portrayals of the collective voice as a conveyor of regimented ideological enthusiasm.

Eliot's chorus also speaks in unison but apparently avoids this rigidity. Both redshirts and blackshirts are presented as militaristic, and their collective utterances are regimented. The chorus concludes:

> There is no help in parties . . .
> There is no help in those whose souls are choked and swaddled
> In . . .
> . . . . the new winding sheets of mass-made thought
> . . .
> We speak to you as individual men;
> As individuals alone with GOD.
> Alone with GOD, you first learn brotherhood with men.[39]

The uniformity offered by modern political ideologies of the left and right (with their "new evangels") does not speak to the people as "individual men," but serves up "mass-made thought," to be spoken in an unthinking and uniform way. Eliot's redshirts and blackshirts seem to have done away with internal hierarchies, at the cost of a loss of individuality. In *Notes Towards the Definition of Culture,* Eliot wrote: "A people should be neither too united nor too divided, if its culture is to flourish. . . . Neither a classless society, nor a society of strict and impenetrable social barriers is good; each class should have constant additions and defections; the classes, while remaining distinct, should be able to mix freely; and they should all have a community of culture with each other which will give them something in common, more fundamental than the community with which each class has with its counterpart in another society."[40] The "something in common" is—at least in *Notes*—to be articulated on a national level. The idea is that the British working class ought to have more culturally in common with the British aristocracy than it does with the French working class. The vernacular English liturgy set out in the Book of Common Prayer is the template for that national cohesion.

A similar approach is taken to cultural variation between the regions of the United Kingdom, as Eliot imagines "a national culture which will draw its vitality from the cultures of its several areas, within each of which again there will be smaller units of culture having their own local peculiarities."[41] He continues: "The ideal reunion of all Christians does not, of course, imply an eventual *uniform* culture the world over: it implies simply a 'Christian culture' of which all local cultures should be variants—and they would and should vary very widely indeed."[42] Consciously or not, Eliot's rejection of the word "uniform" in *Notes Towards the Definition of Culture* gestures back to the Acts of Uniformity that mandated the Book of Common Prayer as the only legitimate form of prayer. While the lasting resonance of the words of the Prayer Book is no doubt partly due to their history as a compulsory ritual, Eliot argues that hegemony requires internal variation and flexibility. So, while his emphasis on the cultural importance of liturgy bears comparison with Gellner's model of the culture of the nation-state, Eliot also emphasizes a significant counterentropic structure of social differentiation and hierarchy, sheltered under the umbrella of a national culture embodied in liturgy. The ideal towards which Eliot's play pushes—the extension of the church, and its liturgy, to all—is not about generating a de-hierarchized, uniform equality: as Esty puts it, he "builds difference back into his model of a self-identical, self-possessed England."[43] All will speak a version of the liturgy, but among the speakers there will be a significant variation in social class and rank—and even theological differences. The "brotherhood" that *The Rock*'s chorus invokes will bring "men" together not through the horizontal solidarity of class politics, but through the vertical integration of a "common culture" in a Christian nation.

The Rock therefore imagines the politics of collective vocalization at two separate levels. First, there are the strident political chants like those of the redshirts and the blackshirts, whose demand for regimented uniformity is itself seen as schismatic, and which are intentionally divisive and oppositional. Eliot thus presents a savage satire of the forms of collective speech described in chapter 2 of this book, under the rubric of protest and engagement. Second, there is liturgical collective speech, which is flexible enough to admit significant local variation within a polity stratified by class and segmented by region, unifying them around a nationally grounded religious ritual culture with a shared vernacular. The kind of variation Eliot practiced in his own ritual life—using the *English Missal* while defending the Book of Common Prayer—is thus reflected on the political level in a vision of a national liturgy that might become universal without being uniform.

T. S. Eliot in the Valley of the Shadow of Death

For Eliot, it was in Christian liturgy that poetry found its true vocation as a cohesive social force, and the Book of Common Prayer was the central instance of this. How can we square Eliot's long-standing belief in the unifying power of liturgy, and his equally long-standing skepticism of efforts to modernize the liturgy, with his decision to join the Archbishops' Commission to Revise the Psalter (1958–63)? This commission worked to "remove obscurities and serious errors of translation" in the Psalms, while promising to "retain, as far as possible, the general character in style and rhythm of Coverdale's version and its suitability for congregational use."[44] The archival records of the commission are revealing of Eliot's late concerns, and shed a new light on his earlier career as a poet and a critic, as, in his later years, he sought to shape the institutions of poetry and of Christian worship. As he put it in an autobiographical note of 1960, "I am much concerned with the problem of saving the London Library, threatened with ruin by the exactions of the Inland Revenue, and with the revision of the Psalter."[45] This may seem somewhat surprising given Eliot's deep attachment to the early modern English of the Book of Common Prayer and the King James Bible ("an exemplar of English prose for successive generations of writers"), and his suspicion of contemporary translations: he deplored the New English Bible (New Testament published in 1961) for its "combination of the vulgar, the trivial, and the pedantic."[46]

To understand these apparent contradictions, we need to trace Eliot's views on the Book of Common Prayer over a longer period. Eliot's conversion in 1927 happed to coincide with the Prayer Book controversy of 1927–28: the first concerted attempt to revise the Book of Common Prayer since 1662. The mass slaughter of the Great War had a destabilizing effect on a liturgy that had become associated with establishment elites. As Jacobs writes, "The intrinsically repetitive character of liturgy reinforces the feeling of mindlessness, of saying without thinking, and the Prayer Book's fixed place in the Establishment connects it with vast, pitiless institutional forces—forces that blithely send young men to their deaths."[47] There was a feeling that the liturgy must change to face these pressures, or fade from significance: "working class soldiers felt alienated by a form of words that they did not understand."[48] As John Maiden has argued in the definitive scholarly account of the Prayer Book controversy, internal church politics also played a role: the rise of the Oxford Movement and then Anglo-Catholicism had led to a perception of "ritualistic lawlessness" within the Anglican community. The revised Prayer Book of

1927 was designed to reestablish a uniformity of ritual practice, compromising with Anglo-Catholic tendencies in order to prevent them from developing independently. As Maiden writes, "A commitment to Anglican comprehensiveness meant a general acceptance of milder Catholic practices." The revised book was presented to Parliament in 1928, but was voted down in the House of Commons that December.[49] The details of the controversy are complicated and beyond the scope of this chapter—and besides, they are expertly explored by Maiden. The important context here is that the proposed revisions to the Prayer Book encompassed some more High Church rituals, but with the aim of restoring a unified single liturgy, and discouraging Anglo-Catholics from practicing separately and according to their own ritual preferences. This complicated politics explains why the Anglo-Catholic T. S. Eliot could object to a revision that was widely viewed as making too many concessions to "Roman sacerdotalism."[50]

Frequently, Eliot used his role on the Archbishops' Commission to Revise the Psalter to defend Coverdale's original translations. Accepting the position, Eliot set limits around the responsibility he would be willing to take for the decisions of the commission. He agreed that he was in a good position to advise on the spiritual grace of the English translations, but not on their accuracy in relation to the original Hebrew—and he implied that there might be a tension between these two things.[51] Robert Sencourt claims in a memoir that "Eliot seldom spoke except to plead for the retention of an old phrase"—but this sounds like mere grumpy conservatism, when the retention of old phrases for collective utterance in the rituals of the church had become an essential element of Eliot's thinking about the social function of poetry. The archival records of the commission confirm that he was deeply engaged with its work over several years.[52] Nevertheless, one might be forgiven for forming the view that he joined this commission not because he agreed with its aims, but because he disagreed with them.

This is the sort of complex motivation that committee work causes us to reflect on, and it has an interesting relationship to the collective voice. When a committee makes a decision, it is in a sense making a collective utterance—but the mechanisms by which this is arrived at form a strong contrast with the shouted slogans at political rallies. Indeed, committee work is often held up as a bulwark of representative democracy against plebiscitary populism. Speech act theorists have paid attention to the ways in which "the committee, the jury, or the community club" can make collective utterances that are performative (in Austin's sense), by establishing a shared illocutionary intention via a process of deliberative discussion.[53] When the foreman of a jury says, "We find the defendant guilty," this is not a collective utterance, as I have defined the term, but it is a group (or collective) speech act in the senses discussed separately by Justin Hughes and Anthonie Meijers.[54] The perlocutionary effect of such an utterance—for example, the imprisonment of a defendant—takes place only when the words spoken by the foreman on behalf of the group express its shared intention, arrived at legitimately by a prescribed method. There may be individuals in the group who do not agree with the group's decision when it is a majority rather than a unanimous one. Yet, by consenting in advance to any decision arrived at by the deliberative process of the group, these individuals nevertheless acknowledge the legitimacy of the speech act made on their behalf, as reflective of a shared intention. Such questions constantly arise when researching the group activities of writers and intellectuals, in committees, conferences, congresses, parties, and campaigns.[55] In writing literary history, one is dealing with independent-minded individuals about whose ideas and motivations we have a great deal of evidence. Yet to watch writers engage in committee work is frequently to confront a contradiction between what was agreed by a committee and the known views of the writer who sat on it. Committee work operates as an important site where, at certain moments, the sovereign individual is temporarily dissolved in a moment of collective decision-making. *Shantih, shantih, shantih.*

So, when Eliot joined the Psalter Commission, it was perhaps partly out of a sense that he might be able to frustrate its implied desire to impose something that he would hate—a tactic no doubt familiar to readers with much experience of university administration. Eliot was skeptical in particular of the scholarly drive for greater "accuracy" in the translation, which offered to put modern Anglican worship back into contact with "Hebrew ideas which are unfamiliar to the ordinary user of the psalms."[56] Eliot's objections to the incorporation of words like "infinite" and "eternal" into the liturgy suggested doubts about the idea that modern idioms could provide access to ancient meanings. Geoffrey Fisher, the archbishop of Canterbury who invited Eliot onto the commission, reassured him that, "while accuracy has its place, discretion in the spiritual grace and elegance of the translation must prevail."[57] In the commission's first meeting, when Eliot was absent, it was "agreed that if the translation of a particular passage was clearly wrong, then a revision must be made, but very careful reference to the Coverdale version must be taken."[58]

In the meeting of 8 January 1960, when Eliot was present, they discussed the preparation of a draft preface, they agreed that Coverdale's words would be used "except where the text is corrupt or meaningless."[59] But what is meant by "meaningless"? As we have seen throughout this book, the meaning of a collective utterance cannot be treated in purely semantic terms. Many obscure phrases in the Coverdale Psalter, as Eliot would insist, had a value that was rooted not in their semantic meaning, but in their repeated ceremonial use. The drive for "accuracy" seemed, to Eliot at least, to miss this vital point.

Tensions of this kind arose in the commission's discussion of the phrase "the valley of the shadow of death," from Psalm 23. This is one of the best-known phrases in the Coverdale Psalter, but it is neither an accurate translation of the Hebrew original, nor an English phrase whose meaning can easily be visualized or glossed. In other words, it is exactly the kind of thing that the commission was tasked to replace. In a list of suggested emendations prepared by Winton Thomas, the Hebrew scholar on the commission, he suggests revising the Prayer Book Psalter's "the shadow of death" to "deep darkness."[60] Eliot cannot have been happy. The effect of the words "valley," "shadow," and "death" in his poem "The Hollow Men" (1925) depends on how they resonate with this vital text in the vernacular culture of English Christianity.[61] The minutes of the commission suggest that there was extensive disagreement and equivocation about how to approach this psalm. In the meeting of 9 December 1959, "Bishop Chase expressed doubts about the revision of Psalm xxiii; he felt that the P[rayer] B[ook] version was so well known, and well liked, that it should be retained."[62] A typescript draft of Psalm 23 from around the same time adopts "the darkest valley," but this has been amended, in red pen, to "the valley of the shadow of death," perhaps during the course of a meeting.[63] Under this Psalm is scrawled something like "Chase's note, v.4. For Convocation. ? Prefer correct translation of v.4." The committee was seemingly unable to decide between Thomas's literal translation and Coverdale's, and Chase even suggested that the commission submit two versions to the Convocations, deferring the decision.[64]

When in 1961 the commission published its first report, including translations of Psalms 1–41, Psalm 23 retained "the valley of the shadow of death," and a footnote indicated: "The Commission agreed that the most probable rendering of this phrase is 'the darkest valley,' and a minority felt that this translation should be incorporated in the text."[65] Eliot seemed to have won the argument. It must have been around this time that Valerie Eliot asked her husband about his day at the Psalter Commission, and Eliot replied: "I think I may have saved the Twenty-Third Psalm."[66] However, the battle for the valley of the shadow of death was not over. In September 1962, Thomas "urged that the correct rendering should be given. After discussion it was agreed to omit the words 'valley of the shadow of death' and to insert 'darkest valley.'"[67] Which version would Bishop Chase eventually present to the Convocation of Canterbury in the commission's final version of the Psalter, in May 1963? The published text gives "darkest valley": Psalm 23 had not been saved—not by Eliot in any case.

This is a minor drama and perhaps it only suggests that attempts by institutions—and ultimately states—to shape the collective utterances of the people are prone to failure. Among the circulated materials that Eliot and the commission discussed is a letter from Canon Hopkins that begins, "At the risk of being regarded as a hopeless reactionary . . ." Hopkins dwells on the question of "the valley of the shadow of death." He writes: "As a parish priest who has the responsibility of trying to help the man in the pew in the difficult art of worshipping by means of what are often archaic and oriental metaphors, I cannot refrain from a plea that your scholars stretch a point in Psalm 23 and allow us to retain 'the valley of the shadow of death.' I do not deny that 'the darkest valley' is clear and understandable, but the present version is so well-known and well-loved that to change it may prejudice the popularity of the whole new version." Hopkins goes on to argue that the phrase is one of the best known in the whole Bible and Prayer Book, that it has become frequently used in funerals (though this is a vernacular adaptation: Psalm 23 does not appear in the funeral service in the Book of Common Prayer), and that it therefore offers a "pastoral opportunity" for the pastor to "touch some cord of familiarity with those he only sees on such occasions." He also argues that "these words have a strong emotional content and have brought to so many passing through the darkest valley a freedom from the fear of death."[68]

In a special submission to the committee that responds to this extraordinary letter, Eliot asserted that he was the only member of the committee who begged to retain "the valley of the shadow of death," and argued that the press was on his side.[69] Eliot felt that the obscurity in some of Coverdale's phrases was generative—perhaps for similar reasons that he argued, in "The Metaphysical Poets," that "poets in our civilization, as it exists at present, must be *difficult*." In a complex modern society, the poet is bound to "become more allusive, more indirect, in order to force, to dislocate if necessary, language into meaning."[70] Coverdale's resonant but sometimes obscure phrasing achieved this end, and crucially it did so not for just for the coterie readership of difficult modernist poetry, but for the Anglican community as a whole. It was, across the United Kingdom and beyond, often spoken or chanted in unison by people who did not and perhaps could not know what it meant, but felt its power. Here is a rather concrete example of what might be meant by Eliot's "belief in a national language as the genuine spirit of a people."[71] It acts as an embodiment of the social function of liturgical language, unifying its speakers without homogenizing them.

Eliot's critical attitude to liturgical reform is an important context for any understanding of his work on the Archbishops' Commission to Revise the Psalter. But the papers show that he was not only there to block revisions to the Coverdale Psalter. He supported most of the changes that were eventually made and seemed satisfied with the commission's work.[72] If liturgy was to serve the social functions that Eliot imagined for it, as a unifying force in the context of a wider cultural disintegration, then some adaptation and variation may well be required. But his pessimistic view of the decay of the English language implied that a simple shift into contemporary English, or even an attempt to meet it half way, risked compounding the problem. If the English nation was to be brought together through collective speech rituals, then these would need to be built on the sixteenth- and seventeenth-century language of the Book of Common Prayer, and of the Reformation that Eliot was in other ways seeking to reverse.

I have discussed Eliot's thinking about the Anglican liturgy at some length, because he is the most significant and representative advocate for this form of collective vocalization. Most modern writers who grapple with the collective voice in a hegemonic and liturgical position tend to see it as an oppressive force associated with the glorification of state power, or with small-minded conformity. A deeper look inside the state apparatus itself would afford new insights of a different kind, but the collective voice is never exclusively political, and always *cultural*. Stalin grasped this when he invited Soviet poets and composers to develop a new national anthem after the message of "L'Internationale" became inconvenient (as I touched on in the bridge between chapters 2 and 3). By drafting Eliot and C. S. Lewis onto the Archbishops' Commission to Revise the Psalter, the Church of England also signaled its understanding of the importance of cultural and poetic forms in establishing hegemonic collective speech. Modern writers have tended to be a rebellious breed, not least because of the vital influence of romanticism in shaping our understandings of what makes a good writer, and Eliot's early work fits that description. Because of his trajectory after his conversion, and notably with works such as *The Rock*, Eliot stands out as a significant literary writer who was willing to make the case for, and to reflect on the art of, hegemonic collective speech.

Peter Grimes: Liturgy and Social Conformity

If Eliot plays the role of the writer who sought to defend, refine, and promulgate hegemonic collective speech in the form of liturgy, then the other figures discussed in this chapter had more ambivalent, and sometimes outright hostile, attitudes to it. This includes Benjamin Britten, a composer who was steeped in centuries of religious music, and participated in the attempts to revive collective political singing in the 1930s left that I have already discussed. Yet, he was a homosexual at a time when gay sex was illegal in the United Kingdom, and he alienated himself not only from the British establishment, but also from his friends on the British left in its most patriotic Popular Front moment, by becoming a conscientious objector during the Second World War, moving to America. He felt like, and in a sense he was, an outsider. In Britten we find an artist who reflected deeply on the capacity of liturgical collective speech to create social cohesion and stability, but one who paid attention, above all, to the people who were excluded by such apparent displays of consensus.

Britten's 1945 opera *Peter Grimes* makes extensive use of a chorus to reflect on the oppressive force of public opinion, which is linked in the piece to the Anglican liturgy. *Grimes*'s chorus is a representation of the people of "The Borough"—the name of George Crabbe's narrative poem of 1810 from which the bones of the opera's plot are taken. The Borough is a coastal fishing town based on Aldeburgh in Suffolk, where both Britten and Crabbe lived. Outside of the chorus, but an inhabitant of the Borough, is the fisherman Peter Grimes, whose apprentices keep dying of unknown causes, and who is suspected by the townsfolk—by turns drunk and pious—of brutalizing and murdering them. Grimes is an outsider figure who has often been connected with Britten himself, and Britten encouraged the connection. In an interview in 1963, Britten described his close collaboration with his lover the tenor Peter Pears, who would play Grimes in the inaugural production at Sadler's Wells: "A central feeling for us was that of the individual against the crowd, with ironic overtones for our own situation. As conscientious objectors we were out of it. . . . I think it was partly this feeling which led us to make Grimes a character of vision and conflict, the tortured idealist he is, rather than the villain he was in Crabbe."[73] Grimes is accordingly recast in Montagu Slater's libretto in the aspect of a troubled romantic who refuses to play along with certain agreed social scripts, and who is condemned for it.

This effect is produced partly by introducing some ambiguity about whether Grimes does in fact murder the apprentices. The coroners' inquest in the opera's prologue finds that Grimes's most recent apprentice died in "accidental circumstances," but Swallow, the coroner, notes ominously, "That's the kind of thing people are apt to remember," and advises Peter not to take another apprentice. Peter's response anticipates his continued persecution by the gossiping chorus:

> The case goes on in people's minds
> And charges that no court has made
> Will be shouted at my head.[74]

And indeed, Peter's subsequent actions are met with relentless suspicion, as the chorus unites around a moralizing consensus:

> Who lets us down must take the rap
> The borough keeps its standards up.[75]

The piece does not exonerate its protagonist. Even Ellen, the good-hearted woman who operates as a potential source of redemption for Grimes, questions his cruel treatment of his new apprentice, and he strikes her.[76] The point is that there is no stable point of truth in the Borough: only a consensus, made of judgmental gossip and moralizing supposition, and embodied in the chorus.

This chorus is explicitly linked to the liturgy of the Book of Common Prayer in a remarkable scene at the beginning of act 2. It is Sunday morning and the borough is at church, offstage, singing the hymn "Now that the Daylight Fills the Sky." Onstage, Ellen is talking to Peter's new boy, a few weeks into his apprenticeship, and trying to coax him into speech. The chorus chants the general confession from the 1662 Book of Common Prayer: "Almighty and most merciful father; We have erred and strayed from your ways like lost sheep."[77] The reason for the boy's reticence becomes clear when Ellen finds a tear on his coat and a bruise on his neck, immediately suspecting Peter of mistreating the child. When Peter arrives, eager to break the sabbath and take the exhausted boy out to sea again, they fight, and Peter strikes her. These interactions between the principal characters are juxtaposed against the congregation in the background, working through the liturgy.

This passage is "composed of five sections corresponding to the phases of the church service, each of which in turn marks a stage in the drama of Ellen, Grimes, and the child."[78] Eric Crozier, who directed the Sadler's Wells premiere of *Peter Grimes,* describes how Mrs. Sedley (one of the townsfolk) arrives late to church, sees Ellen discovering the bruise, and then "passes into the church, impatient to retail this fresh bit of scandal as soon as the service has ended." As the congregation emerges from church, having chanted the Benedicite from the Book of Common Prayer ("O all ye Works of the Lord, bless ye the Lord"), it quickly morphs into an angry mob, "infected by the rumours of new excesses in Grimes's behaviour," and then "hurrying to arm themselves with sticks and cudgels."[79] The seamlessness of this transition, emphasized in Crozier's staging, frames the Anglican liturgy as an oppressive force. The prayers give way to a repeated refrain: "Grimes is at his exercise," one of the few phrases Slater took directly from Crabbe, and which has a strangely ominous character. It is not just that the chanted prayers about love and forgiveness appear hypocritical in this context. The pious content of the liturgy should not be extrapolated as if we could assume it guides the actions of the townsfolk. The liturgy must be considered a speech act that creates cohesion among the townsfolk, excludes Grimes, and underpins the sense of social conformity that pervades the opera: a "socially binding Anglicanism," as Peter Garvie put it.[80]

Britten's relationship with Anglicanism is complex. He expressed a variety of views over his life, but was raised in the church and deeply embedded in the traditions of religious music, and—with an abiding interest in choral music in particular—he wrote church music, including liturgical settings. Across his career he scored a number of key psalms and canticles from the Book of Common Prayer. His wonderful settings of Psalm 150 and the prayers Te Deum and Jubilate Deo (usually known by their Latin names) have entered the repertoire of church music.[81] The Te Deum—a nonscriptural Latin hymn supposed by legend to have been sung for the first time by inspiration at the baptism of St. Augustine in 387—is discussed by Agamben as a particularly condensed example of glorification by acclamation.[82] The words of the 1662 Prayer Book are also used in Britten's *Te Deum in C* (1934):

> We praise thee, O God: we acknowledge thee to be the Lord.
> All the earth doth worship thee: the Father everlasting.

> To thee all Angels cry aloud: the Heavens, and all the Powers
> therein.
> To thee Cherubin and Seraphin: continually do cry,
> Holy, Holy, Holy: Lord God of Sabaoth.
> Heaven, and Earth are full of the Majesty: of thy glory.[83]

More than just an example of a collective utterance whose function is glorify God, the Te Deum is also a metacommentary on the centrality of glorification to the Christian faith. It is a hymn about hymning, that adds angels, cherubim, and seraphim to the earthly choir.

Scholars disagree over the importance of religion in Britten's own life, and as a driving force for his music. While Graham Elliott has made the case for seeing Britten as a profoundly religious composer, and argued that the importance of Britten's homosexuality and pacifism have been overplayed, most scholars follow the secularizing line of Humphrey Carpenter's biography.[84] This dispute will not be resolved here, but it perhaps encourages us to hold two things in view: Britten had a profound interest in the emotional and spiritual power of the Anglican liturgy; he also displayed (in *Peter Grimes*) an understanding of what it meant to be excluded from these rituals.

The libretto for *Peter Grimes* is also a product of Britten's collaboration with Montagu Slater, who based it on a draft scenario developed by Britten and Pears. Slater was a veteran of the interwar communist culture I examined in chapter 2, and a founding editor of *The Left Review,* who worked closely with Jack Lindsay, Randall Swingler, and W. H. Auden, involved with their work to revive and reinvigorate the chorus as a medium for poetry and drama.[85] Britten and Slater had collaborated on plays for the Unity Theatre (where several mass declamations were staged), and Slater scripted the Communist Manifesto Centenary Pageant, performed at the Royal Albert Hall a few years after *Peter Grimes.* The fiction he published in the 1930s saw him "drawn particularly to showing characters (not always attractive characters) under pressure from political and social forces."[86] For Philip Brett, it was Slater who completely transformed the opera, from "what might have been a horrifyingly sentimentalized attempt to recuperate a child abuser" in the Britten-Pears scenario into "a taut localized social drama with universal implications about the precarious balance of responsibility between society and the individual."

The two crucial choral scenes that Slater added to the Britten-Pears drafts—the mob's angry procession, after church, to Grimes's hut, and the manhunt in the final act—"force the character of Grimes beyond its lurking pathology and give moral license to the audience to identify with the victim."[87] When the boy dies, he is under Grimes's care, but in a hurry to flee the angry chorus banging at the door of the hut and singing, "We shall strike and strike to kill / At the slander or the sin."[88] The Borough, therefore, as Brett notes, shares responsibility, distracting Peter as the boy climbs out of the hut and falls down the cliff to his death.[89] While Slater was interested, in his other work, in the liberatory potential of collective speech as protest and engagement (the concerns of chapter 2), his signal contribution to *Peter Grimes,* Brett argues, was to shape its chorus as "a narrow-minded, hypocritical community . . . obsessed with conformity and enforcing 'standards' to its own arbitrary liking."[90] Eliot's conception of the social cohesion that might be achieved through the rituals of the Book of Common Prayer is cruelly subverted here. The distinction Eliot promoted in *The Rock,* between ominously authoritarian and regimented collective speech and that of a unifying national liturgy, breaks down in *Peter Grimes.* In this opera, the rituals of the church provide community and pious fellow feeling, but these underpin the group solidarity of an angry mob.

From Aldeburgh to Africa

Montagu Slater—"one of the leading left-wing writers and intellectuals of the 1930s"—had a wide-ranging fascination with the collective voice, and across his work he imagined it in different relationships to the polis, in different media, and in different national contexts.[91] He was a veteran of the GPO Film Unit, working with Auden and Britten on *Coal Face* (1935), and he became head of production in the Films Division of the Ministry of Information during the war.[92] After the war, and after *Peter Grimes,* he became increasingly interested in Africa. He wrote several African films, including *Man of Africa* (1954) and the Crown Film Unit's *Daybreak in Udi* (1949), traveled to Nigeria and Uganda, and wrote *The Trial of Jomo Kenyatta* (1955)—a still often-cited account of the trial that saw Jomo Kenyatta and the other leaders of the Kenyan national resistance (the Kenya Africa Union, or KAU) imprisoned for supposed terrorist activities. While purporting to offer a balanced and objective view of the trial, Slater, with justification, saw the accused as "the leaders of an open, constitutional, and in every sense legal political movement," who were falsely linked in the course of the proceedings with the "dark, barbarous and terrorist Mau Mau."[93] Slater's career is a winding road: from interwar communist pageantry, to the investigation of romantic outsiderdom in *Peter Grimes,* to the romance of colonial development in Nigeria, to the celebration of anticolonial resistance in Kenya. Where T. S. Eliot's turn from fragmentary modernist poetics to liturgy and choral drama as forces of social cohesion can be represented as a broadly linear trajectory, Slater moves in multiple directions.

But reading Slater's heterogeneous oeuvre is an invitation to reflect on the ways in which hegemonic collective speech relates to the refusing or protesting forms discussed in chapters 1 and 2, and how it mutates in these different contexts. Turning to colonial Africa—the subject of both *Daybreak in Udi* and *The Trial of Jomo Kenyatta*—the Anglican liturgy played an important role and was fundamental to the missionary attempt to establish hegemony via religion. As Cummings writes, in the British Empire, "*The Book of Common Prayer* took on the mantle of colonial acculturation": its rituals were widely practiced, and linked with practices of conversion, turning indigenous people into British subjects.[94] From the 1960s, missionaries began to use the term "inculturation," which signals the way in which Prayer Book rituals were indigenized and changed in the process. The inculturation of the Anglican liturgy was a process of adaptation to vernacular languages and ritual practices.[95] This capacity for flexible adaptation can then be seen to be important to the establishment and maintenance of hegemony. Arguably more important still were the more modern hymns, largely composed and woven into church liturgies over the course of the nineteenth century, and which became central to the missionary project. In *Things Fall Apart,* Achebe depicts a young African man drawn towards Christianity as the missionaries sing:

> There was a young lad who had been captivated. His name was Nwoye, Okonkwo's first son. It was not the mad logic of the Trinity that captivated him. He did not understand it. It was the poetry of the new religion, something felt in the marrow. The hymn about brothers who sat in darkness and in fear seemed to answer a vague and persistent question that haunted his young soul. . . . He felt a relief when the hymn poured into his parched soul. The words of the hymn were like drops of frozen rain melting on the dry plate of the panting earth.[96]

This episode highlights the peculiar power of liturgical language—"the poetry of the new religion"—to generate solidarities that are "felt in the marrow," but that also seem to imply an acceptance of the hegemony of the colonial state.

However, devotion to the Anglican liturgy did not always signal an acceptance of British colonial rule, nor did it fade away in the period of African decolonization. Indeed, in Kenya (whose liberation struggles Slater influentially documented), "the Prayer Book continued to dominate Anglicanism in the region even after political independence was achieved" and indeed "the 1662 Prayer Book is still widely used."[97] On Kenya's road to independence, both in Slater's eyes and in those of Ngũgĩ wa Thiong'o, the anticolonial struggle and the postcolonial state found uses for hymn culture and for the Book of Common Prayer. Inevitably, forms of protest that would belong in chapter 2 will occasionally emerge in the course of this discussion, but I want to show how, in the texts I discuss, thinking about the Anglican liturgy as an almost idealized site of cultural hegemony crosses the lines of race and ethnicity.

Slater's script for *Daybreak in Udi* (set in Nigeria) does not include discussion of Prayer Book rites, and indeed offers a notably secular view of the functioning of the colonial state, though one in which collective vocalization remains important. Presented as a documentary, but heavily scripted by Slater, the film takes on the classic theme of development, exploring how an "ancient African tribe, the Abaja Ibos . . . are teaching themselves to read and write, and are building schools, maternity homes, co-operative shops, and many miles of roads." The principal focus is on the building of a maternity hospital, which progressive villagers want, but which is opposed by some village elders who use witchcraft to subvert the project. In line with the postwar Labour government's policy on Africa, the film emphasizes that development is something Africans must do for themselves in order to work towards independence, while the British district officer offers advice and support. "With few resources but their own strength and spirit," the opening titles announce, "they are starting to bridge the centuries dividing their way of life and ours."[98] The ideology of development inevitably adopts the attitudes of evolutionist anthropology.

The opening scene in *Daybreak in Udi* depicts an outdoor school, with hundreds of boys and men, sitting in a big circle and chanting in Igbo, in a call-and-response with a man who points to writing on a blackboard. This scene is intercut with a similar scene featuring women and girls. This represents a common form of collective vocalization that I have not yet had occasion to discuss in this book: the repetition of a teacher's words by a group of pupils or students in schools and educational contexts. The forms of learning that were available in colonial contexts emerged from discussions that went along with the gradual extension of formal education to the children of the poor in eighteenth- and nineteenth-century Britain.

In educational contexts, collective speech practices were widespread, diverse, significantly embedded in the liturgy of the Book of Common Prayer, and much debated. For example, the educational reformer Sarah Trimmer (1741–1810) was critical of what she called "the prevailing method of exercising the memories of children in learning by rote lessons greatly above their capacities," recommending instead "initiating them by such simple instructions as would gradually unfold their understandings."[99] But Trimmer's solution was to change the style of question, not to move away from the basic pattern according to which teachers ask questions, and students provide set responses in unison. Indeed, Trimmer was a key figure in the development of the catechistic method, which derived its question-and-answer format from the catechisms of the Book of Common Prayer, and which subsequent educationalists and critics tended to view as an extension of rote learning rather than an alternative to it. Eric G. Lorentzen sees Trimmer as the "most unapologetically marginalizing" of the advocates of the catechistic method, and—partly through the lens of Dickens's frequent satires on Victorian education—as the author of rigidly inflexible "indoctrinating scripts."[100]

Trimmer's books do indeed view the education of the poor as fundamentally concerned with the inculcation of Christian morality as well as social and political obedience, and Lorentzen quotes some passages from Trimmer that illustrate this well: "*Questions.*—Are those who honour the king contented with his government? [*Ans.* Yes.] What do they quietly obey? [*Ans.* The laws.] What will they not suffer themselves to be persuaded to join in? [*Ans.* Riots and mobs to disturb the government.] What will they pay cheerfully? [*Ans.* The taxes.] How will they discharge the offices of soldiers, sailors, constables, and watchmen? [*Ans.* Faithfully.]"[101] Trimmer's instructions to teachers suggested that this form of catechistic questioning should be applied individually to the children, "one after the other," rather than treating them only as a collectively speaking bloc.[102] But collective vocalization was part of the mode of instruction that books like *The Teacher's Assistant* helped to institutionalize. And Trimmer—a keen advocate of the 1662 Prayer Book—saw the education of the poor as an extension of the Christian liturgy into the classroom. As she noted in her *Companion to the Book of Common Prayer*, "It appears from scripture that it is the will of God that his people should frequently assemble together, and offer up their prayers and praises, with one heart and one voice."[103]

In colonial Africa, the drive to expand literacy was linked with Christian conversion and this combination has been seen as "the core of a hegemonic colonial project."[104] Critical accounts of colonial education in Africa emphasize "parrot-like repetition" and an excessive emphasis on Bible stories.[105] The Anglican liturgy becomes in many cases explicitly associated with colonial power, a system of ritual and belief imposed on the indigenous population by white colonists. The outdoor schools in *Daybreak in Udi* do not fit this pattern, however. They are led by Black Africans, conducted in both English and Igbo, and with no mention of Christianity. The film reflects on the interesting position of formal education in colonial Africa, as historically and institutionally linked to the fact of colonial domination. However, "rather than being simply imposed by colonial planners," this education "could be a freely chosen and potentially liberating path."[106] Education in Africa was not only imposed but also sought, not only religious but also secular.

Daybreak in Udi is a piece of pro-British propaganda, and as such, it promotes a benign image of an empire that is there to assist the Africans in building an independent future, through the shared goal of development. The district officer, Chadwick, says as much in a speech at the opening ceremony for the new maternity hospital. This comes after a ceremonial dance, entirely in the local style, but which takes place under Union Jack bunting. After the speech, the village starts work on building a road, singing a collective work song in Igbo. Chadwick asks for a translation as the song proceeds:

> We are stronger than the next town.
> Our road goes far.
> I speak true word which is really true.
> When we strike a tree it falls to the ground like a dead man.
> When we dig, the earth crumbles away.
> The tree falls and the earth shakes with our strength.
> When we dig, the earth falls to the mouths of the men behind.
> We are stronger than the next town.
> We have power and we have spirit.
> A thousand men dig and the dust from their hoes rises to the sky.
> Our road goes far.
> Who knows where it will go.
> Who knows.[107]

The liturgical aspiration of *Daybreak at Udi*, then, is not the missionary project to extend Christian rituals across Africa. The impetus—perhaps I should say the fantasy—is to foster independent African expression, while marrying it to a project of development. As Ben Page has argued, the building of the road is "portrayed as a revival of West African customs of social collaboration, which were being applied to new challenges."[108] The nationalist press saw it, by contrast, as more of the same: "yet another film unit come out to our country to depict us as naked savages and unfit to rule ourselves."[109]

Slater's work on the script for *Daybreak in Udi* involved traveling to Nigeria to discuss the development agenda with Chadwick himself. It was Slater who, in the interests of creating plot tension, developed the idea of village elders using witchcraft to forestall the building of the maternity hospital.[110] Their unthinking attachment to ritual links them to the chorus in *Peter Grimes*—but here they are a minority, overcome by the community's embrace of development and change, in a West African key. It is the witches who become the pariahs, explicitly mocked by Chadwick as "foolish people." A new chorus is formed that is authentically Igbo, not Christian but suspicious of pagan "superstitious rubbish" (as one character puts it), and above all wedded to the agenda of development.

In *The Trial of Jomo Kenyatta,* Slater was more overtly critical of the British Empire's role in Africa. The book was banned from circulation in Kenya, as the secretary of state for the colonies explained, because it "deals with the trial of Jomo Kenyatta in a manner which, in the opinion of the Governor in Council, makes its importation and circulation undesirable in the public interest."[111] Slater's account condenses the full transcript of the trial, running to over 2,000 pages, into 252 pages that include his summary and commentary alongside excerpts from the verbatim transcript. While Slater claimed that his presentation of the trial was "as fair as I can make it," he was also open about the process of selection, and, as Peter Leman puts it, "his own socialist politics lead him to sympathize with Kenyatta's nationalist organization, but not Mau Mau."[112]

The defense sought to distinguish the activities of the Kenya African Union (KAU) as a legal nationalist organization from illegal Mau Mau violence. The Christian beliefs of KAU leaders became a dividing line that separated them from the Mau Mau, who were associated with "animal sacrifice, ritual recitations" and so on, rituals—if they happened at all—that were no doubt made to seem more lurid through the lens of British racism.[113] The prosecution sought to challenge the legitimacy of the KAU's Christian faith. Kenyatta is asked, on account of his "undenominational form of Christianity," whether he regarded the oath he took in court as valid. Kaggia, one of the codefendants, was asked, "How do you reconcile your religious convictions with your position in politics?" To which he responded: "Jesus Christ himself was always fighting for the rights of his people by every peaceful means or way and he stood for the rights of human kind and as a Christian I stand for the rights of my people."[114] The prosecution promotes a narrow-minded conception of Christianity aligned with political obedience and social conformity—like the churchgoing chorus in *Peter Grimes*. But here, Kaggia and Kenyatta suggest the possibility (hardly new) that Christianity might motivate anticolonial resistance, and become woven into a newly hegemonic postcolonial order.

This debate has a liturgical dimension which revolves around the "hymn books" that circulated within the KAU rebellion and which formed a significant element of the prosecution's evidence. The Crown "attached a good deal of importance" to these hymn books, and their ability to link the leaders of the KAU with the violent Mau Mau rebellion.[115] The relationship of these hymns to Christian liturgy is often at issue in Slater's account of the trial. D. N. Pritt—Britain's leading communist-sympathizing lawyer—was defending the accused, and he argued that "these really ought to be called songs—not that I have any religious squeamishness."[116] Slater also sees them as expressive of a secular nationalism, calling them "poems of a kind familiar in many a nationalist movement" that "bring to mind Irish songs like 'The Bold Robert Emmett,' or even 'The Wearing of the Green.' "[117] But the prosecution insisted that "they are sung as hymns."[118] In fact, the rebellion often adapted the lyric forms of the missionary Christian church to its own ends. Robert Edgerton shows that a "Mau Mau" version of "Onward Christian Soldiers" circulated:

> Onward Mau Mau soldiers,
> Marching as to war.
> Looking unto Jomo,
> Who has gone before.[119]

"Onward Christian Soldiers" was, of course, not present in the Book of Common Prayer, but part of the canon of Victorian hymns that were prominent in the collective speech arsenal of missionaries. As Slater reports, in the Kenyatta trial, the Crown argued in its closing statements that the hymns "are actually Christian hymns lifted from the Church of Scotland and other hymn books, with the name of Kenyatta substituted for that of the deity."[120] These uses of hymn culture underline the link between collectively uttered rituals and hegemony, but they also show that liturgical forms may flex rather than break, accommodating new solidarities and making room for postcolonial national consciousness. The pessimistic view of the liturgy in Slater's libretto for *Peter Grimes* is moderated in *The Trial of Jomo Kenyatta* by a more capacious understanding of liturgy's affordances.

Ngũgĩ wa Thiong'o's Liturgical Formations

Ngũgĩ wa Thiong'o is a writer who was formed in the same Kenyan struggle for independence documented in Slater's *The Trial of Jomo Kenyatta.* Ngũgĩ had read that book (despite the ban on it) during his time at the University of Makerere.[121] However, in *A Grain of Wheat* (1967, rev. 1987), Ngũgĩ is much less interested than were Slater or Kenyatta in drawing a distinction between violent Mau Mau terrorism and the legal activities of the KAU. Slater had already shown that liturgical forms moved in a complicated way beyond the religion of colonial missionaries to became active in the rebellion. Ngũgĩ goes further in making Christian practice a motivating force for Mau Mau and shows how it became incorporated, in a modified form, into the state liturgy of the newly independent Kenya.

Kihika, the revolutionary hero whose death and legacy hangs over the action of *A Grain of Wheat,* was a committed Christian, though of a very specific kind. After joining the Mau Mau, he assassinated the British district officer, Robson, only to be betrayed by Mugo, the novel's conflicted Conradian protagonist, and publicly hanged by the British authorities. Kihika "believed in prayer," and "even read the Bible every day, and took it with him wherever he went."[122] But these prayers involved animal sacrifice and chanting, and existed at a distance from the rituals of the Book of Common Prayer. Konia, who was also in the forest with the Mau Mau, remembers the practice, at a gathering at Mugo's house (before it becomes known that it was Mugo who betrayed Kihika):

> Oh, we did sacrifice—and ate the meat afterwards. We prayed twice a day and an extra one before any expedition to wrest arms from European farms. We stood up facing Mount Kenya:
>
> Mwenanyaga we pray that you may protect our hideouts.
> Mwenanyaga we pray that you may hold a soft cloud over us.
> Mwenanyaga we pray that you may defend us behind and in front from our enemies.
> Mwenanyaga we pray that you may give us courage in our hearts.
> Thai thathaiya Ngai, Thaai.[123]

This ritual is adapted from one described by Kenyatta himself in his book *Facing Mount Kenya* (1938), to which Ngũgĩ is no doubt referring. This is an ethnographic account of the Gikuyu people: Kenyatta had studied anthropology under Bronisław Malinowski at the London School of Economics. Kenyatta described the ritual, chanted while facing Mount Kenya, in his account of a group called Watu wa Mngu, whose "prayers are a mixture of Gikuyu religion and Christian" and who "proclaim that they belong to the lost tribes of Israel."[124] Mwene-Nyaga (as Kenyatta transcribes it) is a name for God, importing the Christian deity into Gikuyu. This group asserted the value of polygamy on the basis that many biblical figures practiced it and were praised for it: they assumed that the missionaries only promoted monogamy as a means to reduce the indigenous population.[125]

Kenyatta situates this chanted ritual in the early 1930s, and stresses that Watu wa Mngu "do not indulge in politics."[126] He also notes that some of them were arrested for "agitation and incitement" and brought to trial, where, instead of giving evidence, they chanted their prayers in the courtroom.[127] Ngũgĩ transposes the ritual to the more febrile political atmosphere of the 1950s and the Mau Mau uprising, giving it a more political meaning (the reference to "hideouts" is absent in Kenyatta's telling). And Konia notes that the same group also sang:

> We shall never rest
> Without land,
> Without Freedom true
> Kenya is a country of black people.[128]

This overt statement of political nationalism alludes directly to the collective speech practices of the secular revolutionary tradition—and on its own, it would belong to chapter 2's exploration of protest and engagement. "Land and freedom" was a slogan that circulated in nineteenth-century Russian radical circles, and the Mau Mau were also known as the "Kenya Land and Freedom Army." Ngũgĩ thus gives the chant a political meaning that Kenyatta denied it, linking it to the Mau Mau rebellion that Kenyatta would disavow.

But, if the repositioning of this ritual in *A Grain of Wheat* gave it a secular politics, it also, somewhat paradoxically, underlined its continuities with Christian tradition. Kenyatta had complained that "nothing was done to investigate the religious aspects of this group, to show the connection between it and Christianity on the one hand and Gikuyu on the other."[129] Well,

Ngũgĩ brings this dual Christian and Gikuyu inheritance right to the surface, through the devotion of Kihika to his bible. Kihika—the hero of the nationalist movement, who was killed because of Mugo's betrayal—carried this Bible everywhere he went, but on the day he was taken, unusually, he left it at home. General R. produces the Bible for the group in Mugo's room, who leaf through it, finding some lines that Kihika underlined in red. Gikonyo, one of the leaders of the rebellion, reads from Psalm 72: "He shall judge the poor of the people, he shall save the children of the needy, and shall break in pieces the oppressor."[130] Ngũgĩ positions Coverdale's words—as chanted in the Anglican liturgy—in a novel collective speech constellation, aligning them with the Watu wa Mngu prayer, as well as with the secular nationalism of "Kenya is a country of Black people." In *The River Between* (1965), Ngũgĩ had represented Christian converts and African tribal traditionalists as implacably opposed: in that novel it is the protagonist Waiyaki who hopes is might be possible to steer a path between the two, to grasp the benefits of development while "strip[ping] education in Africa of its religious trappings."[131] Waiyaki thinks he can join the voices of Christians and tribalists under the banner of an essentially secular nationalism, aspiring to "lead them in a political movement that would shake the whole country, that would tell the white man 'Go!' "[132] *A Grain of Wheat*, by contrast, imagines the Anglican tradition, condensed in the image of Kihika's Bible and the lines from the Coverdale Psalter, as a crucial node in an expanded, composite liturgical formation.

This formation becomes a chorus that confronts Mugo as an outsider. The day after the group reads the psalm in his room, Coverdale's words resurface in his memory and "thrill him." Their strong message of revolutionary justice makes Mugo fear the others—and fear that they might know the terrible secret of his betrayal of Kihika. Mugo feels the others forming into a hegemonic chorus, and closing ranks around this liturgy. He is celebrated as a hero of the independence movement, and is called upon to speak publicly, but feels uneasy about it. At one event, he speaks about his imprisonment "in a dry monotone." Initially he "enjoyed the distance he had established between himself and the voice," but "soon the voice disgusted him."[133] Mugo betrayed Kihika because he was horrified at the violence of his act, as well as out of fear of the reprisals he may face for abetting it. He recoils from the idea of "singing tributes to the man he had so treacherously betrayed."[134] As Kenya's day of freedom approaches, he feels unable to join in with the new liturgy of the postcolonial nation-state.

This comes to a head at the Uhuru celebrations, Kenya's independence day, when Mugo publicly confesses to his betrayal of Kihika. Ngũgĩ's presentation of the scene emphasizes the togetherness of the gathered crowd. The narrator even descends from his omniscient perch, to join the crowd, deploying, for the first time, the first-person plural: "This was Kihika's day; it was Mugo's day; it was our day."[135] Women in the crowd sing the composite liturgy: "Christian hymns mixed with traditional and Uhuru songs." Kingori takes to the platform and says: "Let us pray. Lord open thou our hearts." And the crowd responds as the Book of Common Prayer commands: "And our mouths shall show forth thy praise."[136] This Cranmerian prayer then becomes mixed with Gikuyu elements, as Kingori invokes the "God of Isaac and Jacob and Abraham, who also created Gikuyu and Mumbi," in a sermon that links British colonialism with Pharoah, and casts the African population as the persecuted Jews. The crowd respond in unison, "Amen."[137] This acclamation, in Agamben's terms, serves to glorify the power of the new nation-state.

Having become united around this composite liturgy, the crowd then turn to Mugo. They want him to speak for the independence movement, and to supply a heroic account of Mau Mau's success: "From one corner, a man shouted for Mugo. The demand was immediately chorused from different parts of the field, until the meeting seethed with Mugo's name in a threatening unison."[138] Mugo cannot speak in these terms, and General R. takes to the microphone instead—but his discourse turns to Kihika's death, and he concludes: "Maybe he who betrayed Kihika is here, now, in this crowd. We ask him to come forward to this platform, to confess and repent before us all."[139] General R. suspects that it is Karanja who is the guilty party, and is as surprised as everybody else when Mugo comes to the stage to declare that it is he who is "Judas." After this confession "nobody said anything"—the seething unison of the crowd fragments and pulls apart: "they rose and started talking, moving away in different directions, as if the meeting ended with Mugo's confession."[140] The imagination of a fully inclusive composite national liturgy, that brings Cranmer and Coverdale into alignment with Gikuyu culture and with secular independence politics, founders because Mugo cannot join in. *A Grain of Wheat* was written before Ngũgĩ's turn to a more militantly secular politics, critical of the neo-colonialism he came to see in embodied in the postindependence Kenyan state. But the beginnings of that critique can be found in this novel, as the problematic outsider figure of Mugo—like Peter Grimes—helps us to see a hegemonic liturgy from the outside.

Katharine Burdekin's Nazi Liturgy

Katharine Burdekin's dystopia *Swastika Night* (1937) opens with the ritual performance of a Nazi liturgy in the Holy Hitler chapel. Seven hundred years after the establishment of the German Empire, Nazism is depicted as a centuries-old religion that abominates Christians and women, celebrates homosexuality, exerts a total control over knowledge by outlawing all books other than technical manuals and the Hitler Bible, and prescribes a devotional practice based on the rote repetition of set prayers, in unison. Orwell was influenced by Burdekin's novel as he wrote *Nineteen Eighty-Four* (1949), and this ritual bears comparison with the Two Minutes Hate.[141] Burdekin's depiction of this Nazi rite alludes to the Nazi *Thingspiel* movement, a vogue for large-scale collective theatrical spectacle that was hugely popular in the early years of the Third Reich (1933–36), reflecting Goebbels's desire to "create a theatre of fifty thousand and hundred thousand."[142] *Thingspiele* could be enormous: in October 1933, seventeen thousand actors performed a play by Gustav Goes for a crowd of sixty thousand; a *Thingspiel* by Heinrich Lersch mobilized a chorus of three thousand.[143] Large, purpose-built outdoor auditoriums were constructed across Germany to accommodate these spectacles. The *Thingspiel* aimed to create a "unity of performers and spectators" by involving the audience in the choruses and the singing of rousing nationalistic and militaristic songs (though there is some doubt about the extent to which this audience participation really took hold).[144] Burdekin's depiction, in *Swastika Night,* of a "mighty and toneful roaring of male voices," raised in unison in praise of the Nazi Reich, suggests that she had some familiarity with the *Thingspiel* movement, which she may have encountered through discussions at Popular Front meetings, or read about in the British press.[145]

Thingspiele, as Erika Fischer-Lichte argues, were "able to trigger quasi-religious feelings, to be directed towards the nation, towards the fatherland."[146] This religious aspect was sometimes made explicit by the use of Christian themes, and Wilhelm von Schramm further underlined this religious dimension when he referred to the *Thingspiel* as a "people's (völkische) liturgy."[147] Burdekin emphasized this liturgical aspect, to the extent that the ritual that opens the novel is an explicitly religious rite that takes place in a church (the Holy Hitler Chapel). The assembled masses sing the creed:

> *I believe,* sang all the men and boys and the Knight in unison, *in God the Thunderer, who made this physical earth on which men march in their*

> *mortal bodies, and in His Heaven where all heroes are, and in His Son our Holy Adolf Hitler, the Only Man. Who was, not begotten, not born of a woman, but Exploded!*[148]

This prayer is adapted from the Apostles' Creed as we find it in the Book of Common Prayer: "I believe in God the Father Almighty, Maker of heaven and earth: And in Jesus Christ his only Son our Lord, Who was conceived by the holy Ghost, Born of the Virgin Mary."[149] *Swastika Night* suggests other parallels between the Nazi ritual and the Anglican liturgy. For example, Cranmer's catechism requires the congregant to recite the Ten Commandments, while in Burdekin's novel, the Knight intones the "fundamental immutable laws of Hitler society."[150] Returning repeatedly to the political as well as the religious debates around the Book of Common Prayer, Burdekin's work encourages us to contemplate the Reformation as an ongoing, incomplete project.

The Prayer Book also plays an important role in Burdekin's rather different novel *The Rebel Passion* (1929), whose narrator is a twelfth-century Norman monk called Giraldus. This narrator is given visions of the past, present and future, from the evolution of man to the thirty-second century, in roughly chronological order, while, in the novel's present, he works in his Glastonbury monastery on a manuscript Mass book. He is led through his visions by a spirit guide who plays Virgil to Giraldus's Dante, "one of the Children of God," referred to throughout simply as "the Child."[151] The novel allows readers to experience the development of the Protestant Reformation, the English Civil War, the Industrial Revolution, and the Great War from the defamiliarizing perspective of a medieval narrator.

The schism in the church is a central theme of the novel, and Giraldus is skeptical of the "heretics" who deny that the blood and body of Christ are literally present in the bread and wine of the Eucharist. Giraldus frequently does not know the modern terms for the thing he describes, so the word "Protestant" is never used: the distinction is between those who say "it is not there" and those who insist "it is there"—"it" being the blood and body of Christ during the eucharistic rite. The heroine in the novel's historiography of English Christianity is Elizabeth I, who says in relation to this question of transubstantiation, "I don't know." Indeed, Elizabeth's revised Book of Common Prayer of 1559 (established as the only legal form of religious observance in an Act of Uniformity that year) deliberately fudged the question: as Alan Jacobs writes, it restored an "ambiguous language" that "allowed worshippers to believe that Christ was, in some way, not specifically defined, truly present in the bread and wine."[152] Or not, depending on the particular preferences of the devotee.

The writing of *The Rebel Passion* coincided with the 1928 attempt to revise the Prayer Book to which, as we have seen, T. S. Eliot objected. In Burdekin's novel, Giraldus describes how "a small and lively section of the heretics who would say—'it is there' [presumably the Anglo-Catholics]—and yet would stay in their own Church and create strife . . . produced a new book for the prayers of the heretics."[153] After explaining the failure of the new book of 1928, the Child shows Giraldus the 1662 Prayer Book:

> So they returned to their old book of prayers, and the Child took me into a vision that I might read it. I have forgotten it now, but I remember that it was written in the deep, strong, resonant English that was its perfection, and that the prayers at their semblance of the Mass were very beautiful, neither could I see why any of them wanted to change a word of it. I remember I said to the Child:
>
> "If a man will pray these prayers with earnestness and humility surely he will find our Lord Christ."
>
> And the Child said: "Surely he will."

After his initial shock at the heretical questioning of transubstantiation, Giraldus comes like T. S. Eliot to sympathize with the spirit of Elizabethan compromise, and in this passage he argues that the venerable 1662 Prayer Book that had been in place since the Restoration will serve as a more than adequate guide for a Christian life: "though it is a heretics' book," he concludes, "there must be in it very much good."[154]

Over the course of the novel, Giraldus's identification with the Protestant heresy deepens to the extent that he becomes wary of deviations from the new Anglican norms, both from High Church Anglo-Catholics (which he associates with the 1928 attempt to revise the Book) and from Puritan dissenters. Puritans—the most important critics of the Book of Common Prayer in the seventeenth century—objected to what Milton called "the servile yoak of liturgy," as we have seen.[155] Giraldus is in general dismissive of the Puritans (whom he calls "the joyless people" in an account of the Cromwellian protectorate), but he finds among them one redeeming figure in John Bunyan, whom the Child commends as "a great man, and a noble, and one the world must thank God for."[156] This is significant because Bunyan was, like Milton, famously critical of set prayers, berating those who were "so hot for the forms and not for the power of praying," and rejecting the Prayer Book entirely in favor of spontaneous and improvised prayer that "bubbleth out of the heart."[157] By celebrating Bunyan, *The Rebel Passion* seems to signal some sympathy for the more individualistic, improvisatory forms of prayer that Puritans valued.

In the final section of *The Rebel Passion,* Giraldus is given a vision of the thirty-second century, which the Child presents as an achieved utopia. Christianity has become radically less hierarchical, so that "the priesthood, as it used to be, is clean passed away."[158] Durham Cathedral is now the only church in the country, and Giraldus makes a pilgrimage there to attend Mass. Giraldus's description of the liturgy explicitly evokes the Elizabethan compromise: "Their form of words I cannot now remember, but I know that the spirit of the words of the Wise Queen was in it, and most humbly, and with utter adoration of our Lord Christ this people said—'I do not know.' "[159] This utopian future is one in which the bloody Reformation debates about the precise "form of words" for set prayers has receded, but Elizabeth's example remains important in preserving ambiguity around the question of transubstantiation. A set liturgy continues to exist, and retains a clear relationship to Elizabeth's Book of Common Prayer, but the sectarian debates that surround it are over: "there are no sects, and no heretics, and all are Christians," the Child reports. "The wound in the Church of Christ is healed."[160]

Despite the continued presence of the Prayer Book in the Durham rite, the utopia that concludes Giraldus's visions is clearly more individualistic than the Anglican liturgy encountered earlier on in the novel. The demise of the priesthood seems crucial here: there is evidence of an agreed script for worship, but without it having been imposed by a church hierarchy. The element of individualism that Giraldus discovers in the utopia of the thirty-second century is also interestingly bound up with the question of print. As Giraldus patiently copies his Mass book in the novel's present, he is shown visions of the printing press, and of a culture based on the widespread circulation of printed books among a literate population. *The Rebel Passion* repeatedly underscores the fact that its twelfth-century narrator is looking across the frontier of a media revolution. During Giraldus's vision of the printing press, the Child points out that its operator "can write a thousand books while you are writing half of one." Giraldus then expresses a concern that if the man "writes ill books with his engine it will be as if the devil had spawned, and for every devil there had been in the world before there would now be ten thousand." A bad book produced on the printing press could have a much more extensive influence than Giraldus's own hand-copied Mass book, he worries. But the Child reassures him: "I will show you a time when two out of every four books written with this writing-engine shall be trivial, blasphemous and lustful, yet I say to you that the good of this writing-engine by far will exceed its harm, and that it is the most blessed invention of man, and will lead to a great growth of pity, and understanding, and a knowledge of man, his virtues and his imperfections."[161] The Child looks forward to a polycentric, literate culture where a wide variety of texts coexist in a variegated intellectual ecosystem. In the long historical trajectory described by *The Rebel Passion,* the Reformation culture in which the state imposed set prayers for joint utterance is only a staging post on the way to something better. Books can be institutionalized in a national church and used as a means to make everyone say the same thing. However, we may hold out for the possibility of a more pluralistic and individualistic high literacy, in which the importance of a single unifying script has receded.

These two novels offer contrasting models for the future of national liturgy, and for the long-term outcomes of the Reformation. A flexible, inclusive, nondogmatic set of collective prayers in *The Rebel Passion* allow citizens a considerable degree of individual agency in an era of what Burdekin would call, in *Proud Man* (1934), "unselfish individualism."[162] This forms a contrast with the brutal Nazi regime in *Swastika Night,* which imposes its liturgy by force, in order to suppress any form of individuality, or indeed collective resistance. Von Hess, a senior Teutonic knight in the regime who is nevertheless its staunchest critic, explains: "That Creed has held this huge empire together for over six hundred years. Nonsense of such endurance value almost ceases to be nonsense."[163] If this Nazi regime is a continuation of the politico-religious impulse of the Reformation, as Burdekin's text implies, then the latter represents anything but the arrival of individualism. Rather, it constitutes an attempt to enforce a more collective kind of observance through the imposition of a state-backed liturgy.

Swastika Night depicts the power of liturgy in its most extreme hegemonic form. There is not much hope in this novel that the dystopian Nazi Empire might be overturned. However, the germs of refusal can be found in the characters' reactions against the rote repetition of set forms of words. The most exploited and oppressed section of society in this dystopia are the women, who are treated as animals only good for breeding and kept in appalling conditions entirely separated from the men. Sons are removed from their mothers as infants in order to be raised in an exclusively male society. Women are also required to participate in the state religion, at a separate women's worship. Burdekin's depiction of this rite is characterized by a tension between the set form of the ceremony and the women's spontaneous outpouring of grief for their estranged sons: "All together, women fell into a sort of mass grief," Burdekin's narrator reports. This cacophony of "feminine squeakings and wailings" is overwritten by an agreed social script, captured by Burdekin in a highly unusual form of narration: "Of course women were not fit to rear men-children, of course it was unseemly for a man to be able to point to a woman and say 'There is my mother'—of course they must be taken away from us, and never see us, and forget us wholly."[164] In a fascinating article on collective narrative, Monika Fludernik investigates the use of free indirect style to depict collective thoughts shared by a group.[165] As in Fludernik's examples, Burdekin's third-person omniscient narrator moves into free indirect discourse, with the repetition of "of course" expressing the first-person plural perspective of the whole group of women. "Of course" moreover suggests the internalized commonsense ideology of an oppressive regime that deprives these same women of their children, and teaches them—by catechistic indoctrination—that this is both inevitable and fair. However, free indirect style by definition retains third-person pronouns while combining them with "the indications of time and place appropriate to direct discourse."[166] To follow the ordinary conventions of free indirect style, this passage from *Swastika Night* would have to read "of course [the children] must be taken away from them, and never see them, and forget them wholly." But Burdekin makes the first-person plural pronouns ("us") break through into the omniscient third-person narration, doing for collective free indirect style what James Joyce and Dorothy Richardson did for its individual variant in *Ulysses* (1922) and *Pilgrimage* (1915–67). We will have to call this "collective interior monologue," a technique that Burdekin may well have invented, or in any case used to striking effect, to explore the relationship between the social scripts internalized by a group, and the individual conscience.

The set words that the women speak in unison as part of the liturgy, and the scripts they have internalized as a result, exist in tension with the possibility of individual self-expression. Like many rites in the Book of Common Prayer, the women's worship involves scripted call-and-response patterns initiated by the minister—in this case, the knight—but the women's grief cannot be fully contained by the rote response:

> "Are you not blessed above all female animals in being allowed to be the mothers of men?"
>
> He paused. In dreary little scattered whispers came the formal response: "Yes, Lord. Yes, Lord. We are blessed." But a renewed burst of weeping followed as the women wondered where were the men they had borne. He is twelve now—he is twenty-five and Rudi twenty-one—if Hans is still alive he's seventy this summer, with a white beard like the Knight. But this last thought was in the mind of a very old and incredibly repulsive hag, far too old to cry.[167]

The formal response is followed by the reassertion of a grief that "bubbleth out of the heart" (in Bunyan's words), and that tends towards the fragmentation of the speaking group into individuals with their essentially private experiences of grief. The sentence that begins "He is twelve now" is in a sort of free indirect style, but instead of being focalized either through the group or through one given individual, it is a composite of multiple individual perspectives: different women who lost different sons. The women's experiences of losing their sons are individual and distinct, and yet bracketed together in a single multiperspectival sentence that paratactically links these disparate experiences and orients them against the imposed unanimity of the public ritual. Mentally, they are already beating a trail out of Thebes, to Mount Cithaeron, on their way to becoming bacchants.

The question about how disparate voices might relate to one another is central to the way in which the novel has been theorized as a genre. What makes the novel novelistic, argued Bakhtin, is its dialogism—its ability to coordinate multiple different voices held in tension: "in the novel," he wrote, "double-voicedness sinks its roots into a fundamental, sociolinguistic speech diversity and multi-languagedness."[168] Where for Bakhtin the unique power of the literary novel is its capacity to make one narratorial voice speak as many, and therefore to mobilize the linguistic diversity of the community, liturgy is designed to make many voices speak as one. In the context of the Reformation debates to which I have drawn attention, the novel as a form might be thought to have taken the side of Milton and Bunyan, steering away from the "servile yoak of liturgy" to invest its attention on a multiplicity of individualistic perspectives in free indirect discourse, that "bubbleth out of the heart." The novel does not lend itself the collective voice, which is perhaps why novelists—like Sembène, Roumain, or Burdekin—who seek to mobilize that voice end up straining and sometimes overleaping the limitations of the form.

In *Swastika Night* there is one more palpable site of potential resistance to the Nazi liturgy, which is to be found in the last vestiges of an English vernacular oral culture where secret rebellious songs, sung in monodic unison, offer a patriotic rejection of German domination:

God send our warrior-king,
God send our valiant king,
God send our king.
Send him victorious,
War-worn but glorious
Long to rule over us,
God send him soon.

Thy choicest arms in store
On us be pleased to pour
On churl and thegn,
Scatter the enemy!
Death to all Germany!
England will yet be free
In that great reign.[169]

This bastardized reworking of "God Save the King" provides a secret source of resistance against Nazism and points to a perceived need for new forms of collective speech, sung or spoken in unison. It connects Burdekin's novel to the politics of the Popular Front, which saw the reactivation of folk cultural forms as a vital source of antifascist resistance.

Burdekin's work—still underappreciated and in many cases out of print—is a rich resource for reflecting on the role of the collective voice in relation to religion, politics, and the state.[170] This chapter has shown how, for writers including Eliot, Slater, and Ngũgĩ, liturgy can play a vital role in glorifying state power, and securing the cultural hegemony of the ruling class. As writers worried about "cultural disintegration," national liturgy could appear as a countervailing force, entropically diffusing a shared culture and extending a homogeneous set of social norms. But as Britten, Slater and Ngũgĩ show, the effect of this homogenization is also to generate exclusion and to create outsider figures like Peter Grimes, or Mugo, who cannot or will not accept the shared social scripts imposed by liturgical means. By linking the Anglican liturgy to Nazi politics, Burdekin suggests that the hegemonic collective voice has an irreducibly authoritarian and oppressive character. However, Burdekin's depiction of the women's internal deviations from the liturgy, and her positioning of vernacular English folk culture as a possible site of resistance to Nazism, gesture towards the politics of refusal and of protest. What starts as an individualistic recoil from liturgical collective vocalization as such, becomes a search for new scripts that might be used in the service of collective refusal, and—perhaps, eventually—of engagement.

CODA

COMPLETING THE CIRCLE

WHEN THE COLLECTIVE VOICE aids in the consolidation of political power by glorifying it, it also creates exclusions, and in so doing, it plants the seeds of resistance to that power. This is often in the first instance the resistance of the individual conscience, heavily emphasized by Puritan radicals as they demurred from the set liturgies of the Catholic and Anglican Churches, intertwined as they were with state power. But the individual rejection of liturgy and hegemony can coalesce into collective refusal, exile, and fugitive sociality. In Katharine Burdekin's *Swastika Night*—which links the liturgical collective voice with fascist authoritarianism—the women, debased and abjected by the state, dissent only mentally, in stuttering and fragmented ways. The narrator of that novel begins to join them together in a collectivity that exists on the level of narrative discourse, but which they cannot themselves yet consciously articulate. Nevertheless, Burdekin is sketching a route to refusal. If the women can join their voices—as foreshadowed formally by the narrator's use of collective interior monologue—they will be on their way to becoming bacchants. This coda completes the circle described in the introduction to this book, before offering some concluding remarks.

Take This Hammer

The John Henry tradition is capacious enough to see the collective voice in every relation to the polis, and it can close the circle that this book has described, from exile/refusal, to protest/engagement, to liturgy/hegemony—and back to refusal again. Collected by Zora Neale Hurston and Alan Lomax, "John Henry" was part of the "Undercommons" described by Fred Moten and seen, as Paul Rekret puts it, as "a down-home expression of pride in craft and the resilience of labour as it confronts mass industry."[1] The work songs I explored in chapter 2 became tied up in a productivist mythology of the worker, and were turned towards the polis by Langston Hughes and others. We see John Henry from another angle in John Fahey's "Nine Pound Hammer," on his 1968 album *The Voice of the Turtle*—a sprawling, experimental record whose extensive liner notes set out a mainly fictional folk mythology around its own origins. Fahey recorded a number of John Henry songs over the course of his career, mainly as instrumentals for solo guitar in his signature style: "John Henry" appears on *Blind Joe Death, Vol. 1* (1959), and on *Death Chants, Breakdowns and Military Waltzes* (1963) the beautiful "John Henry Variations." That 1963 recording breaks out of the frame of the traditional ballad to explore the discordant possibilities of Fahey's open D tuning, and so to access a spacious emotional prairie, as far as you can get from the railroad camp.[2] "Nine Pound Hammer," unusually in Fahey's work, includes a vocal:

> This here hammer that killed John Henry
> Ain't gon' kill me
> Ain't gon' kill me
> Ain't gon' kill me
>
> If the [?]
> Up to my home
> Up to my home
> Up to my home
>
> Take this hammer that killed John Henry
> Ain't gon' kill me
> Ain't gon' kill me
> Ain't gon' kill me
>
> My hammer, it rings like silver
> It shine like gold
> It shine like gold
> Shine like gold
>
> Take this hammer and carry it to my captain
> Tell him I'm gone
> Tell him I'm gone
> Tell him I'm gone[3]

This song combines a number of traditional lyrics that were already in circulation, including most famously on Lead Belly's recording "Take This Hammer," in which he utters a loud grunt at the end of each line—as in Zora Neale Hurston's demonstration of lining rhythms—to show where the hammer falls, and to root the song in the collective labor of the railroad camp. Similar lines were recorded by Joseph "Chinaman" Johnson.[4] In many John Henry songs (including some of Hughes's versions), he is reported to have "died with his hammer in his hand" after proving himself by beating a steam drill in a race. Hughes's wartime adaptations of "John Henry" had sought to put the work song, and the laboring body that it orchestrated, at the service of an international fight against fascism, and a domestic fight against Jim Crow and the Ku Klux Klan.

Fahey's version has a very different emphasis: it is an anti-work song, a "refusal of work," as Rekret puts it.[5] Its last verse—"Take this hammer and carry it to my captain / Tell him I'm gone"—imagines the speaker leaving the railroad camp entirely. It marks a duality within the tradition of the work song. Hughes's John Henry songs are representative of a Popular Front tradition that sought to reintegrate manual labor with the creative and expressive powers of the work song. In the crisis of the Second World War, Hughes reimagined John Henry as a way of harnessing work to a state that was fighting fascism. Fahey's version, recorded against the backdrop of the unfolding nightmare of the Vietnam War, is in tune with the countercultural currents of the late 1960s. Drawing on the traditional lyrics (popularized by Lead Belly), Fahey's singer downs tools, drops out, and joins a fugitive refusal of work, and of social conformity as such. The productivist work song—especially if turned to hegemonic nationalist ends—starts to look potentially fascistic. "Nine Pound Hammer" evinces a fundamentally different orientation to work.

What was happening, in 2016, when the San Francisco 49ers quarterback Colin Kaepernick took the knee during the singing of "The Star-Spangled Banner"?[6] The conventions around that anthem are in any case highly particular, and Kaepernick's gesture can be understood only in the context of these. "The Star-Spangled Banner" is sung with monotonous regularity before the start of sporting events across the US, where in the UK's football culture, for example, "God Save the King" is heard only at appearances of the national team and at the FA Cup Final (after "Abide with Me," since 1927 the traditional FA cup hymn). "God Save the King" (like "Abide with Me") is sung by the crowd, and that is essential to its meaning and effect. But "The Star-Spangled Banner" is typically performed by a professional singer or group, with the crowd listening, standing with hand on heart. The song is notoriously difficult to sing, with a big range and high notes that are often beyond the capacity of untrained voices.[7] And so it lends itself to virtuoso performances, some of which—like those by Marvin Gaye (NBA All-Star Game, 1983), Whitney Houston (Super Bowl XXV), and Beyoncé (Barack Obama's inauguration in 2013)—have attained legendary status. The virtuoso can be thought of as singing on behalf of the assembled crowd, including them in the piece's first-person plural pronouns ("our flag"), as everyone confirms their assent by standing and putting hand to heart, rather than joining in. Viral social media moments occasionally arise when the PA system fails and the spectators take over, confirming that the singing really does happen on their behalf (and that, at least in musical terms, it is a good thing, too, as the high notes prove more than a strain). Metonymically, the singer stands and speaks for the American people as a whole, to glorify the flag and the nation: an archetypal instance of hegemonic and liturgical collective speech.

When Kaepernick took the knee, he refused to assent to the anthem being sung on his behalf. He could not join in, even symbolically, because he associated the anthem with white supremacy, which was most viscerally expressed in the persistence of unpunished police brutality against Black people. So Kaepernick knelt to express his refusal: "Take this hammer," he seemed to say. Others who felt the same started to copy the gesture. This provoked hostile reactions from conservative quarters, which only galvanized others to refuse: soon, there was a movement—perhaps it should be called a protest movement, as it turned towards the polis—led by some prominent Black players, but supported by millions of Americans across racial divides. The refusal to join with the anthem led to another kind of joining, and a kind of countercollective was formed.

What happened in this case was not the transformation of the US state, but the gradual blunting of the gesture itself as it was incorporated, adopted, and even institutionalized. The Dallas Cowboys—"America's team," not known for their radicalism—agreed to kneel all together as a team, along with Cowboys owner Jerry Jones, *before* the anthem was played, in order to do so without actually disrespecting the flag. Jones had brokered an agreement that the whole team would then all stand together, hand on heart, for the anthem itself.[8] Meanwhile, the gesture of taking the knee spread around the world. In the English Premier League, it is now performed by all players at the first and last match of the season, "as well as dedicated No Room For Racism fixtures in October and April." Announcing the arrangements for the 2024–25 season, the league noted: "The Premier League supports the players' decision and will continue to work with clubs this season to reiterate anti-discrimination messaging and promote the action taken as part of the League's No Room For Racism Action Plan."[9] At this point it would be disruptive *not* to take the knee: the gesture itself (albeit a collective action rather than a vocalization) has completed its path from refusal, to protest, to liturgy.

Conclusion

The collective voice remains a vital cultural force, linking political solidarity with embodied collectivity, ethnic belonging, and spiritual succor. Writers, critics, and theorists of modern literature, regretting their own individualism and that which they see around them in capitalist societies, have often mourned the passing of this voice, and sought to revive it in the service of a range of cultural-political projects.

The variety of texts and performances I have discussed in this book tend to confirm the importance of taking an expansive view of the collective voice, which acknowledges that it has several different political functions. Secondary collective vocalization has proved a rich and capacious category. It is notable that in the two examples I have discussed in this coda—Fahey's versions of John Henry, and Kaepernick's refusal to stand for "The Star-Spangled Banner"—the definition of collective vocalization with which I started the book is not met. Yet they can and should be understood as being continuous with the broader phenomenon of collective speech. Fahey's percussive guitar picking on "John Henry Variations" no longer literally includes the grunts of the railroad workers, and it is an ostentatiously individual solo performance. But the sound of hammers driving steel are behind it: it is underpinned and to an extent determined by its relationship to the collective speech practice from which it ultimately derives. The effect and meaning of such works are brought into a new focus by understanding how they invoke the collective voice, and by situating them in the collective speech traditions traced in this book. By sharpening our awareness of the mediation of primary collective speech through layers of cultural representation, this book has tried to show how modern literature and drama are consciously positioned in relation to the antagonistic realm of collective politics. Fredric Jameson's formalist emphasis on the "hidden kindling of a collective spark" in a literary text can be extended and supplemented by a more literal attention to that text's relationship with overtly collective forms of art and politics.[10]

The collective voice has turned out to be a useful way of thinking about the general relationship between politics and culture, in both of the two senses of "culture" influentially discussed by Raymond Williams.[11] First, collective speech is woven into culture seen as a "whole way of life" and is an important element of how that anthropological sense of culture is mobilized politically. As we have seen, collective vocalizations of various kinds have often been positioned as the primal and authentic expressions of an ethnic or cultural group. As such they can embody a fugitive and antipolitical sociality, or be travestied by racist representation, used to promote the interests of a group or cause, or be claimed as expressions of the cultural essence of a nation-state, and recast as anthems used to glorify power. Sometimes all of these things can happen to the same set of words. As such, a focus on the politics of collective vocalization underlines the importance of contextual factors, and the limitations of purely semantic ones, for any understanding of language in use.

Second, the collective voice holds an important place within the sphere of culture in the more specialized sense of "the arts and learning." Pointed deployments of theatrical and operatic choruses, the invention of mass declamation poetry, the careful crafting of liturgical language, and attempts to activate the collectively speaking mass within prose narrative, show writers and dramatists trying to channel the power of the collective voice for political ends. These creative inventions build on the importance of collective voicing in religious, political, and sporting settings, and draw strength from the ways they channel or reinvent these. Williams is rightly inclined to "insist on both" of these meanings of culture, and on the "significance of their conjunction." Human creativity and imagination surge through collective utterances that would not normally be designated as art, such as football songs, protest chants, or prayers. And self-consciously artistic uses of the collective voice gain meaning, force, and beauty, when they are understood in relationship to this wider field of collective utterances.

The more self-consciously artistic the collective utterance, the more likely it is to draw attention to its own formal qualities, and to the formal possibilities of collective vocalization as such. The texts and performances I have discussed in this book offer a rich archive for observing these formal possibilities, across a variety of media. Discussions about the meaning and status of the theatrical chorus, to take one prominent example discussed in chapter 2, show how literary and dramatic forms were adapted, in the wake of the American and French Revolutions, to encompass a new, modern conception of politics in which "the people" were a key player. Prose fiction is the site of significant formal ingenuity in its evocations of the collective voice, which are in this context secondary by definition. Georg Lukács imagined the realist novel as containing a modern equivalent to Greek tragic chorus, its figuration of social totality via omniscient third-person narration seeming to encode a form of secondary collective speech. Katharine Burdekin's experiments in *Swastika Night* with what I called collective interior monologue, or Ousmane Sembène's recourse to the collective protagonist in *God's Bits of Wood,* showed that novelists continued to innovate in their attempts to represent collective political action within the apparently individualistic form of the bourgeois novel. To attend to the formal qualities of the collective voice in context is an education in conceptions of collective life.

As I suggested in the introduction, the formal qualities of a collective utterance are no sure guide to its political morality. Taking a step back, this book has attempted instead a speculative mapping of the collective voice in its different relationships to the polis. But are the three positions I have described—of exile/refusal, protest/engagement, and liturgy/hegemony—associated with different formal properties in collective speech? Musical qualities—pitch, melody, harmony, polyphony, rhythm—are often defining formal features of the collective voice, and vital to its contextual meaning. Are these things in any sense correlated with the positionalities I have mapped?

Weakly, perhaps, but not insignificantly. In the position of refusal, complex polyphonic and harmonic arrangements *are* unusual: collective utterances that refuse the polis often deliberately invoke primitivism and orality, and, like Zora Neale Hurston, tend to revel in a rough-and-ready aesthetic that can be embodied in repetitive chanting, monodic unison, and nonsemantic or untranslatable vocalization. These often (though not always) involve small groups of speakers. Meanwhile, more elaborate musical and narrative forms (often with more participants) make a virtue of the high level of premeditated structural organization that is made possible by the printed score: these suggest analogies with organized political life that resonate with the liturgical and hegemonic position. In between, some engaged protest chants (like "Black lives matter!" and "Lock her up!") are primitive in form, emphasizing that they are the authentic vocal expressions of the people while turning this energy towards the polis. Other engaged forms adopt elaborate structures to hold larger groups together, while polyphonically emphasizing significant internal variation (like the chorus in *Lohengrin*), or even signaling a readiness for government. Meanwhile, some hegemonic forms—like the national anthem, or chants of "Four more years!" that are formally very close to "Lock her up!"—run contrary to this weak correlation, being deliberately monodic and formally simple, underscoring a "volkish" quality by setting aside polyphony's internal hierarchization. If there is indeed a correlation of the kind I have suggested, it is anything but a hard-and-fast rule. But we learn something about national anthems (to persist with that example) if we recognize that they often invoke in their formal qualities modes of solidarity that are commonly associated with refusal or protest.

The map in figure 1 is my own invention, but it is not simply fanciful. The work of this book suggests that the figure is latent in the texts I examine, and in the modern culture of which they form a part. Literary and dramatic works in modern times tend to imagine the practice of collective voicing in the spatial terms I have described. And the nineteenth and twentieth centuries mark the historical point at which positionality becomes an indispensable tool for thinking about the affordances of collective speech. These two centuries saw the consolidation of a conception of the political as a closed system. Capitalism, empire, the nation-state, and ethno-cultural identities started increasingly in this period to be thought of, and even experienced as, what Caroline Levine calls "bounded wholes."[12] This context therefore calls forth an understanding of the collective voice in terms of its spatial relationship to these formations. I have used the idea of the polis as a capacious means of capturing and comparing the ways in which human collectivity has organized itself in relation to such wholes. The literature and drama of this period helps to bring to the surface a pervasive logic of inside and outside, towards and away from, that governs the cultural and political operations of the collective voice.

NOTES

Introduction

1. Steven Connor, "Choralities," in *Twentieth-Century Music* 13:1 (2016), 3–23, 6.

2. Fred Cummins, *The Ground from Which We Speak: Joint Speech and the Collective Subject* (Newcastle: Cambridge Scholars Press, 2018), 6.

3. The persistence of this evolutionist narrative, and the weight of the evidence against it, has been explored in depth in David Graeber and David Wengrow, *The Dawn of Everything: A New History of Humanity* (London: Penguin, 2021), see esp. 446–49.

4. Judith Butler, *Notes Toward a Performative Theory of Assembly* (Cambridge: Harvard University Press, 2015), 5.

5. See Elias Canetti, *Crowds and Power* (trans. Carol Stewart) (New York: Seabury Press, 1978); Sigmund Freud, *Mass Psychology and the Analysis of the "I"* (trans. J. A. Underwood), in *Mass Psychology and Other Writings* (London: Penguin, 2004), 17–106; Gustave Le Bon, *The Crowd: A Study of the Popular Mind* (New York: Macmillan, 1896); José Ortega y Gasset, *The Revolt of the Masses* (authorized translation from the Spanish) (New York: Norton, 1993).

6. Hans Ulrich Gumbrecht, *Crowds: The Stadium as a Ritual of Intensity* (Stanford: Stanford University Press, 2021), 30–44; Dan Hancox, *Multitudes: How Crowds Made the Modern World* (London: Verso, 2024).

7. Spike Lee, dir., *BlacKkKlansman* (2018).

8. Amelia Saunders, "Not Just Talk: The Politics of Enunciation in *BlacKkKlansman*," *Black Camera* 13:2 (2022), 234–54, 236.

9. Luke Turner, "HEWILLNOTDIVIDE.US" digital video, color, sound, 3:15, displayed at *Milk*, Wellcome Collection, London, 30 March–10 September 2023.

10. Cummins, *The Ground from Which We Speak*, 6.

11. Chantal Mouffe, *For a Left Populism* (London: Verso, 2018), 1–2.

12. "Kamala Harris Shuts Down 'Lock Him Up!' Chant About Trump," YouTube video, https://www.youtube.com/watch?v=BSoU2-zpAco.

13. Mouffe, *For a Left Populism*, 22.

14. Ousmane Sembène, *God's Bits of Wood* (trans. Francis Price) (London: Heinemann, 1976), 241, 216.

15. Butler, *Notes*, 155.

16. Adriana Cavarero, *For More Than One Voice: Toward a Philosophy of Vocal Expression* (trans. Paul A. Kottman) (Stanford: Stanford University Press, 2005), 42.

17. Cavarero, *For More*, 9, 42.

18. Cavarero, *For More*, 3.

19. Adriana Cavarero, *Surging Democracy: Notes on Hannah Arendt's Political Thought* (Stanford: Stanford University Press, 2021), 61.

20. Cavarero, *Surging Democracy*, 62.

21. Cavarero, *Surging Democracy*, 73.

22. J. L. Austin, *How to Do Things with Words* (Oxford: Oxford University Press, 1975), 14.

23. Fredric Jameson, "Schematizations, or How to Draw a Thought," *Critical Inquiry* 50:1 (2023), 31–53, 31.

24. Bonnie Honig, *A Feminist Theory of Refusal* (Cambridge: Harvard University Press, 2021), 1.

25. For an invaluable recent discussion the British reformist tradition and its proto-Gramscian elements, see Benjamin Kohlmann, *British Literature and the Life of Institutions: Speculative States* (Oxford: Oxford University Press, 2021), 68. While the Communist Manifesto did not use the term "dictatorship of the proletariat," the idea that the proletariat would seize the state for a transitional period is already laid out there. Karl Marx and Friedrich Engels, *The Communist Manifesto* (trans. Samuel Moore) (London: Penguin, 1985), 104. The "dictatorship of the proletariat" entered the Marxist lexicon shortly after, in a series of articles republished as Karl Marx, *The Class Struggles in France, 1848–1850* (New York: New York Labor News Co., 1924). Lenin elaborated the theory further in *The State and Revolution* (trans. Robert Service) (London: Penguin, 1992), 81. The implications of the Soviet Constitution, and its departure from the idea of the dictatorship of the proletariat as a "transitional" phase, is described in Étienne Balibar, *On the Dictatorship of the Proletariat* (trans. Graham Locke) (London: NLB, 1977), 50, emphasis in original.

26. Euripides, *Bacchae* (trans. John Davie), in *The Bacchae and Other Plays* (London: Penguin, 2005), 128–65.

27. Bonnie Honig, *A Feminist Theory of Refusal* (Cambridge: Harvard University Press, 2021), 2.

28. The term "fugitive sociality" is suggested in Fred Moten, *The Universal Machine (Consent Not to Be a Single Being)* (Durham: Duke University Press, 2018), 100.

29. Fred Moten, *Black and Blur (Consent Not to Be a Single Being)* (Durham: Duke University Press, 2017), 256.

30. George Shulman, "Fred Moten's Refusals and Consents: The Politics of Fugitivity," *Political Theory* 49:2 (2021), 272–313, 292.

31. For Moten's critique of Arendt, see Fred Moten, *The Universal Machine (Consent*

Not to Be a Single Being) (Durham: Duke University Press, 2018), 65–139. Importantly, Moten has also emphasized the specificity of Black struggle, so he might object to the way my book (and Honig's for that matter) puts this into a comparative dialogue with other struggles and suggests that we can learn from such a comparison. I am not trying to say that all struggles are the same, and my book aims to capture the specificity of different instances of collective speech and to map some schematic correspondences.

32. Euripides, *Bacchae,* 160–63.

33. Honig, *Refusal,* 77–84.

34. Nancy Fraser, "Rethinking Recognition," *New Left Review* 3 (May–June 2000), 107–20.

35. Kate Bowen and Paul A. Pickering, *Songs of Liberty: Music, Radicalism and Reform in the Anglophone World, 1790–1914* (Manchester: Manchester University Press, 2017), 32.

36. Michael Hardt and Antonio Negri, *Assembly* (Oxford: Oxford University Press, 2017), 274.

37. Cummins, *The Ground from Which We Speak,* 21–2.

38. Caroline Levine, "Literary Studies and Collective Life," *New Literary History* 54:1 (2022), 693–720, 694.

39. Fredric Jameson, "Criticism and Categories," *PMLA* 137:3 (2022), 563–67, 564.

40. H. Rider Haggard, *King Solomon's Mines* (London: Penguin, 2007), 106.

41. Levine, *Forms.*

42. Simon Goldhill, "The Greek Chorus: Our German Eye," in Joshua Billings, Felix Budelmann, and Fiona Macintosh (eds.), *Choruses, Ancient and Modern* (Oxford: Oxford University Press, 2013), 35–52.

Chapter 1

1. Friedrich Nietzsche, *The Birth of Tragedy out of the Spirit of Music* (trans. Shaun Whiteside) (London: Penguin, 1993), 36–37.

2. Nietzsche, *Tragedy,* 39.

3. Nietzsche, *Tragedy,* 39.

4. Nietzsche, *Tragedy,* 18.

5. There is a case to be made that the chorus (in Greek tragedy and beyond) does sometimes aspire to work through and with the apparatus of the state as a representative of "the people," or of some subgroup thereof, and I discuss this tradition of thinking about the chorus in chapter 2.

6. Bonnie Honig, *A Feminist Theory of Refusal* (Cambridge: Harvard University Press, 2021), 1.

7. Saidiya Hartman, "Intimate History, Radical Narrative," *Black Perspectives* (May 2022), https://www.aaihs.org/intimate-history-radical-narrative/.

8. Lindsey Stewart, *The Politics of Black Joy: Zora Neale Hurston and Neo-Abolitionism* (Evanston: Northwestern University Press, 2021), 33.

9. William Shakespeare, *Macbeth* IV.i.20–21, in Stephen Greenblatt et al. (eds.), *The Norton Shakespeare* (New York: Norton, 1997), 2555–2618, 2597.

10. Shakespeare, *Macbeth,* I.i.10, I.iii.36.

11. Jean Rouch, dir., *Yenendi: Les hommes qui font la pluie* (1951).

12. H. Rider Haggard, *King Solomon's Mines* (London: Penguin, 2007), 247n.

13. Haggard, *King Solomon's Mines,* 86.

14. David Pocock, speaking in *Strange Beliefs: Sir Edward Evans-Pritchard* (TV documentary first screened 1986), YouTube video, https://www.youtube.com/watch?v=hXyoOyEcQnk.

15. Haggard, *King Solomon's Mines,* 106.

16. Rachel Blau DuPlessis, "'HOO, HOO, HOO': Some Episodes in the Construction of Modern Whiteness," *American Literature* 67:4 (1995), 667–700, 668.

17. T. S. Eliot, *Sweeney Agonistes: Fragments of an Aristophanic Melodrama* (London: Faber & Faber, 1932), 30–31.

18. DuPlessis, "'HOO, HOO, HOO,'" 668.

19. Haggard, *King Solomon's Mines,* 84.

20. Haggard, *King Solomon's Mines,* 121.

21. Haggard, *King Solomon's Mines,* 120.

22. Shakespeare, *Macbeth,* IV.i.96 (2598), V.iii.4 (2610).

23. The different significance of some of these terms, the history of their use, and the "politics of spelling" is mapped in Alasdair Pettinger, "From Vaudoux to Voodoo," *Forum of Modern Language Studies* 40:4 (2004), 415–25, 415. Albert J. Raboteau's discussion "From *Vaudou* to Conjuring," makes a distinction between "voodoo as a religious cult and voodoo as a system of magic," arguing that the system of magic (often referred to as "hoodoo," "root work," or "conjure") outlived the religious cult (more often called "voudou," "vadou," or "voodoo"), in the United States. Albert J. Raboteau, *Slave Religion: The "Invisible Institution" in the Antebellum South,* rev. ed. (1978; Oxford: Oxford University Press, 2004), 75 and 75–87.

24. Ahmad Greene-Hayes, "'A Very Queer Case': Clementine Barnabet and the Erotics of a Sensationalized Voodoo Religion," *Nova Religio: The Journal of Alternative and Emergent Religions* 26:4 (2023), 58–84, 65.

25. Greene-Hayes, "Queer Case," 60.

26. DuPlessis, "'HOO, HOO, HOO,'" 670.

27. Adam McGee, "Haitian Vodou and Voodoo: Imagined Religion and Popular Culture" *Studies in Religion / Sciences Religieuses* 41:2 (2012), 231–56, 232, 239.

28. Raboteau, *Slave Religion,* 81–82.

29. Judith Weisenfeld, ""A Rare Human Document": LoBagola's African American Humbug Religion," *American Religion,* 1:1 (October 2019), 27–48, 47.

30. Tomoko Masuzawa, *The Invention of World Religions: Or, How European Universalism Was Preserved in the Language of Pluralism* (Chicago: University of Chicago Press, 2005), 16.

31. Bill Schwarz, "Breaking Bread with History: C. L. R. James and *The Black Jacobins*" (interview of Stuart Hall), *History Workshop Journal* 46:1 (1998), 17–32, 18. Mark Christian Thompson links the 1930s obsession with Haiti more specifically with black nationalism, arguing that the Haitian War of Independence "signified race pride and

the possibility of Black revolutionary change." Mark Christian Thompson, *Black Fascisms: African American Literature & Culture Between the Wars* (Charlottesville: University of Virginia Press, 2007), 15.

32. David Scott, *Conscripts of Modernity: The Tragedy of Colonial Enlightenment* (Durham: Duke University Press, 2004), 101. Scott sets out the terms of the debate over several insightful pages (101–5).

33. C. L. R. James, *The Black Jacobins: Toussaint L'Ouverture and the San Domingo Revolution* (London: Penguin, 2001), 161.

34. James, *Black Jacobins*, 14.

35. Crystal Nicole Eddins, *Rituals, Runaways, and the Haitian Revolution: Collective Action in the African Diaspora*, 2nd ed. (Cambridge: Cambridge University Press, 2022), 293.

36. Eddins, *Rituals*, 131.

37. Alasdair Pettinger, "'Eh! eh! Bomba, hen! hen!': Making Sense of a Vodou Chant," in Diana Paton and Maarit Forde (eds.), *Obeah and Other Powers: The Politics of Caribbean Religion and Healing* (Durham: Duke University Press, 2012), 80–102, 80.

38. This sense of an "indigenous" Haitian culture, with voodoo as its religion, had recently been theorized by the group of writers who rallied against the US occupation of Haiti (1915–34) under the banner of *indigènisme*. See also Amanda T. Perry, "Becoming Indigenous in Haiti, from Dessalines to *La Revue Indigène*," *Small Axe* 21:2.53 (2017), 45–61.

39. James, *Black Jacobins*, 14. James added a note in a later edition that seemed to acknowledge the speculative nature of these claims: "Such observations, written in 1938, were intended to use the San Domingo revolution as a forecast of the future of colonial Africa" (339n).

40. Pettinger, "'Eh! eh!,'" 94.

41. Jean Price-Mars (trans. Magdaline W. Shannon), *So Spoke the Uncle: Ethnographic Essays (Ainsi parla l'oncle)* (Washington, DC: Three Continents Press, 1983), 111n.

42. Price-Mars, *So Spoke the Uncle*, 53.

43. Scott, *Conscripts*, 129.

44. James, *Black Jacobins*, 69; Pettinger, "'Eh! eh!,'" 88. Stuart Hall made a similar point about James's dialectical interest in historical moments when Enlightenment ideas are expressed in popular political action: "His presentation of Toussaint L'Ouverture in *The Black Jacobins* is of a man who is a thinker and a reader, as well as a political leader, so he never venerated insurrectionary irrationalism. But he was absorbed by those moments when the masses enter history, in their own person as it were." Hall, "Breaking Bread," 21–22.

45. Douglas Robinson suggests in *Translation and Empire* that "a hegemonic culture only translates those works by authors in a dominated culture that fit the former's preconceived notions of the latter"—i.e., that seem typical of the culture being translated. This claim is complicated by cases—often found particularly in collectively chanted or sung ritual speech—where the very foreignness, indeed the potential untranslatabil-

ity, of the utterance is what makes it seem typical. Douglas Robinson, *Translation and Empire: Postcolonial Theories Explained* (London: Routledge, 2014), 32.

46. Langston Hughes, "Emperor of Haiti," in *The Collected Works of Langston Hughes,* vol. 5, *Plays to 1942: Mulatto to the Sun Do Move,* ed. Leslie Sanders and Nancy Johnston (Columbia: University of Missouri Press, 2002), 278–332, 283, 285.

47. After the revolution, when he is emperor, Dessalines becomes reliant on mulatto servants to read his correspondence aloud and write down the replies. Hughes, "Emperor of Haiti," 300. "Mulatto" was an important designation in revolutionary Haiti, and a term used freely by both James and Hughes.

48. Hughes, "Emperor of Haiti," 283.

49. Hughes, "Emperor of Haiti," 292.

50. Hughes, "Emperor of Haiti," 295–96.

51. Shane Graham, "'It Cancels the Slave Ship!': Africa, Slavery, and the Haitian Revolution in Langston Hughes's *Emperor of Haiti* and Aimé Césaire's *The Tragedy of King Christophe*" in *Modern Drama* 62:4 (2019), 458–82, 465.

52. Hughes, "Emperor of Haiti," 317.

53. Langston Hughes, *I Wander as I Wander: An Autobiographical Journey* (New York: Hill and Wang, 1964), 28.

54. Welles says of the setting that it was intended to be "suggestive of Haiti at the time of the Black Emperor Henri Christophe." Citizen Welles, "Orson Welles, Sketch Book—Episode 2: Critics," YouTube video, https://www.youtube.com/watch?v=NL3ZoUJ-Tek. Christophe became ruler following the assassination of Dessalines.

55. Robert Sawyer, "'All's Well That Ends Welles': Orson Welles and the 'Voodoo' Macbeth" in *Multicultural Shakespeare: Translation, Appropriation and Performance* 13:28 (2016), 87–103, 94.

56. Atkinson, qtd. in Sawyer, "All's Well," 97.

57. Clifford Mason, *Macbeth in Harlem: Black Theater in America from the Beginning to Raisin in the Sun* (New Brunswick: Rutgers University Press, 2020), 163. Mason's account of the production, its contexts, and reception (152–65) is the most vivid I have found, and ranges over a rich array of press responses.

58. Richard France, preface to *Macbeth,* in Richard France (ed.), *Orson Welles on Shakespeare: The W.P.A. and Mercury Theatre Playscripts* (Westport: Greenwood Press, 1990), 29–36, 32–33.

59. Orson Welles, *Macbeth (Negro Version),* p. 24, Federal Theatre Project Materials Collection, George Mason University, https://mars.gmu.edu/handle/1920/4494.

60. Welles, *Macbeth,* 25. The version of the script held in the Lilly Library, University of Indiana, consists of a roughly identical typescript, but with many more indications for voodoo drumming and chanting penciled on. See Orson Welles, *Macbeth (Apr. 14 1936),* Welles mss., 1930–1950, Lilly Library, Indiana University, Bloomington. It is reasonable to assume that this was a production copy and that these annotations (and many details of how the voodoo elements would be staged) accumulated during rehearsals. Both versions include a typescript comment at the top of act 3, scene 3, indicating: "This scene is entirely incomplete. It's [*sic*] setting and arrangement depend on physical production decision" (47).

61. Marguerite H. Rippy, *Orson Welles and the Unfinished RKO Projects: A Postmodern Perspective* (Carbondale: Southern Illinois University Press, 2009), 72.

62. Rippy, *Orson Welles,* 76; Mason, *Macbeth,* 153.

63. Michael Denning, *The Cultural Front: The Labouring of American Culture in the Twentieth Century* (London: Verso, 1997), 396.

64. Benjamin Hilb, "Afro-Haitian-American Ritual Power: *Vodou* in the Welles-FTP *Voodoo Macbeth,*" *Shakespeare Bulletin* 32:4 (Winter 2014), 649–81, 651.

65. Welles, "Orson Welles, Sketch Book."

66. Mason, *Macbeth,* 154.

67. Welles, "Orson Welles, Sketch Book."

68. Houseman, quoted and discussed at length in Mason, *Macbeth,* 158.

69. Welles, "Sketch Book."

70. H. P. Lovecraft, "The Call of Cthulhu," in *The Complete Cthulhu Mythos Tales* (New York: Barnes & Noble, 2016), 36–61, 43.

71. Lovecraft, "The Call," 43–47.

72. Many scholars have documented how Lovecraft invokes racial tropes in his fiction, which reflect racist views that he expressed elsewhere. See, e.g., Timothy H. Evans, "A Last Defense Against the Dark: Folklore, Horror, and the Uses of Tradition in the Works of H. P. Lovecraft," *Journal of Folklore Research* 42:1 (2005), 99–135; Michel Houellebecq, *H. P. Lovecraft: Against the World, Against Life* (trans. Dorna Khazeni) (London: Gollancz, 2008); David Punter and Glennis Byron, *The Gothic* (Oxford: Blackwell, 2004), 144.

73. S. T. Joshi, *A Dreamer and a Visionary : H P Lovecraft in His Time* (Liverpool: Liverpool University Press, 2001), 242.

74. Lovecraft, "The Call," 44–45.

75. Lovecraft, "The Call," 49.

76. Lovecraft, qtd. in Joshi, *Dreamer,* 244.

77. Jeanne-Marie Jackson, *The African Novel of Ideas: Philosophy and Individualism in the Age of Global Writing* (Princeton: Princeton University Press, 2021), 96, 15. Jackson has deepened her critique of anthropological approaches to African fiction in "Against Ethnography: On Teaching Minority Literature," in Ato Quayson and Ankhi Mukherjee (eds.), *Decolonizing the English Literary Curriculum* (Cambridge: Cambridge University Press, 2023), 200–213.

78. Henry Louis Gates Jr., "Criticism in the Jungle," in Henry Louis Gates Jr. (ed.), *Black Literature and Literary Theory* (New York: Methuen, 1984), 1–24, 5.

79. Lewis R. Gordon, *Fear of Black Consciousness* (London: Penguin, 2022), 133.

80. Conrad, qtd. (and discussed) in Chinua Achebe, "An Image of Africa: Racism in Conrad's *Heart of Darkness,*" *Massachusetts Review* 57:1 (2016), 14–27, 17.

81. Chinua Achebe, *Things Fall Apart* (London: Penguin, 2001), 122.

82. David Richards, "At Other Times: Modernism and the 'Primitive,'" in Vincent Sherry (ed.), *The Cambridge History of Modernism* (Cambridge: Cambridge University Press, 2017), 64–82, 79.

83. Ben Etherington, *Literary Primitivism* (Stanford: Stanford University Press, 2017), xii.

84. Etherington, *Primitivism,* 25, 38.

85. Zora Neale Hurston, *Dust Tracks on a Road,* in Zora Neale Hurston, *Folklore, Memoirs, and Other Writings,* ed. Cheryl Wall (New York: Library of America, 1995), 557–809, 683.

86. Franz Boas, "Psychological Problems in Anthropology," in George W. Stocking (ed.), *A Franz Boas Reader: The Shaping of American Anthropology, 1883–1911* (Chicago: University of Chicago Press, 1974), 243–54. Modern readers are likely to pick up on the persistence of racist categories in Boas's work, despite his relative position within his contemporary anthropological community. Stronger remnants of an essentialist conception of race were present in earlier works such as "Human Faculty as Determined by Race" in Stocking's *Boas Reader,* 221–42.

87. Zora Neale Hurston, *Mules and Men* (New York: Harper Perennial, 1990), 185.

88. Hurston, *Mules and Men,* 191.

89. Hurston, *Mules and Men,* 193.

90. Hurston, *Mules and Men,* 239.

91. Franz Boas, *Race, Language and Culture* (New York: Free Press, 1966), 281.

92. Franz Boas, "The History of Anthropology," in George W. Stocking Jr. (ed.), *A Franz Boas Reader: The Shaping of American Anthropology, 1883–1911* (Chicago: University of Chicago Press, 1974), 23–36, 27.

93. On cultural relativism, see Sean O'Neill, "The Boasian Legacy in Ethnomusicology: Cultural Relativism, Narrative Texts, and the Role of Comparison," in Regna Darnell, Joshua Smith, Michelle Hamilton, and Robert L. A. Hancock (eds.), *The Franz Boas Papers,* vol. 1, *Franz Boas as Public Intellectual—Theory, Ethnography, Activism* (Lincoln: University of Nebraska Press, 2015), 129–60.

94. Boas, "The History of Anthropology," 34.

95. Hurston, *Dust Tracks,* 687.

96. Franz Boas, preface to Zora Neale Hurston, *Mules and Men* (New York: Harper Perennial, 1990), xiii–xiv, xiii.

97. Zora Neale Hurston, *Mules and Men* (New York: Harper Perennial, 1990), 8.

98. Hurston, *Mules and Men,* 273.

99. Hurston, *Mules and Men,* 202.

100. Pettinger, "'Eh! eh!,'" 94.

101. Gore Vidal, qtd. in Kwame Anthony Appiah, *The Lies That Bind: Rethinking Identity* (London: Profile, 2018), 38–39.

102. Appiah, *Lies,* 39.

103. Zora Neale Hurston, *Jonah's Gourd Vine* (London: Virago, 1987), 252.

104. Zora Neale Hurston, "Spunk," in *Spunk: The Selected Short Stories of Zora Neale Hurston* (Berkeley: Turtle Island, 1985), 1–8, 1.

105. Hurston, "Spunk," 6.

106. Hurston, "Spunk," 8.

107. Zora Neale Hurston, "Spunk," in Jean Lee Cole and Charles Mitchell (eds.), *Zora Neale Hurston: Collected Plays* (New Brunswick: Rutgers University Press, 2008), 227–68, 245.

108. Hurston, "Spunk" (play), 246.

109. Hurston, "Spunk" (play), 261.

110. Hurston, "Spunk" (play), 265.

111. Zora Neale Hurston, *Spunk,* in Jean Lee Cole and Charles Mitchell (eds.), *Zora Neale Hurston: Collected Plays* (New Brunswick: Rutgers University Press, 2008), 227–68, 264.

112. Alain Locke, text from handbill for *The Great Day* (1932), reproduced in Hurston, *Collected Plays,* 363–65, 365.

113. Hurston, *Mules and Men,* 215.

114. Anthea Kraut, *Choreographing the Folk: the Dance Stagings of Zora Neale Hurston* (Minneapolis: University of Minnesota Press, 2008). Kraut's fascinating account is based on analyses of draft playscripts held in the archives at Howard University, which are inaccessible at the time of writing.

115. Kraut, *Choreographing the Folk,* 141.

116. Zora Neale Hurston, *Dust Tracks on a Road: An Autobiography* (London: Virago, 1986), 208.

117. Kraut, *Choreographing the Folk,* 21–22.

118. Hurston, *Jonah's,* 59.

119. Zora Neale Hurston, *Tell My Horse: Voodoo and Life in Haiti and Jamaica* (New York: Harper and Row), 39, 54.

120. Hurston, *Tell My Horse,* 113, 205.

121. Scott, *Conscripts,* 111.

122. Lindsey Stewart, *The Politics of Black Joy: Zora Neale Hurston and Neo-Abolitionism* (Evanston: Northwestern University Press, 2021), 33. Stewart builds, in part, on the work of Saidiya Hartman, who has advocated "the rejection of a politics of recognition" and a "clear refusal to offer Black suffering as the raw material of white pedagogy and enjoyment." Saidiya Hartman, "Intimate History, Radical Narrative," *Black Perspectives* (May 2022), https://www.aaihs.org/intimate-history-radical-narrative/. Honig's argument in *A Feminist Theory of Refusal,* which advocates for the importance of a return to the polis, is conceived in part as a response to Hartman. See *A Feminist Theory of Refusal,* ch. 3.

123. Zora Neale Hurston, "Spirituals and Neo-Spirituals," in Nancy Cunard (ed.), *Negro: An Anthology* (London: Wishart & Co., 1934), 359–61, 359.

124. Hurston, "Spirituals," 361.

125. Hurston, "Spirituals," 360–61.

126. Jean Lee Cole and Charles Mitchell, "Introduction: Zora Neale Hurston—a Theatrical Life," in Jean Lee Cole and Charles Mitchell (eds.), *Zora Neale Hurston: Collected Plays* (New Brunswick: Rutgers University Press, 2008), xv–xxxi, xxii.

127. Hurston, *Jonah's,* 281.

128. James Baldwin, *The Fire Next Time* (London: Penguin, 2017), 36.

129. Baldwin, *The Fire,* 36.

130. Baldwin, *The Fire,* 40.

131. Zora Neale Hurston, "Art and Such," in Henry Louis Gates Jr. (ed.), *Reading*

Black, Reading Feminist: A Critical Anthology (New York: Meridian, 1990), 21–26, 23.

132. Hurston, "Spirituals," 359.

133. W. E. B. Du Bois, *The Souls of Black Folk* (Oxford: Oxford University Press, 2007), 169.

134. Du Bois, *Souls,* 170.

135. Du Bois, *Souls,* 175.

136. Stewart, *Black Joy,* 65.

137. Stewart, *Black Joy,* 55.

138. Stewart, *Black Joy,* 60. See also Fred Moten, *In the Break: The Aesthetics of the Black Radical Tradition* (Minneapolis: University of Minnesota Press, 2003), 6.

139. Du Bois, *Souls,* 169.

140. W. E. B. Du Bois, "The Talented Tenth," in Booker T. Washington (ed.), *The Negro Problem: A Series of Articles by Representative Negroes of Today* (New York: James Pott & Co., 1903), 33–75, 33.

141. Du Bois, "Talented Tenth," 45.

142. Hurston, "Spirituals," 360.

143. Paul Gilroy, *The Black Atlantic: Modernity and Double Consciousness* (London: Verso, 2022), 92.

144. Thompson, *Black Fascisms,* 122, 118. Thompson is applying to Hurston's work some of the arguments made in Paul Gilroy, "Black Fascism," *Transition* 81–82 (2000), 70–91.

145. Hurston, "Spirituals," 359–60.

146. Stefano Harney and Fred Moten, *The Undercommons: Fugitive Planning and Black Study* (Wivenhoe: Minor Compositions, 2013), 19.

Bridge: Towards the Polis

1. See Steven Connor, *A History of Asking* (London: Open Humanities Press, 2023), 96–147, esp. 113–14.

2. Jacques Roumain, *Masters of the Dew* (trans. Langston Hughes and Mercer Cook) (London: Heinemann, 1978), 66–67.

3. Roumain, *Masters,* 67.

4. Roumain, *Masters,* 70.

5. Roumain, *Masters,* 71.

6. Roumain, *Masters,* 71–72.

7. Price-Mars spells it "vaudou" in his original French version, and Shannon translates this as "voodoo" in her English translation. Jean Price-Mars, *Ainsi parla l'oncle* (Ottawa: Lemeac, 1973), 78 and *passim*; Jean Price-Mars, *So Spoke the Uncle: Ainsi parla l'oncle* (trans. Magdaline W. Shannon) (Washington, DC: Three Continents Press, 1983). Shannon explains her choice of "voodoo" in her introduction, ix–xxvi, xxiii–xxv.

8. Celucien L. Joseph, "The Religious Philosophy of Jean Price-Mars," *Journal of Black Studies* 43:6 (September 2012), 620–45, 621.

9. Price-Mars, *So Spoke the Uncle,* 7–8.

10. Price-Mars, *So Spoke the Uncle,* 39, 43.

11. Price-Mars, *So Spoke the Uncle,* 48, 49.

12. Price-Mars, *So Spoke the Uncle,* 115.

13. Laura Marcus, *Rhythmical Subjects: The Measures of the Modern* (Oxford: Oxford University Press, 2023), 9.

14. Quoted and discussed by Marcus in *Rhythmical Subjects,* 72–73.

15. Marcus, *Rhythmical Subjects,* 9.

16. Etherington, *Literary Primitivism,* xiii.

17. Carolyn Fowler, *A Knot in the Thread: The Life and Work of Jacques Roumain* (Washington, DC: Howard University Press, 1980), 214.

18. Fowler, *A Knot in the Thread,* 215.

19. Jacques Roumain, *Le Sacrifice du tambour-assoto(r)* (Port au Prince: Imprimerie de L'État, 1943), 7. My translation: "La religion est intimement associée au chant, à la danse, à la musique." An example of a Legba chant is on 22.

20. Fowler, *A Knot in the Thread,* 216–19.

21. Celucien L. Joseph, *Thinking in Public: Faith, Secular Humanism, and Development in Jacques Roumain* (Eugene: Pickwick Publications, 2017), 4.

22. Jacques Roumain, *A propos de la campagne "antisuperstitieuse,"* in Léon-François Hoffmann and Yves Chemla (eds.), *Jacques Romain: Œuvres complètes,* critical ed. (Paris: CNRS Éditions, 2018), 750. My translation: "Ce qu'il faut mener en Haiti, ce n'est pas une campagne anti-superstitieuse, mais une campagne anti-misère."

23. Roumain, *Masters,* 88–89.

24. Roumain, *Masters,* 27–28.

25. Langston Hughes, "Masters of the Dew, drafts, typescript and carbon, corrected, 1945–46." Langston Hughes Papers, James Weldon Johnson Collection, Yale Collection of American Literature, Beinecke Rare Book and Manuscript Library, Box 426, Folder 9474.

26. Fernando Ortiz, *Cuban Counterpoint: Tobacco and Sugar* (trans. Harriet De Onís) (New York: A. A. Knopf, 1947), 88–89.

27. Richard Sennett, *The Craftsman* (London: Penguin, 2009), 74–80.

28. Roumain, *Masters,* 89–90.

29. Roumain, *Masters,* 75.

30. Ira De Augustine Reid to Langston Hughes, 18 October 1945, Langston Hughes Papers, Box 136, Folder 2526.

31. Jacques Roumain, "Filthy Negroes" (trans. Joanne Fungaroli and Ronald Sauer), in *When the Tom-Tom Beats: Selected Prose and Poems* (Washington, DC: Azul Editions, 1995), 84–97.

32. Langston Hughes, "Damned Nigger," typescript poem, translated from Jacques Roumain, "Sales Nègres," 1945, Langston Hughes Papers, Box 426, Folder 9471.

33. T. S. Eliot, "East Coker," in Christopher Ricks and Jim McCue (eds.), *The Poems of T. S. Eliot* (London: Faber & Faber, 2015), 185–92, 188 (ll. 47–48).

34. Peter Womack, "Pronouns: We/Us/Our," *Critical Quarterly* 64:2 (2022), 93–99, 94.

35. Bonnie Costello, *The Plural of Us: Poetry and Community in Auden and Others* (Princeton: Princeton University Press, 2017), 2.

36. Jacques Roumain, "Poetry as a Weapon" (trans. Joanne Fungaroli and Ronald Sauer), in *When the Tom-Tom Beats,* 105–9, 108.

37. Richard Wright, *Twelve Million Black Voices: A Folk History of the Negro in the United States* (London: Lindsay Drummond Ltd., 1947), 14.

38. Adolph L. Reed Jr., *The South: Jim Crow and Its Afterlives* (London: Verso, 2022), 94.

39. Hughes, "Damned Nigger."

40. Eugène Pottier, "L'Internationale," in *Chants révolutionnaires* (Paris: Dentu, 1887), 13–15, 13.

41. Albert Cervoni, "A Historic Confrontation in 1965 Between Jean Rouch and Ousmane Sembène: 'You Look at Us as If We Were Insects,'" in Annett Busch and Max Annas, *Ousmane Sembène: Interviews* (Jackson: University of Mississippi Press, 2008), 3–6, 3–4.

42. Jean Jonassaint, qtd. in Jamie Berthe, "Beyond the Entomological Critique: Re-Thinking Rouch and African Cinema," *Studies in French Cinema* 18:3 (2018), 267–77, 269.

43. Jean Jonassaint, "Le cinéma de Sembène Ousmane, une (double) contre-ethnographie: (Notes pour une recherche)," *Ethnologies* 31:2 (2010), 241–86, 255. My translation: "un renversement radical, ce n'est pas le dominant qui s'approprie des outils ou savoirs du dominé, mais le dominé, l'Africain, qui fait sien les outils et savoirs des colonisateurs français pour parler de lui, de sa rencontre avec cette France qui devient objet d'investigation."

44. Jonassaint, "Le cinéma," 272–73.

45. Claude Lévi-Strauss, *Structural Anthropology* (trans. Claire Jacobson and Brooke Grundfest Schoepf) (New York: Basic Books, 1963), 18.

46. Ousmane Sembene, *God's Bits of Wood* (trans. Francis Price) (London: Heinemann, 1976), 8–9.

47. Samba Gadjigo, *Ousmane Sembène: The Making of a Militant Artist* (trans. Moustapha Diop) (Bloomington: Indiana University Press, 2010), 147. Sembène paid tribute to Roumain in his war film *Camp de Thiaroye* (1988), when the sergeant of the Senegalese regiment at the center of the story is (anachronistically) reading *Masters of the Dew.*

48. David Murphy, *Sembene: Imagining Alternatives in Film & Fiction* (Oxford: James Currey, 2000), 7.

49. Sembène, *God's Bits of Wood,* 77.

50. Sembène, *God's Bits of Wood,* 75–76.

51. Gadjigo, *Ousmane Sembène,* 143.

52. Murphy, *Sembene,* 112.

53. Interview with Léopold Sédar Senghor, found in "Senghor et les arts, réinventer l'universel," RFI podcast, 8 February 2023, https://www.rfi.fr/fr/podcasts/vous-m-en-direz-des-nouvelles/20230208-senghor-et-les-arts-r%C3%A9inventer-l-universel.

My translation: "La Négritude, c'est l'ensemble des valeurs de civilization de monde noir. Les noirs ont une certain facon de danser, de chanter, de sculpter . . . de rire, de pleurer. C'est toute là, la Negritude. Plus precisement, la Negritude se characterise par certains valeurs. Dans les meurs socials et politiques par example, par une certaine forme de democracie qui s'exprime dans la palabres. [. . .] Mais pour nous la Negritude s'exprime essentiellement dans le domain de l'art."

54. Patrick Delices, "Price-Mars and Black Public Intellectual Tradition in Haiti: Cementing Scholarship with Service," in Celucien L. Joseph, Jean Eddy Saint Paul, and Glodel Mezilas (eds.), *Between Two Worlds: Jean Price-Mars, Haiti, and Africa* (Lanham: Lexington Books, 2018), 31–58, 49.

55. Senghor, qtd. in Murphy, *Sembene,* 13.

56. Murphy, *Sembene,* 12.

57. Sembène quoted in Gadjigo, *Ousmane Sembène,* 142–43.

58. Nancy Fraser, in Fraser and Axel Honneth, *Redistribution or Recognition? A Political-Philosophical Exchange* (London: Verso, 2003), 13.

59. Sembène, interviewed by David Murphy, in Murphy, *Sembene,* 227–40, 229.

60. Eileen Julien, "African Literature," in Phyllis M. Martin and Patrick O'Meara (eds.), *Africa,* 3rd ed. (Bloomington: Indiana University Press, 1995), 295–312, 299.

61. Murphy, *Sembene,* 41.

62. Simon Gikandi, *Reading the African Novel* (London: James Currey, 1987), 116.

63. Sembène, *God's Bits of Wood,* 172.

64. This extended scene bears comparison to the political pilgrimage in Ngũgĩ wa Thiong'o's *Petals of Blood* (1977), which also includes a great deal of collective speech.

65. Sembène, *God's Bits of Wood,* 124.

66. Sembène, *God's Bits of Wood,* 215.

67. Sembène, *God's Bits of Wood,* 179.

68. Sembène, *God's Bits of Wood,* 183.

69. Sembène, *God's Bits of Wood,* 178–79.

70. Sembène, interviewed by David Murphy, in Murphy, *Sembene,* 227–40, 239.

71. Sembène, interviewed by David Murphy, in Murphy, *Sembene,* 227–40, 228.

72. Ousmane Sembène, speaking in Gerald Peary and Patrick McGilligan, "Ousmane Sembène: An Interview (1972)," in Annett Busch and Max Annas (eds.), *Ousmane Sembène: Interviews* (Jackson: University of Mississippi Press, 2008), 41–51, 49.

73. Sembène, speaking in Peary and McGilligan, "An Interview," 50.

74. Pfaff sees this as evidence that Sembène "not only denounces colonialism and its fascist methods of fighting fascism, but he also criticizes traditional African religions." Françoise Pfaff, "Myths, Traditions and Colonialism in Ousmane Sembène's Emitai," *CLA Journal* 24:3 (1981), 336–46, 345.

75. Nathalie Dompnier, "Entre *La Marseillaise* et *Maréchal, nous voilà!* quel hymne pour le régime de Vichy?," in Myriam Chimènes (ed.), *La vie musicale sous Vichy* (Brussels: Éditions Complexe, 2001), 69–83.

76. My translation:

Une flamme sacrée
Monte du sol natal,
Et la France enivrée
Te salue, Maréchal!
Maréchal, nous voilà!
Devant toi, le sauveur de la France,
Nous jurons, nous tes gars,
De servir et de suivre tes pas.

77. Murphy has explored the effects of Sembène's creative reworkings of history in "Fighting for the Homeland? The Second World War in the Films of Ousmane Sembene," *L'Esprit Créateur* 47:1 (2007), 56–67, 59.

78. Sembène, speaking in Peary and McGilligan, "An Interview," 50–51.

Chapter 2

1. Bonnie Honig, *A Feminist Theory of Refusal* (Cambridge: Harvard University Press, 2021), 1.

2. Aeschylus, *The Oresteia* (trans. Ted Hughes) (London: Faber & Faber, 1999), 193.

3. Nietzsche, *Tragedy*, 36.

4. Simon Goldhill, "The Greek Chorus: Our German Eye," in Joshua Billings, Felix Budelmann, and Fiona Macintosh (eds.), *Choruses, Ancient and Modern* (Oxford: Oxford University Press, 2013), 35–52.

5. Goldhill, "The Greek Chorus," 51–52.

6. Goldhill, "The Greek Chorus," 36.

7. Joshua Billings, "Choral Dialectics: Hölderlin and Hegel," in Renaud Gagné and Marianne Govers Hopman (eds.), *Choral Mediations in Greek Tragedy* (Cambridge: Cambridge University Press, 2013), 317–38, 318.

8. Augustus Wilhelm Schlegel, *A Course of Lectures on Dramatic Art and Literature* (trans. John Black; 2nd ed.) (London: J. Templeman, 1840), 1:80.

9. Joshua Billings, *Genealogy of the Tragic: Greek Tragedy and German Philosophy* (Princeton: Princeton University Press, 2014), 40.

10. Friedrich Schiller, "Über den Gebrauch des Chors in der Tragödie / On the Use of the Chorus in Tragedy" (trans. by Guido Avezzù), in "The Chorus in Drama," special issue, *Skenè: Journal of Theatre and Drama Studies* 1:1 (2015), 135–66, 149.

11. L. C. Knights, *The Wheel of Fire: Essays in Interpretation of Shakespeare's Sombre Tragedies* (London: Oxford University Press, 1930), 178.

12. Schiller, qtd. in Billings, "Choral Dialectics," 322.

13. Billings, "Choral Dialectics," 322.

14. Friedrich Hölderlin, *Hölderlin's Sophocles: Oedipus and Antigone* (trans. David Constantine) (Northumberland: Bloodaxe Books, 2001), 116.

15. Hölderlin, *Hölderlin's Sophocles*, 67.

16. Billings, "Choral Dialectics," 328.

17. Georg Wilhelm Friedrich Hegel, *The Phenomenology of Spirit* (trans. Terry

Pinkard and Michael Baur) (Cambridge: Cambridge University Press, 2018), 422. Billings generates a slightly different emphasis by translating "Alters" as "old men."

18. Kornél Mundruczó, interviewed by Malte Krasting, "Die Imagination des Helden: Ein Gespräch vor Probenbeginn mit dem Regisseur Kornél Mundruczó," in *Lohengrin: Oper in drei Acten,* concert program, Bayerische Staatsoper, München, Spielzeit 2022–23, 50–63, 53. In German: "populistische Figur" and "menschengemachtes Idol." Quotations from *Lohengrin* come from Richard Wagner, *Lohengrin* (London: John Calder, 1993), 54, 56–57.

19. Tim Blanning, "Richard Wagner and the German Nation," *Transactions of the Royal Historical Society* 25 (2015), 95–112, 106.

20. See, e.g., Mark Berry, "Characters in the 'World' of the Ring," in Mark Berry and Nicholas Vazsonyi (eds.), *The Cambridge Companion to Wagner's Der Ring Des Nibelungen* (Cambridge: Cambridge University Press, 2020), 159–84.

21. Blanning "Richard Wagner," 107.

22. Richard Wagner, *Opera and Drama* (trans. Edwin Evans) (London: W. M. Reeves, 1913), 100.

23. Thomas S. Grey, "Wagner's 'Lohengrin': Between *Grand Opéra* and *Musikdrama,*" in Richard Wagner, *Lohengrin* (opera guide) (London: Overture, 2011), 15–32, 21.

24. Yunn-Shan Ma, "The Chorus as a Dramatic Force in Wagner's Operas," *Choral Journal* 60:11 (2020), 20–33, 27.

25. Grey, "Wagner's 'Lohengrin,'" 21.

26. This might help explain what Simon Goldhill calls a "tension within Wagner's thinking," on the chorus, which oscillates between the "ideal of absolute music as an expression of the true inwardness of emotion" on the one hand, and "the chorus as a potentially idealized form of the voice of the People, linked intimately to the nationalist ideals of *das Volk,*" on the other. Goldhill, "The Greek Chorus," 44.

27. Wagner, *Opera and Drama,* 97.

28. Qtd. in Karol Berger, *Beyond Reason: Wagner contra Nietzsche* (Oakland: University of California Press, 2017), 168.

29. Qtd. in Goldhill, "The Greek Chorus," 43.

30. Georg Lukács, *The Historical Novel* (trans. Hannah Mitchell and Stanley Mitchell) (Harmondsworth: Penguin Books, 1976), 157.

31. Lukács, *Historical Novel,* 158.

32. Lukács, *Historical Novel,* 158.

33. Georg Lukács, *The Theory of the Novel: A Historico-Philosophical Essay on the Forms of Great Epic Literature* (trans. Anna Bostock) (Cambridge: MIT Press, 1971), 42.

34. William Shakespeare, *The Tragedy of Julius Caesar,* in *The Norton Shakespeare,* 1525–89, III.ii.25–32, 1564.

35. Shakespeare, *Julius Caesar,* III.ii.41–44, 1565.

36. Shakespeare, *Julius Caesar,* III.ii.222, 1568.

37. Shakespeare, *Julius Caesar,* III.ii.233, 1569.

38. Lukács, *Theory of the Novel,* 43.

39. See Mary McCarthy, *Ideas and the Novel* (London: Weidenfeld and Nicholson, 1981), 73; Matthew Taunton, "Chorus and Agon in the Political Novel: Staging Left-Wing Arguments in H. G. Wells, Iris Murdoch, and Doris Lessing," *MFS: Modern Fiction Studies* 67:2 (2021), 247–71, 252–54.

40. Fredric Jameson, "Criticism and Categories," *PMLA/Publications of the Modern Language Association of America* 137:3 (2022), 563–67.

41. Raymond Williams, *Modern Tragedy* (London: Chatto & Windus, 1966), 18.

42. Williams, *Modern Tragedy,* 55.

43. Butler, *Notes,* 166.

44. Eve Kosofsky Sedgwick, *Touching Feeling: Affect, Pedagogy, Performativity* (Duke University Press, 2003), 28–31.

45. Steven Connor, *Styles of Seriousness* (Stanford: Stanford University Press, 2023), 1.

46. Edith Hall and Henry Stead, *A People's History of Classics: Class and Greco-Roman Antiquity in Britain and Ireland 1689 to 1939* (Abingdon: Routledge, 2020), 482–83.

47. An excellent summary of the state of scholarship on Jack Lindsay appears in Anne Cranny-Francis, *Jack Lindsay: Writer, Romantic, Revolutionary* (Cham: Palgrave Macmillan, 2024), 11–13.

48. Jack Lindsay, "The Fullness of Life" (unpublished autocriticism), ch. 3, p. 30, https://jacklindsayproject.com/the-fullness-of-life/. All references to this work are to Anne Cranny-Francis's edited transcriptions.

49. Colin Chambers, *The Story of Unity Theatre* (London: Lawrence and Wishart, 1989), 82.

50. Ben Harker, "'Communism is English': Edgell Rickword, Jack Lindsay and the Cultural Politics of the Popular Front," *Literature and History* 20:2 (2011), 16–24, 25. Elinor Taylor makes a similar point in a discussion of Lindsay's historical novel *1649,* describing a "Popular Front endorsement of the nation state as a form in which capitalism could be resisted." Elinor Taylor, "'The Voice Speaking, Desired, Awaited': Jack Lindsay's *1649,* Textual Form and Communist Historiography," *Twentieth Century Communism* 12 (2017), 15–36, 26.

51. Derek Kahn, "Theatre Notes," *Left Review* 2:15 (1936), 833.

52. Nancy Cunard (ed.), *Authors Take Sides on the Spanish War* (London: Left Review, 1937).

53. Don Watson, "Jack Lindsay: Poetry and the Spanish Civil War," in Robert Mackie (ed.), *Jack Lindsay: the Thirties and Forties,* Occasional Seminar Paper No. 4 (London: University of London Institute of Commonwealth Studies Australian Studies Centre, 1984), 61–72, 67. Evidence about these performances is scattered and piecemeal. Watson's interesting account cites some published accounts as well as acknowledging conversations with Lindsay himself as a useful source of information.

54. Elinor Taylor, "Experiments in Left Populism: British Literature Between the Wars," in Benjamin Kohlmann and Matthew Taunton (eds.), *"The People" and British*

Literature: Belonging, Exclusion, and Democracy (Cambridge: Cambridge University Press, 2025), 141–56, 154–55.

55. Jack Lindsay, "On Guard for Spain: A Massed Chant" (c. 1938), p. 1, Papers of the Bristol Unity Players Club, University of Warwick Archives, MSS.212/L/1/8/2, Warwick Digital Collections, https://wdc.contentdm.oclc.org/digital/collection/scw/id/14403.

56. Lindsay, *The Fullness of Life,* ch. 4, 26.

57. Lindsay, *On Guard,* 1.

58. Randall Swingler and Edgar Criddle, "Spain: A Drama of Modern History," in Simon Breden (ed.), *El Unity Theatre y la Guerra Civil española: Propaganda literaria y teatral en el Reino Unido* (Madrid: Guillermo Escolar Editor, 2020), 269–89.

59. Watson, "Jack Lindsay," 71.

60. Lindsay, *The Fullness of Life,* ch. 4, 30.

61. Harker, "'Communism Is English,'" 23.

62. Jack Lindsay, "A Plea for Mass Declamation," *Left Review* 3:9 (1937), 511–19, 511, 512.

63. Lindsay, "A Plea," 512n.

64. Lindsay, "A Plea," 516.

65. Chambers, *Unity Theatre,* 82.

66. Watson, "Jack Lindsay," 71.

67. Adriana Cavarero, *Surging Democracy: Notes on Hannah Arendt's Political Thought* (trans. Matthew Gervase) (Stanford: Stanford University Press, 2021), 73.

68. See Ben Harker, *The Chronology of Revolution: Communism, Culture, and Civil Society in Twentieth-Century Britain* (Toronto: University of Toronto Press, 2021), 28–37.

69. Andy Croft, *The Years of Anger: The Life of Randall Swingler* (London: Routledge, 2020), 85–6. An excellent survey of the editorial aims of these publications, including details about their changing casts of editors, is in Peter Marks, "Art and Politics in the 1930s: *The European Quarterly* (1934–5), *Left Review* (1934–8), and *Poetry and the People* (1938–40)," in Peter Brooker and Andrew Thacker (eds.), *The Oxford Critical and Cultural History of Modernist Magazines,* vol. 1, *Britain and Ireland 1880–1955* (Oxford: Oxford University Press, 2013), 623–46. As Ben Harker puts it, "The cultural politics of the Popular Front formation of the Swingler circle were sustained through the journal *Poetry and the People* (1938–1940). Most significant, however, was the new cultural journal that superseded it, *Our Time,* launched by the group behind Fore Publications in February 1941 and positioned as an egalitarian corrective to Cyril Connolly's elitist *Horizon* to which 'the ghosts of literary values long defunct' had allegedly retreated." Harker, *Chronology,* 46.

70. William T. Nettlefold, "Song for a Choir of Agricultural Workers to Sing at Covent Garden," *Poetry and the People* 9 (1939).

71. Elizabeth Carolyn Miller, *Slow Print: Literary Radicalism and Late Victorian Print Culture* (Stanford: Stanford University Press, 2013), 197.

72. Jack Lindsay, *A Short History of Culture from Prehistory to the Renascence* (London: Studio Books, 1962), 403.

73. Jack Lindsay, introduction to Jane Harrison, *Ancient Art and Ritual* (Bradford-on-Avon: Moonraker Press, 1978), v–xii, viii.

74. Lindsay, *Short History,* 231; Lindsay, introduction to Harrison, *Ancient Art and Ritual,* xii. Lindsay also recorded, in *A Short History of Culture,* "In many ways I have been working at this book, on paper or in my head, ever since 1919 when I first read Jane Harrison's writings" (7).

75. Lindsay, *Short History,* 236–37.

76. Jane Harrison, *Ancient Art and Ritual* (Bradford-on-Avon: Moonraker Press, 1978), 64.

77. Jane Ellen Harrison, *Reminiscences of a Student's Life* (London: Hogarth Press, 1925), 84.

78. Lindsay, introduction to Harrison, *Ancient Art and Ritual.*

79. Harrison, *Ancient Art,* 12.

80. Harrison, *Ancient Art,* 66.

81. Harrison, *Ancient Art,* 68.

82. C. L. R. James, *Every Cook Can Govern: A Study of Democracy in Ancient Greece, Its Meaning for Today,* in *A New Notion: Two Works By C. L. R. James* (Oakland: PA Press, 2010), 129–55, 141.

83. Bim Mason, *Street Theatre and Other Outdoor Performance* (London: Routledge, 1992), 3.

84. Mason, *Street Theatre,* 87.

85. Anna Kornbluh, *Immediacy, or The Style of Too Late Capitalism* (London: Verso, 2024), 10.

86. See J. L. Austin, *How to Do Things with Words,* 2nd ed. (Oxford: Oxford University Press, 1975), 5.

87. Matthew Chrisman and Graham Hubbs, "Protest and Speech Act Theory," in *The Routledge Handbook of Social and Political Philosophy of Language* (New York: Routledge, 2021), 179–92, 182. See also Matthew Chrisman and Graham Hubbs, "'The Language of the Unheard': Rioting as a Speech Act," in *Philosophy and Public Affairs* 49 (2021), 379–401.

88. Austin, *How to Do Things with Words,* 22. See also the illuminating discussion in Connor, *A History of Asking,* 114–15.

89. Jan Cohen-Cruz, "General Introduction," in Jan Cohen-Cruz (ed.), *Radical Street Performance: An International Anthology* (London: Routledge, 1998), 1–8, 1.

90. Account of early performances in Chambers, *The Story,* 84.

91. Jack Lindsay, "Five Thousand Years of Poetry," typescript with holograph annotations by an unknown hand, Unity Theater Records, Special Collections Research Center, Southern University Carbondale, Box 8, Folder 19.

92. Lindsay, *Five Thousand Years,* 1.

93. Ben Harker, "Communism Is English," 23.

94. Lindsay, *Five Thousand Years,* 21–24.

95. Jack Lindsay, "The May-Day Tradition," *Left Review* 3:16 (May 1938), 963–66, 966.

96. Lindsay, *Five Thousand Years*, 1, 6.

97. Lindsay, "The May Day Tradition," 966.

98. Lindsay, *Five Thousand Years*, 26.

99. Harrison, *Ancient Art*, 27.

100. Raymond Williams, *Culture & Society: Coleridge to Orwell* (London: Hogarth Press, 1993).

101. Christopher Caudwell, *Illusion and Reality: A Study of the Sources of Poetry* (London: Lawrence & Wishart, 1946), 14; Edith Hall, "Christopher Caudwell's Greek and Latin Classics," in Henry Stead and Edith Hall (eds.), *Greek and Roman Classics in the British Struggle for Social Reform* (London: Bloomsbury, 2015), 235–55, 251.

102. Caudwell, *Illusion*, 26.

103. Caudwell, *Illusion*, 27.

104. Theodor Adorno, "Commitment," *New Left Review* 87–88 (1974), 75–89.

105. George Thomson, *Marxism and Poetry* (New York: International Publishers, 1946), 8–9.

106. Thomson, *Marxism*, 9.

107. Thomson, *Marxism*, 19.

108. Thomson, *Marxism*, 18.

109. Thomson, *Marxism*, 19.

110. Thomson, *Marxism*, 58.

111. Ted Gioia, *Work Songs* (Durham: Duke University Press, 2006) xiii.

112. Gioia, *Work Songs*, 4.

113. Gioia, *Work Songs*, 54.

114. Gioia, *Work Songs*, 44.

115. A. L. Lloyd, "Sing Out, America!," *Keynote: The Progressive Music Quarterly* 1:1 (Autumn 1945), 18–19, 18.

116. "Festival of Music for the People," print program (London: Workers' Music Association, 1939), 9, consulted in Alan Bush Papers, British Library.

117. Alan Bush, "The Crisis of Modern Music," *Keynote* 1/4 (1946), 4–7, 5.

118. "Festival," 7.

119. "Festival," 10.

120. "Festival," 7.

121. Hurston, *Mules and Men*, 55, 248.

122. Hurston, *Mules and Men*, 65.

123. A. L. Lloyd, *Folk Song in England* (New York: International Publishers, 1967), 89.

124. See Guy B. Johnson, *John Henry: Tracking Down a Negro Legend* (Chapel Hill: University of North Carolina Press, 1929); Louis Chappell, *John Henry: A Folk-Lore Study* (Jena: W. Biedermann, 1933). Roark Bradford published a novel called *John Henry* in 1931 and turned it into a Broadway musical, starring Paul Robeson, in 1940. These are brought together in Steven Tracey, *John Henry: Roark Bradford's Novel and Play* (Oxford: Oxford University Press, 2008), along with some invaluable bibliographies and discographies of written and recorded versions of the John Henry myth

and its musical life. A recent scholarly reconstruction of the wider tradition is in Scott Reynolds Nelson, *Steel Drivin' Man: John Henry, the Untold Story of an American Legend* (New York: Oxford University Press, 2006).

125. Johnson, *John Henry,* 69.

126. Hurston, *Mules and Men,* 264.

127. Hurston, *Mules and Men,* 264.

128. Hurston speaking on Stetson Kennedy, Herbert Halpert, and Zora Neale Hurston, "Shove It Over," recorded in Jacksonville, Florida, 1939, Herbert Halpert 1939 Southern States Recording Expedition, Library of Congress, https://www.loc.gov/item/flwpa000006/.

129. Brendan Kibbee, "Black Labor and the Deep South in Hurston's *The Great Day* and Ellington's *Black, Brown, and Beige*," *Current Musicology* 101 (Fall 2017), 81–97, 81.

130. Anthea Kraut, *Choreographing the Folk: The Dance Stagings of Zora Neale Hurston* (Minneapolis: University of Minnesota Press, 2008), 120–22.

131. Sophie Abramowitz, "'Trained and Taught This Song by Zora Hurston': Dramatic Ethnography and Zora Neale Hurston's *The Great Day*," *American Quarterly* 72:4 (2020), 881–908, 901.

132. Credit list for *The Man Who Went to War* (typescript dated 1944), Langston Hughes Papers, Beinecke Rare Book and Manuscript Library, Yale University, JWJ MSS 26, Box 537, Folder 13195.

133. Langston Hughes, *The Man Who Went to War: A Ballad Opera* (typescript dated 1944), Langston Hughes Papers, Beinecke Rare Book and Manuscript Library, Yale University, JWJ MSS 26, Box 273, Folder 4452, p. 1.

134. Nicholas Grant, "Patriotism and Black Internationalism," *Modern American History* 6 (2023), 322–40, 324. The phrase was coined in Kwame Anthony Appiah, "Cosmopolitan Patriots," *Critical Inquiry* 23:3 (1997), 617–39.

135. Zora Neale Hurston, "Spunk," in Jean Lee Cole and Charles Mitchell (eds.), *Zora Neale Hurston: Collected Plays* (New Brunswick: Rutgers University Press, 2008), 227–68, 230.

136. Hughes, *The Man Who Went to War,* 15.

137. Hughes, *The Man Who Went to War,* 15.

138. Hughes, *The Man Who Went to War,* 15–16.

139. Langston Hughes, *Scottsboro, Limited: A One Act Play,* in Leslie Sanders and Nancy Johnston (eds.), *The Collected Works of Langston Hughes,* vol. 5, *Plays to 1942:* Mulatto *to* The Sun Do Move (Columbia: University of Missouri Press, 2002), 116–29, 122–23.

140. Michael Thurston, "Black Christ, Red Flag: Langston Hughes on Scottsboro," *College Literature* 22:3 (1995), 30–49, 40.

141. Hughes, *Scottsboro,* 117–18.

142. Marc Ferris, *Star Spangled Banner: The Unlikely Story of America's National Anthem* (Baltimore: Johns Hopkins University Press, 2014), 160.

143. Hughes, *Scottsboro,* 129.

144. Langston Hughes, *Labor for Victory: John Henry Hammers It Out,* typescript

play for radio, broadcast June 27 1943, Langston Hughes Papers, JWJ MSS 26, Box 401, Folder 8048, p. 1.

145. Hughes, *Labor,* 1–2.

146. Hughes, *Labor,* 3.

147. Hughes, *Labor,* 5.

148. Hughes, *Labor,* 6.

149. Hughes, *Labor,* n.p.

150. Hughes, *Labor,* 6–7.

151. Anthony Dawahare, "Langston Hughes's Radical Poetry and the 'End of Race,'" *MELUS* 23:3 (1998), 21–41, 33.

152. Imani Perr, *May We Forever Stand: A History of the Black National Anthem* (Chapel Hill: University of North Carolina Press, 2018), 32, 62.

153. Judith Butler and Gayatri Spivak, *Who Sings the Nation-State? Language, Politics, Belonging* (London: Seagull, 2007), 58–59, 69.

154. Fred Moten, *Black and Blur* (Durham: Duke University Press, 2017), 294n.

Bridge: Becoming Hegemonic

1. Adriana Cavarero, *Surging Democracy: Notes on Hannah Arendt's Political Thought* (Stanford: Stanford University Press, 2021), 70.

2. Benedict Anderson, *Imagined Communities: Reflections on the Origin and Spread of Nationalism,* rev. ed. (London: Verso, 1991), 145.

3. Eugène Pottier, "L'Internationale," in *Chants révolutionnaires* (Paris: Dentu,1887), 13–15, 15.

4. Georges Bossi and Jacques Estager, *L'Internationale, 1888–1988* (Paris: Messidor, Éditions Sociales), 125–29.

5. N. A. Soboleva, "The Composition of State Anthems of the Russian Empire and the Soviet Union," *Russian Social Science Review* 50:2 (2009), 67–94, 80.

6. Nicolai Evreinov (trans. David Riff), "The Storming of the Winter Palace: an Article by the Production's Director-in-Chief" (1920) in Inke Arns, Sylvia Sasse, Igor Chubarov (eds.), *The Storming of the Winter Palace* (Chicago: Chicago University Press, 2017), 23–25, 24–25.

7. Nikola Shubski, "On Uritski Square (Impression of a Muscovite)" (trans. David Riff and ed. Arns et al., 1920), *The Storming of the Winter Palace,* 143–47, 147.

8. Kate Bowan and Paul A. Pickering, *Sounds of Liberty: Music, Radicalism and Reform in the Anglophone World, 1790–1914* (Manchester: Manchester University Press, 2017), 32–33.

9. Quoted in Gerald Stanton Smith, *Songs to Seven Strings: Russian Guitar Poetry and Soviet "Mass Song"* (Bloomington: Indiana University Press, 1984), 15.

10. Sheila Fitzpatrick, *The Russian Revolution,* 4th ed. (Oxford: Oxford University Press, 2017), 116.

11. Stanton Smith, *Songs,* 15.

12. Ben Harker, "'Workers' Music': Communism and the British Folk Revival," in *Red Strains: Music and Communism Outside the Communist Bloc* (Oxford: Oxford

University Press, 2013), 89–104, 89; *Soviet Airmen's Song: Unison Song with Piano Accompaniment,* words adapted by Randall Swingler, tune arranged by G.M.S. and J.T. (London: Worker's Music Association, 1939).

13. Alan Bush and Randall Swingler, introduction to *Left Song Book* (London: Victor Gollancz, 1938), 3.

14. Clare Warden, *Migrating Modernist Performance: British Theatrical Travels Through Russia* (Basingstoke: Palgrave Macmillan, 2016), 93.

15. "Soviet Day," *The Listener* 30:773 (4 November 1943), 520. This article, along with various broadcast scripts and schedules, was discussed by Claire Davison in " 'Never More Close, Intimate and Cordial': The 'Projection of Russia Campaign' on the BBC Home Service, 1941–45," unpublished paper, delivered at the Anglo Russian Research Network Reading Group, Pushkin House, 3 March 2017.

16. Soboleva, "Composition," 83.

17. George Orwell, *Animal Farm: A Fairy Story* (London: Penguin, 1989), 7.

18. Orwell, *Animal Farm,* 59–60.

19. Ernest Gellner, *Nations and Nationalism,* 2nd ed. (Oxford: Blackwell, 2006), 9.

20. Gellner, *Nations,* 47.

21. Gellner, *Nations,* 11.

22. Alan Jacobs, *The Book of Common Prayer: A Biography* (Princeton: Princeton University Press, 2013), 31.

23. Gellner, *Nations,* 16.

24. Gellner, *Nations,* 17.

25. Gellner, *Nations,* 33.

26. See, e.g., Stuart Hall and Tony Jefferson, *Resistance Through Rituals: Youth Subcultures in Postwar Britain (*Birmingham: University of Birmingham, Centre for Contemporary Cultural Studies, 1976); Raymond Williams, *Marxism and Literature* (Oxford: Oxford University Press, 1977), 121–27; Dick Hebdige, *Subculture: The Meaning of Style* (London: Routledge, 2003).

27. Gellner, *Nations,* 63.

28. George Orwell, *The Lion and the Unicorn: Socialism and the English Genius,* in Peter Davison (ed.), *The Complete Works of George Orwell,* vol. 12, *A Patriot After All,* 391–432, 432.

29. The link with Nkrumah and Banda is made, for example, in Mpalive-Hangson Msiska, *Wole Soyinka* (Plymouth: Northcote House, 1998), 30. Soyinka's desire to distance the play from such a direct allegorical interpretation is well documented in Josef Gugler, "Wole Soyinka's Kongi's Harvest from Stage to Screen: Four Endings to Tyranny," *Canadian Journal of African Studies/La Revue canadienne des études africaines* 31:1 (1997), 32–49, 36.

30. Versions of the New Yam Festival are celebrated by a number of ethnic groups in West Africa. For example, its importance to the Aro people is explored in Eli Bentor, "Challenges to Rural Festivals with the Return to Democratic Rule in Southeastern Nigeria," *African Arts* 38:4 (2005), 38–93.

31. Wole Soyinka, *Kongi's Harvest,* in *Collected Plays 2* (Oxford: Oxford University Press, 1974), 59–141, 81.

32. Soyinka, *Kongi's Harvest*, 129–30.

33. Soyinka, *Kongi's Harvest*, 130.

34. Soyinka, *Kongi's Harvest*, 130, 131.

35. Euripides, *Bacchae*, 165.

36. Honig, *A Feminist Politics of Refusal*, 78.

37. Honig, *A Feminist Politics of Refusal*, 83.

38. Wole Soyinka, "Drama and the Revolutionary Ideal," in Karen L. Morrell (ed.), *In Person: Achebe, Awoonor, and Soyinka at the University of Washington* (Seattle: University of Washington African Studies Programme, 1975), 61–88, 65.

39. Soyinka was familiar with the debates about the chorus I outlined in chapter 2. For example, he discussed Nietzsche's *Birth of Tragedy* in Wole Soyinka, *Myth, Literature and the African World* (Cambridge: Cambridge University Press, 1978), 140–43.

40. Wole Soyinka, *The Bacchae of Euripides*, in *Collected Plays 1* (Oxford: Oxford University Press, 1973), 233–307, 234.

41. Soyinka, *Bacchae*, 246.

42. Soyinka, *Bacchae*, 240.

43. Soyinka, *Bacchae*, 256.

44. Soyinka, *Bacchae*, 294.

45. Soyinka, *Bacchae*, 295.

46. Euripides, *Bacchae*, 154.

47. Soyinka, *Bacchae*, 307.

48. Msiska, *Wole Soyinka*, 67.

49. Soyinka, *Bacchae*, 307.

50. Soyinka, *Kongi's Harvest*, 115.

51. Soyinka, *Kongi's Harvest*, 116.

52. Wole Soyinka, *The Climate of Fear: the Reith Lectures 2004* (London: Profile Books, 2004), 59, 65.

53. Soyinka, *Climate*, 82.

54. Soyinka, *Climate*, 82–83.

Chapter 3

1. In Chantal Mouffe's reading of Gramsci, she emphasizes "expansive hegemony," meaning not simply the imposition of working-class values on the subordinate classes, but a genuine synthesis. Chantal Mouffe, "Hegemony and Ideology in Gramsci" (trans. Denise Derôme), in Chantal Mouffe (ed.), *Gramsci and Marxist Theory*, 169–205, 182–83.

2. Antonio Gramsci, *Selections from the Prison Notebooks* (ed. and trans. Quintin Hoare and Geoffrey Nowell Smith) (London: Lawrence and Wishart), 349.

3. Eric Hobsbawm, "Introduction: Inventing Traditions," in Eric Hobsbawm and Terence Ranger, *The Invention of Tradition* (Cambridge: Cambridge University Press, 1983), 1–14, 1.

4. See, for example, the invaluable discussion in Steven Lukes, "Political Ritual and Social Integration," *Sociology* 9:2 (1975), 289–308.

5. Eric Hobsbawm, "Mass Producing Traditions: Europe, 1870–1914," in Eric

Hobsbawm and Terence Ranger, *The Invention of Tradition* (Cambridge: Cambridge University Press, 1983), 263–307, 269.

6. Giorgio Agamben, *The Kingdom and the Glory: For a Theological Genealogy of Economy and Government* (trans. Lorenzo Chiesa with Matteo Mandarini) (Stanford: Stanford University Press, 2011) xii.

7. Agamben, *Kingdom,* 230.

8. Agamben, *Kingdom,* 230–32.

9. Agamben, *Kingdom,* 231–32, 254.

10. Gellner, too, noted the "fascinating relationship between the Reformation and nationalism." He writes: "The stress of the Reformation on literacy and scripturalism, its onslaught on a monopolistic priesthood (or, as Weber clearly saw, its universalization rather than abolition of priesthood), its individualism and links with mobile urban populations, all made it a kind of harbinger of social features and attitudes which, according to our model, produce the national age." Gellner, *Nations and Nationalism,* 39–40.

11. See Elizabeth L. Eisenstein, *The Printing Press as an Agent of Change: Communications and Cultural Transformations in Early-Modern Europe,* 2 vols. (Cambridge: Cambridge University Press, 2009); Alasdair MacIntyre, *A Short History of Ethics: A History of Moral Philosophy from the Homeric Age to the Twentieth Century* (London: Routledge Classics, 2002); Walter J. Ong, *Orality and Literacy: The Technologizing of the Word* (London: Routledge, 2002); Max Weber, *The Protestant Ethic and the Spirit of Capitalism (*trans. Talcott Parsons) (London: Routledge, 2001); Ian Watt, *The Rise of the Novel: Studies in Defoe, Richardson and Fielding (*London: Pimlico, 2000).

12. Quotation from Ramie Targoff, *Common Prayer: The Language of Public Devotion in Early Modern England* (Chicago: University of Chicago Press, 2001), 4. See also more generally Brian Cummings, *The Book of Common Prayer: A Very Short Introduction* (Oxford: Oxford University Press, 2018); Alan Jacobs, *The Book of Common Prayer: A Biography* (Princeton: Princeton University Press, 2013).

13. Brian Cummings, introduction to *The Book of Common Prayer: The Texts of 1549, 1559, and 1662 (*Oxford: Oxford University Press, 2013) ix–lii, x.

14. Cummings, *The Book of Common Prayer: A Very Short Introduction,* 2.

15. Jacobs, *Book of Common Prayer,* 24.

16. Gramsci, *Prison Notebooks,* 239.

17. John Milton, *Eikonoklastes,* in *The Complete Prose Works of John Milton,* ed. Merritt Y. Hughes, vol. 3, *1648–1649* (New Haven, CT: Yale University Press, 1962), 335–601, 505.

18. Barry Spurr, *Anglo-Catholic in Religion: T. S. Eliot and Christianity* (Cambridge: Lutterworth Press, 2010), 86.

19. Jamie Callison, *Modernism and Religion: Between Mysticism and Orthodoxy* (Edinburgh: Edinburgh University Press, 2023), 37.

20. Spurr, *Anglo-Catholic,* 235.

21. While making Becket speak Cranmer's words is striking, it expresses a familiar instinct within the Anglican tradition. As Paul Avis affirms, "Anglican apologists trace

the English church back through the Reformation, through medieval Christendom, to the fathers and the apostles themselves." Paul Avis, "Anglican Ecclesiology," in Paul Avis (ed.), *The Oxford Handbook of Ecclesiology* (Oxford: Oxford University Press, 2018), 239–62, 247.

22. Jacobs, *Book of Common Prayer,* 95.

23. Jacobs, *Book of Common Prayer,* 100.

24. T. S. Eliot, "A Dialogue on Dramatic Poetry: With the Original Preface," in *The Complete Prose of T. S. Eliot: The Critical Edition,* vol. 3, *Literature, Politics, Belief, 1927–1929,* ed. Frances Dickey, Jennifer Formichelli and Ronald Schuchard (Baltimore: Johns Hopkins University Press and Faber & Faber Ltd., 2015), 396–412, 400.

25. Eliot set out more programmatically the case for a rejuvenated religious drama in T. S. Eliot, "Religious Drama: Medieval and Modern" in Iman Javadi, Ronald Schuchard and Jayme Stayer, *The Complete Prose of T. S. Eliot* vol. 5, *Tradition and Orthodoxy, 1934–1939* (Baltimore: Johns Hopkins University Press, 2021), 519–30.

26. Jed Esty, *A Shrinking Island: Modernism and National Culture in England* (Princeton: Princeton University Press, 2004), 70.

27. T. S. Eliot, *The Rock: A Pageant Play Written for Performance at Sadler's Wells Theatre 28 May—9 June 1934 on Behalf of the Forty-Five Churches Fund of the Diocese of London* (London: Faber & Faber, 1934), 73.

28. Eliot, *The Rock,* 73–74.

29. Eliot, *The Rock,* 73–74.

30. T. S. Eliot, *Notes Towards the Definition of Culture,* in *The Complete Prose of T. S. Eliot: The Critical Edition,* vol. 7, *A European Society, 1947–1953,* ed. by Iman Javadi and Ronald Schuchard (London: Johns Hopkins University Press and Faber & Faber Ltd., 2018), 194–287, 204.

31. T. S. Eliot, *The Rock,* 8.

32. T. S. Eliot, "The Three Voices of Poetry," in Iman Javadi and Ronald Schuchard (eds.), *The Complete Prose of T. S. Eliot: The Critical Edition,* vol. 7, *A European Society, 1947–1953* (Baltimore: Johns Hopkins University Press and Faber & Faber Ltd., 2018), 817–33.

33. Eliot, "Three Voices," 819.

34. T. S. Eliot to Robert Doone, typescript letter, 5 March 1936, Henry W. and Albert A. Berg Collection of English and American Literature, New York Public Library, Berg Coll MSS Eliot, TS, Folder 2.

35. Eliot, "Three Voices," 819.

36. Eliot, *The Rock,* 43.

37. Eliot, *The Rock,* 32.

38. Eliot, *The Rock,* 44.

39. Eliot, *The Rock,* 46.

40. Eliot, *Notes,* 222.

41. Eliot, *Notes,* 234.

42. Eliot, *Notes,* 243.

43. Esty, *Shrinking Island,* 127.

44. "Terms of Reference," in Minutes of the Archbishops' Commission to Revise

the Psalter, 22 January 1959 (typescript minutes), Church of England Record Centre, Bermondsey ACRP/2.

45. T. S. Eliot, "Autobiographical Note: *Harvard Class of 1910 Fiftieth Anniversary Report*," in *The Complete Prose of T. S. Eliot: The Critical Edition*, vol. 8, *Still and Still Moving, 1954–1965*, ed. Jewel Spears Brooker and Ronald Schuchard (Baltimore: Johns Hopkins University Press and Faber & Faber Ltd., 2019), 419–22, 421.

46. T. S. Eliot, "T. S. Eliot on the Language of the New English Bible," in *The Complete Prose of T. S. Eliot: The Critical Edition*, vol. 8, *Still and Still Moving, 1954–1965*, ed. Jewel Spears Brooker and Ronald Schuchard (Baltimore: Johns Hopkins University Press and Faber & Faber Ltd., 2019), 530–36, 530.

47. Jacobs, *Book of Common Prayer*, 157–58.

48. Cummings, *Book of Common Prayer*, 106.

49. John Maiden, *National Religion and the Prayer Book Controversy, 1927–1928* (Woodbridge: Boydell & Brewer, 2009), 9.

50. T. S. Eliot, "Parliament and the New Prayer Book: To the Editor of *The New Adelphi*," in Frances Dickey, Jennifer Formichelli, and Ronald Schuchard (eds.), *The Complete Prose of T. S. Eliot: The Critical Edition*, vol. 3, *Literature, Politics, Belief, 1927–1929* (Baltimore: Johns Hopkins University Press, 2015), 431–34.

51. T. S. Eliot to Geoffrey Fisher (Archbishop of Canterbury), 19 November 1958, Fisher Papers, Lambeth Palace Library, f. 273.

52. Robert Sencourt, *T. S. Eliot: A Memoir*, ed. Donald Adamson (London: Garstone Press, 1971), 172.

53. Justin Hughes, "Group Speech Acts," in *Linguistics and Philosophy* 7:4 (November 1984), 379–95, 380.

54. Hughes, "Group Speech Acts"; Anthonie Meijers, "Collective Speech Acts," in Savas L. Tsohatzidis (ed.), *Intentional Acts and Institutional Facts: Essays on John Searle's Social Ontology* (Dordrecht: Springer, 2007), 93–110.

55. Research by scholars such as Rachel Potter and Jini Kim Watson has insightfully investigated writers' work on committees, and some of the historiographical challenges of this. See Rachel Potter, "International PEN: Writers, Free Expression, Organisations," in Benjamin Kohlmann and Matthew Taunton (eds.), *A History of 1930s British Literature* (Cambridge: Cambridge University Press, 2019), 120–33; Jini Kim Watson, *Cold War Reckonings: Authoritarianism and the Genres of Decolonization* (New York: Fordham University Press, 2021). Watson's first chapter, "Writing Freedom from Bandung to PEN International" (29–58), reads writers' congresses as "a distinctly Cold War-postcolonial genre" (58).

56. G. A. Chase, *A Companion to the Revised Psalter* (London: S.P.C.K., 1963), 4–5.

57. Geoffrey Fisher to T. S. Eliot, 20 November 1958, Fisher Papers, Lambeth Palace Library, f. 274.

58. Minutes of the Archbishops' Commission to Revise the Psalter, 22 January 1959 (typescript minutes), Church of England Record Centre, Bermondsey ACRP/2.

59. Minutes of the Archbishops' Commission to Revise the Psalter, 8 January 1960 (typescript minutes), Church of England Record Centre, Bermondsey ACRP/2.

60. Notes and Suggestions on Psalms xvi–xxx by Professor Winton Thomas, Papers

of the Archbishops' Commission to Revise the Psalter, Church of England Record Centre, Bermondsey, ACRP/5.

61. T. S. Eliot, "The Hollow Men," in *Collected Poems of T. S. Eliot,* vol. 1, *Collected and Uncollected Poems,* ed. Christopher Ricks and Jim McCue (London: Faber & Faber, 2015), 81–84.

62. Minutes of the Archbishops' Commission to Revise the Psalter, 9 December 1959 (typescript minutes), Church of England Record Centre, Bermondsey ACRP/2.

63. Typescript draft of Psalm 23 with manuscript annotations (marked 28–30 December 1960), Papers of the Archbishops' Commission to Revise the Psalter, Church of England Record Centre, Bermondsey, ACRP/6.

64. Minutes of the Archbishops' Commission to Revise the Psalter, 9 December 1959 (typescript minutes), Church of England Record Centre, Bermondsey ACRP/2.

65. *The Revised Psalter: The First Report of the Commission to Revise the Psalter appointed by the Archbishops of Canterbury and York* (London: S.P.C.K.,1961), 31.

66. Brian Cummings, *The Book of Common Prayer: A Very Short Introduction* (Oxford: Oxford University Press, 2018), 107.

67. Psalter Commission Minutes, Residential Meeting at Addington Palace, Croydon, 13–15 September 1962, Papers of the Archbishops' Commission to Revise the Psalter, Church of England Record Centre, Bermondsey, ACRP/2.

68. Copy of letter from Canon H.E. Hopkins [n.d., but 1963], Papers of the Archbishops' Commission to Revise the Psalter, Church of England Record Centre, Bermondsey, ACRP/2.

69. T. S. Eliot, paper circulated to the ACRP, 2 September 1963, Papers of the Archbishops' Commission to Revise the Psalter, Church of England Record Centre, Bermondsey, ACRP/2.

70. T. S. Eliot, "The Metaphysical Poets," in *Selected Essays* (London: Faber & Faber, 1999), 281–91.

71. The phrase is Colin MacCabe's, in *T. S. Eliot* (Liverpool: Liverpool University Press, 2006), 67. The significance of this belief, as it played out in Eliot's later career as a "public intellectual," including briefly his work on the Archbishops' Commission to Revise the Psalter, is insightfully parsed in Jeremy Noel-Tod, "Eliot as Public Intellectual," in Megan Quigley and David E. Chinitz, *Eliot Now* (London: Bloomsbury Academic, 2024), 51–63, 61.

72. For example, he explicitly supports replacing "leasing" with "lying" or "falsehood," and some other changes in T. S. Eliot to Bishop G. A. Chase, typescript letter, 29 August 1962, Papers of the Archbishops' Commission to Revise the Psalter, Church of England Record Centre, Bermondsey, ACRP/30. Eliot's warm memories of the commission are found in T. S. Eliot to Bishop G.A. Chase, typescript letter, 6 November 1963, Papers of the Archbishops' Commission to Revise the Psalter, Church of England Record Centre, Bermondsey, ACRP/30.

73. Murray Schafer, *British Composers in Interview* (London: Faber & Faber, 1963), 116–17.

74. Benjamin Britten and Montagu Slater, *Peter Grimes: An Opera in Three Acts and a Prologue* (new corrected ed.) (London: Boosey and Hawkes, 1972), 4.

75. Britten and Slater, *Peter Grimes,* 28.

76. Britten and Slater, *Peter Grimes,* 24.

77. Britten and Slater, *Peter Grimes,* 21.

78. Britten and Slater, *Peter Grimes,* 22; Edward Sackville-West, "The Musical and Dramatic Structure," in Eric Crozier (ed.), *Peter Grimes: Essays* (London: John Lane the Bodley Head, for The Governors of Sadler's Wells, 1945), 27–55, 39.

79. Eric Crozier, "Notes on the Production of Benjamin Britten's *Peter Grimes,*" in Paul Banks (ed.), *The Making of Peter Grimes (*Woodbridge: Boydell Press, 1996), 2:7–20, 14–15.

80. Peter Garvie, "Plausible Darkness: *Peter Grimes* After a Quarter of a Century," *Tempo,* no. 100 (1972), 9–14, 13.

81. These are discussed in Graham Elliott, *Benjamin Britten: The Spiritual Dimension* (Oxford: Oxford University Press, 2006), esp. ch. 7, 74–92.

82. See Cummings, *Book of Common Prayer,* 692n; Agamben, *The Power,* 222–24.

83. Cummings, *Book of Common Prayer,* 243.

84. Elliott, *Benjamin Britten,* 3. For a staunch critique of Elliott's argument, see Edward Venn, "*Benjamin Britten: The Spiritual Dimension.* By Graham Elliott," review in *Music and Letters* 89:1 (2008), 143–48. Carpenter quotes Peter Pears's claim "I am not sure that [Britten] would really have called himself a Christian," and tends to foreground Britten's sexuality over spirituality. Humphrey Carpenter, *Benjamin Britten: A Biography* (London: Faber & Faber 1992), 113.

85. Montagu Slater and Randall Swingler were "great friends," according to Slater's widow. Enid Slater, speaking in Donald Mitchell, "Montagu Slater (1902–1956): Who Was He?," in Philip Brett (ed.), *Benjamin Britain: Peter Grimes* (Cambridge: Cambridge University Press, 1983), 22–46, 31.

86. Ian Patterson, "Two Librettists: Montagu Slater and Ronald Duncan," in Vicki P. Stroeher and Justin Vickers (eds.), *Benjamin Britten in Context* (Cambridge: Cambridge University Press, 2022), 232–40, 232.

87. Philip Brett, "*Peter Grimes:* The Growth of the Libretto," in Paul Banks (ed.), *The Making of* Peter Grimes (Woodbridge: Boydell Press, 1996), 2:53–78, 62–63.

88. Britten and Slater, *Peter Grimes,* 32.

89. Brett, "The Growth of the Libretto," 64.

90. Brett, "The Growth of the Libretto," 65.

91. Patterson, "Two Librettists," 232.

92. Montagu Slater, *The Trial of Jomo Kenyatta* (London: Secker and Warburg, 1955), 257.

93. Slater, *The Trial,* 14.

94. Cummings, *Book of Common Prayer,* 97.

95. See Ian T. Douglas, "Inculturation and Anglican Worship," in Charles Hefling and Cynthia Shattuck (eds.), *The Oxford Guide to the Book of Common Prayer: A Worldwide Survey* (Oxford: Oxford University Press, 2006), 271–6.

96. Chinua Achebe, *Things Fall Apart,* 139.

97. Esther Mombo, "Anglican Liturgies in Eastern Africa," in Charles Hefling and

Cynthia Shattuck (eds.), *The Oxford Guide to the Book of Common Prayer: A Worldwide Survey* (Oxford: Oxford University Press, 2006), 277–86, 277.

98. Terry Bishop, dir., *Daybreak in Udi* (1949), http://www.colonialfilm.org.uk/node/252.

99. Sarah Trimmer, *Reflections on the Education of Children in Charity Schools with the Outline of a Plan of Appropriate Instruction for the Children of the Poor Submitted to the Consideration of the Patrons of Schools of Every Denomination Supported by Charity* (London: T. Longman, 1792), 34.

100. Eric G. Lorentzen, "'This Schoolroom Is a Nation': Subverting the Catechistic Method in Dickens," *Dickens Studies Annual* 49:2 (2018), 279–329.

101. Sarah Trimmer, *The Teacher's Assistant: Consisting of Lectures in the Catechetical Form, Being Part of a Plan of Appropriate Instruction for the Children of the Poor* (London: F.C. and J. Rivington, 1812), 171.

102. Trimmer, *Teacher's Assistant,* 1.

103. Sarah Trimmer, *A Companion to the Book of Common Prayer of the Church of England: Containing a Comment on the Service for Sundays; Including the Collects, Epistles, and Gospels* (London: T. Longman, 1791), v.

104. Carol Summers, "Education and Literacy," in John Parker (ed.), *The Oxford Handbook of Modern African History* (Oxford: Oxford University Press, 2013), 319–37, 321.

105. Government inspectors in Southern Rhodesia in 1923, quoted in Summers, "Education and Literacy," 322.

106. Summers, "Education and Literacy," 329.

107. Bishop, *Daybreak in Udi.*

108. Ben Page, "'And the Oscar Goes to . . . *Daybreak in Udi*': Understanding Late Colonial Community Development and Its Legacy Through Film," *Development and Change* 45:5 (2014), 813–68, 842.

109. T. Bishop writing in *Spectator,* quoted in Rosaleen Smyth, "The Post-War Career of the Colonial Film Unit in Africa: 1946–1955," *Historical Journal of Film, Radio and Television* 12:2 (1992), 163–77, 167.

110. Rosaleen Smyth, "Grierson, the British Documentary Movement, and Colonial Cinema in British Colonial Africa," *Film History* 25:4 (2013), 82–113, 94.

111. *House of Commons, Hansard's Parliamentary Debates: The Official Report* (14 December 1955, vol. 547, col. 16), https://hansard.parliament.uk/commons/1955-12-14/debates/f0346ea4-e1ca-49d5-a3f1-7bdc3858f692/Book(Prohibition). The member of Parliament who asked the question about the ban on this book was the Labour MP Stephen Swingler, the brother of Randall, and presumably known to Slater.

112. Peter Leman, "African Oral Law and the Critique of Colonial Modernity in *The Trial of Jomo Kenyatta,*" *Law & Literature* 23:1 (2011), 26–47, 34.

113. Leman, "African Oral Law," 35.

114. Slater, *The Trial,* 161, 192.

115. Slater, *The Trial,* 23.

116. Pritt, qtd. in Slater, *The Trial,* 88.

117. Slater, *The Trial,* 24.

118. Slater, *The Trial*, 88.

119. Robert B. Edgerton, *Mau Mau: An African Crucible* (New York: Free Press, 1989), 93–94.

120. Slater, *The Trial*, 232.

121. Carol Sicherman, "Ngugi's Colonial Education: 'The Subversion . . . of the African Mind,'" *African Studies Review* 38:3 (1995), 11–41, 19.

122. Ngũgĩ wa Thiong'o, *A Grain of Wheat* (London: Penguin, 2002), 22.

123. Ngũgĩ, *A Grain*, 21.

124. Jomo Kenyatta, *Facing Mount Kenya: The Tribal Life of the Gikuyu* (London: Secker & Warburg, 1938), 274.

125. Kenyatta, *Facing*, 276.

126. Kenyatta, *Facing*, 278.

127. Kenyatta, *Facing*, 277.

128. Ngũgĩ, *A Grain*, 21.

129. Kenyatta, *Facing*, 277.

130. Ngũgĩ, *A Grain*, 22.

131. Lupenga Mphande, "Ngugi and the World of Christianity: A Dialectic," *Journal of Asian and African Studies* 39:5 (2004), 357–78, 361.

132. Ngũgĩ wa Thiong'o, *The River Between* (London: Penguin, 2002), 144.

133. Ngũgĩ, *A Grain*, 64.

134. Ngũgĩ, *A Grain*, 65.

135. Ngũgĩ, *A Grain*, 65.

136. Ngũgĩ, *A Grain*, 213. See Cummings (ed.), *Book of Common Prayer*. The 1549 text has priest: "O Lorde, open thou my lyppes." And answer: "And my mouthe shall shewe forth thy prayse" (7). The 1662 text has "O Lord open thou our lips," and answer: "And our mouth shall shew forth thy praise" (241).

137. Ngũgĩ, *A Grain*, 213–14.

138. Ngũgĩ, *A Grain*, 215.

139. Ngũgĩ, *A Grain*, 217.

140. Ngũgĩ, *A Grain*, 218–19.

141. Burdekin's influence on Orwell is excavated in detail in Elizabeth English, "Orwell and Katharine Burdekin," in Nathan Waddell (ed.), *The Oxford Handbook of George Orwell* (Oxford: Oxford University Press, 2025), 560–76.

142. Joseph Goebbels, qtd. Erika Fischer-Lichte, *Theatre, Sacrifice, Ritual: Exploring Forms of Political Theatre* (Abingdon: Routledge, 2005), 128.

143. Henning Eichberg "The Nazi *Thingspiel:* Theater for the Masses in Fascism and Proletarian Culture" (trans. Robert A. Jones), *New German Critique* 11 (1977), 133–50, 140.

144. Fischer-Lichte, *Theatre, Sacrifice, Ritual*, 155.

145. Katharine Burdekin, *Swastika Night* (New York: Feminist Press 1985), 5. Examples of press reporting of *Thingspiele* include A Correspondent, "Propaganda in the Theatre," *The Times*, 4 December 1935, 12 and J.M.D.P., "Art in Nazi Germany," *Manchester Guardian*, 16 March 1937, 11.

146. Fischer-Lichte, *Theatre, Sacrifice, Ritual,* 126.

147. Wilhelm von Schramm, qtd. Fischer-Lichte, *Theatre, Sacrifice, Ritual,* 128.

148. Burdekin, *Swastika Night,* 5.

149. Cummings (ed.), *Book of Common Prayer,* 247.

150. Burdekin, *Swastika Night,* 7.

151. Katharine Burdekin, *The Rebel Passion* (London: Thornton Butterworth, 1929), 24.

152. Jacobs, *The Book of Common Prayer,* 58.

153. Burdekin, *The Rebel Passion,* 240. Giraldus, and presumably Burdekin, have misunderstood the complex politics around the 1928 Prayer Book revision. See my earlier discussion of this controversy, and above all, Maiden, *National Religion.*

154. Burdekin, *The Rebel Passion,* 240–41.

155. John Milton, *Eikonoklastes* in *The Complete Prose Works of John Milton,* ed. Merritt Y. Hughes, vol. 3, *1648–1649* (New Haven, CT: Yale University Press, 1962), 504.

156. Burdekin, *The Rebel Passion,* 135.

157. John Bunyan, *A Discourse on Prayer,* in *The Complete Works of John Bunyan with an Introduction by Rev. John P. Gulliver,* pt. 4 (Philadelphia: Bradley, Garrettson & Co.: 1872), 656–57.

158. Burdekin, *The Rebel Passion,* 271.

159. Burdekin, *The Rebel Passion,* 304.

160. Burdekin, *The Rebel Passion,* 271.

161. Burdekin, *The Rebel Passion,* 123–24.

162. Katharine Burdekin, *Proud Man* (New York: Feminist Press, 1993), 149. For an expanded discussion of this novel's thinking about the Prayer Book and collective speech, see Matthew Taunton, "Katharine Burdekin and Collective Speech: Politics, Chorus and Liturgy," *Women: A Cultural Review* 31:4 (2020), 384–400, 391–94.

163. Burdekin, *Swastika Night,* 138.

164. Burdekin, *Swastika Night,* 10.

165. Monika Fludernik, "The Many in Action and Thought: Towards a Poetics of the Collective in Narrative," *Narrative* 25:2 (2017), 139–63, 142.

166. Chris Baldick, "Free Indirect Style," in *The Oxford Dictionary of Literary Terms,* online ed. (Oxford University Press, 2015).

167. Burdekin, *Swastika Night,* 12.

168. M. M. Bakhtin, *The Dialogic Imagination: Four Essays* (trans. Caryl Emerson and Michael Holquist) (Austin: University of Texas Press, 1981), 325–26.

169. Burdekin, *Swastika Night,* 124.

170. One reason for this neglect is that Burdekin wrote novels of ideas. For a general diagnosis of the critical rejection of that form, see Rachel Potter and Matthew Taunton, "Introduction: The British Novel of Ideas," in *The British Novel of Ideas: George Eliot to Zadie Smith* (Cambridge: Cambridge University Press, 2025), 1–25. For a reading of Burdekin as a novelist of ideas, see Glyn Salton-Cox, "Katharine Burdekin: Self and Not-Self," in Potter and Taunton, *The British Novel of Ideas,* 180–91.

Coda

1. Paul Rekret, *Take This Hammer: Work, Song, Crisis* (London: Goldsmiths Press, 2024), 9–10.

2. John Fahey, "John Henry Variations," *Death Chants, Breakdowns and Military Waltzes* (Takoma, 1999).

3. John Fahey, "Nine Pound Hammer," *The Voice of the Turtle* (Takoma, 1968).

4. Joseph "Chinaman" Johnson and Group, "This Old Hammer Killed John Henry," in Bruce Jackson (ed.), *Wake Up Dead Man: Afro-American Prison Worksongs from Texas Prisons* (Cambridge: Harvard University Press, 1972), 238–39. As discussed in Rekret, *Take This Hammer*, 9–10.

5. Rekret, "Take This Hammer," 10.

6. Steph Doehler, "Taking the Star-Spangled Knee: The Media Framing of Colin Kaepernick," *Sport in Society* 26:1 (2023), 45–60.

7. Marc Ferris, *Star Spangled Banner: The Unlikely Story of America's National Anthem* (Baltimore: Johns Hopkins University Press, 2014), 26. Ferris notes that it has long been considered difficult, and that it was originally composed for a solo voice, with the chorus joining in for the last two lines of each verse.

8. A fascinating take on the controversy, including documentation of the discussions within the Dallas Cowboys team and wider organization, is presented in *All or Nothing*, season 3, episode 2 (Amazon Prime Video, 2018).

9. "Premier League Statement: Players to Take the Knee Again in 2024/25," https://www.premierleague.com/news/4089060.

10. Jameson, "Criticism and Categories," 564.

11. Raymond Williams, "Culture is Ordinary," in *Resources of Hope: Culture, Democracy, Socialism* (London: Verso, 1989), 3–18, 4.

12. Caroline Levine, *Forms: Whole, Rhythm, Hierarchy, Network* (Princeton: Princeton University Press, 2015), 27.

BIBLIOGRAPHY

Sophie Abramowitz, "'Trained and Taught This Song by Zora Hurston': Dramatic Ethnography and Zora Neale Hurston's *The Great Day*." *American Quarterly* 72:4 (2020), 881–908.

Chinua Achebe, "An Image of Africa: Racism in Conrad's *Heart of Darkness*." *Massachusetts Review* 57:1 (2016), 14–27.

Chinua Achebe, *Things Fall Apart* (London: Penguin, 2001).

Theodor Adorno, "Commitment." *New Left Review* 87–88 (1974), 75–89.

Aeschylus, *The Oresteia* (trans. Ted Hughes) (London: Faber & Faber, 1999).

Giorgio Agamben, *The Kingdom and the Glory: For a Theological Genealogy of Economy and Government* (trans. Lorenzo Chiesa with Matteo Mandarini) (Stanford: Stanford University Press, 2011).

Benedict Anderson, *Imagined Communities: Reflections on the Origin and Spread of Nationalism*, rev. ed. (London: Verso, 1991).

Kwame Anthony Appiah, "Cosmopolitan Patriots." *Critical Inquiry* 23:3 (1997), 617–39.

Kwame Anthony Appiah, *The Lies That Bind: Rethinking Identity* (London: Profile, 2018), 38–39.

J. L. Austin, *How to Do Things with Words* (Oxford: Oxford University Press, 1975).

Paul Avis, "Anglican Ecclesiology." In Paul Avis (ed.), *The Oxford Handbook of Ecclesiology* (Oxford: Oxford University Press, 2018), 239–62.

M. M. Bakhtin, *The Dialogic Imagination: Four Essays* (trans. Caryl Emerson and Michael Holquist) (Austin: University of Texas Press, 1981), 325–26.

Chris Baldick, "Free Indirect Style," in *The Oxford Dictionary of Literary Terms*, online ed. (Oxford University Press, 2015).

James Baldwin, *The Fire Next Time* (London: Penguin, 2017).

Étienne Balibar, *On the Dictatorship of the Proletariat* (trans. Graham Locke) (London: NLB, 1977).

Eli Bentor, "Challenges to Rural Festivals with the Return to Democratic Rule in Southeastern Nigeria" *African Arts* 38:4 (2005), 38–93.

Mark Berry, "Characters in the 'World' of the Ring." In Mark Berry and Nicholas Vazsonyi (eds.), *The Cambridge Companion to Wagner's Der Ring Des Nibelungen* (Cambridge: Cambridge University Press, 2020), 159–84.

Jamie Berthe, "Beyond the Entomological Critique: Re-Thinking Rouch and African Cinema." *Studies in French Cinema* 18:3 (2018), 267–77.

Joshua Billings, "Choral Dialectics: Hölderlin and Hegel." In Renaud Gagné and Marianne Govers Hopman (eds.), *Choral Mediations in Greek Tragedy* (Cambridge: Cambridge University Press, 2013), 317–38.

Joshua Billings, *Genealogy of the Tragic: Greek Tragedy and German Philosophy* (Princeton: Princeton University Press, 2014).

Tim Blanning, "Richard Wagner and the German Nation." *Transactions of the Royal Historical Society* 25 (2015), 95–112.

Franz Boas, "The History of Anthropology." In George W. Stocking Jr. (ed.), *A Franz Boas Reader: The Shaping of American Anthropology, 1883–1911* (Chicago: University of Chicago Press, 1974), 23–36.

Franz Boas, "Human Faculty as Determined by Race." In George W. Stocking (ed.), *A Franz Boas Reader: The Shaping of American Anthropology, 1883–1911* (Chicago: University of Chicago Press, 1974), 221–42.

Franz Boas, preface to *Mules and Men*, by Zora Neale Hurston (New York: Harper Perennial, 1990), xiii–xiv.

Franz Boas, "Psychological Problems in Anthropology." In George W. Stocking (ed.), *A Franz Boas Reader: The Shaping of American Anthropology, 1883–1911* (Chicago: University of Chicago Press, 1974), 243–54.

Franz Boas, *Race, Language and Culture* (New York: Free Press, 1966).

Georges Bossi and Jacques Estager, *L'Internationale, 1888–1988* (Paris: Messidor, Éditions sociales).

Kate Bowen and Paul A. Pickering, *Songs of Liberty: Music, Radicalism and Reform in the Anglophone World, 1790–1914* (Manchester: Manchester University Press, 2017).

Philip Brett, "*Peter Grimes:* The Growth of the Libretto." In Paul Banks (ed.), *The Making of* Peter Grimes (Woodbridge: Boydell Press, 1996), 2:53–78.

Benjamin Britten and Montagu Slater, *Peter Grimes: An Opera in Three Acts and a Prologue*, rev. ed. (London: Boosey and Hawkes, 1972).

John Bunyan, *A Discourse on Prayer* in *The Complete Works of John Bunyan with an Introduction by Rev. John P. Gulliver* (Philadelphia: Bradley, Garrettson & Co., 1872), pt. 4, 656–57.

Katharine Burdekin, *The Rebel Passion* (London: Thornton Butterworth, 1929).

Katharine Burdekin, *Swastika Night* (New York: Feminist Press, 1985).

Katharine Burdekin, *Proud Man* (New York: Feminist Press, 1993).

Alan Bush, "The Crisis of Modern Music," *Keynote*, 1/4 (1946), 4–7.

Alan Bush and Randall Swingler, introduction to *Left Song Book* (London: Victor Gollancz, 1938).

Judith Butler, *Notes Toward a Performative Theory of Assembly* (Cambridge: Harvard University Press, 2015).

Judith Butler and Gayatri Spivak, *Who Sings the Nation-State? Language, Politics, Belonging* (London: Seagull, 2007).
Jamie Callison, *Modernism and Religion: Between Mysticism and Orthodoxy* (Edinburgh: Edinburgh University Press, 2023).
Elias Canetti, *Crowds and Power* (trans. Carol Stewart) (New York: Seabury Press, 1978).
Humphrey Carpenter, *Benjamin Britten: A Biography* (London: Faber & Faber, 1992).
Christopher Caudwell, *Illusion and Reality: A Study of the Sources of Poetry* (London: Lawrence & Wishart, 1946).
Adriana Cavarero, *For More than One Voice: Toward a Philosophy of Vocal Expression* (trans. Paul A. Kottman) (Stanford: Stanford University Press, 2005).
Adriana Cavarero, *Surging Democracy: Notes on Hannah Arendt's Political Thought* (trans. Matthew Gervase) (Stanford: Stanford University Press, 2021).
Albert Cervoni, "A Historic Confrontation in 1965 Between Jean Rouch and Ousmane Sembène: 'You Look at Us as If We Were Insects.'" In Annett Busch and Max Annas, *Ousmane Sembène: Interviews* (Jackson: University of Mississippi Press, 2008), 3–6.
Colin Chambers, *The Story of Unity Theatre* (London: Lawrence and Wishart, 1989).
Louis Chappell, *John Henry: A Folk-Lore Study* (Jena: W. Biedermann, 1933).
G. A. Chase, *A Companion to the Revised Psalter* (London: S.P.C.K., 1963).
Matthew Chrisman and Graham Hubbs, "'The Language of the Unheard': Rioting as a Speech Act." In *Philosophy and Public Affairs* 49 (2021), 379–401.
Matthew Chrisman and Graham Hubbs, "Protest and Speech Act Theory." In *The Routledge Handbook of Social and Political Philosophy of Language* (New York: Routledge, 2021), 179–92.
Jan Cohen-Cruz, "General Introduction." In Jan Cohen-Cruz (ed.), *Radical Street Performance: An International Anthology* (London: Routledge, 1998), 1–8.
Jean Lee Cole and Charles Mitchell, "Introduction: Zora Neale Hurston—A Theatrical Life." In Jean Lee Cole and Charles Mitchell (eds.), *Zora Neale Hurston: Collected Plays* (New Brunswick: Rutgers University Press, 2008), xv–xxxi.
Steven Connor, "Choralities." *Twentieth-Century Music* 13:1 (2016), 3–23.
Steven Connor, *A History of Asking* (London: Open Humanities Press, 2023).
Steven Connor, *Styles of Seriousness* (Stanford: Stanford University Press, 2023).
A Correspondent, "Propaganda in the Theatre," *The Times*, 12 April 1935, 12.
Bonnie Costello, *The Plural of Us: Poetry and Community in Auden and Others* (Princeton: Princeton University Press, 2017).
Anne Cranny-Francis, *Jack Lindsay: Writer, Romantic, Revolutionary* (Cham: Palgrave Macmillan, 2024).
Andy Croft, *The Years of Anger: The Life of Randall Swingler* (London: Routledge, 2020).
Eric Crozier, "Notes on the Production of Benjamin Britten's *Peter Grimes*." In Paul Banks (ed.), *The Making of* Peter Grimes (Woodbridge: Boydell Press, 1996), 2:7–20.
Brian Cummings, *The Book of Common Prayer: A Very Short Introduction* (Oxford: Oxford University Press, 2018).

Brian Cummings (ed.), *The Book of Common Prayer: The Texts of 1549, 1559, and 1662* (Oxford: Oxford University Press, 2013).

Brian Cummings, introduction to *The Book of Common Prayer: The Texts of 1549, 1559, and 1662*, ed. Brian Cummings (Oxford: Oxford University Press, 2013), ix–lii.

Fred Cummins, *The Ground from Which We Speak: Joint Speech and the Collective Subject* (Newcastle: Cambridge Scholars Press, 2018), 6.

Nancy Cunard (ed.), *Authors Take Sides on the Spanish War* (London: Left Review, 1937).

Claire Davison, "'Never More Close, Intimate and Cordial": The 'Projection of Russia Campaign' on the BBC Home Service, 1941–45," unpublished paper delivered at the Anglo Russian Research Network Reading Group, Pushkin House, 3 March 2017.

Anthony Dawahare, "Langston Hughes's Radical Poetry and the 'End of Race.'" *MELUS* 23:3 (1998), 21–41.

Patrick Delices, "Price-Mars and Black Public Intellectual Tradition in Haiti: Cementing Scholarship with Service." In Celucien L. Joseph, Jean Eddy Saint Paul, and Glodel Mezilas (eds.), *Between Two Worlds: Jean Price-Mars, Haiti, and Africa* (Lanham: Lexington Books, 2018), 31–58.

Michael Denning, *The Cultural Front: The Labouring of American Culture in the Twentieth Century* (London: Verso, 1997).

Steph Doehler, "Taking the Star-Spangled Knee: The Media Framing of Colin Kaepernick." *Sport in Society* 26:1 (2023), 45–60.

Nathalie Dompnier, "Entre *La Marseillaise* et *Maréchal, nous voilà!* quel hymne pour le régime de Vichy?" In Myriam Chimènes (ed.), *La vie musicale sous Vichy* (Brussels: Éditions Complexe, 2001), 69–83.

Ian T. Douglas, "Inculturation and Anglican Worship." In Charles Heffing and Cynthia Shattuck (eds.), *The Oxford Guide to the Book of Common Prayer: A Worldwide Survey* (Oxford: Oxford University Press, 2006), 271–76.

W. E. B. Du Bois, *The Souls of Black Folk* (Oxford: Oxford University Press, 2007).

W. E. B. Du Bois, "The Talented Tenth." In Booker T. Washington (ed.), *The Negro Problem: A Series of Articles by Representative Negroes of Today* (New York: James Pott & Co., 1903), 33–75.

Rachel Blau DuPlessis, "'HOO, HOO, HOO': Some Episodes in the Construction of Modern Whiteness." *American Literature* 67:4 (1995), 667–700.

Crystal Nicole Eddins, *Rituals, Runaways, and the Haitian Revolution: Collective Action in the African Diaspora*, 2nd ed. (Cambridge: Cambridge University Press, 2022).

Robert B. Edgerton, *Mau Mau: An African Crucible* (New York: Free Press, 1989).

Henning Eichberg, "The Nazi *Thingspiel*: Theater for the Masses in Fascism and Proletarian Culture" (trans. Robert A. Jones), *New German Critique* 11 (1977), 133–50.

Elizabeth L. Eisenstein, *The Printing Press as an Agent of Change: Communications and Cultural Transformations in Early-Modern Europe*, 2 vols. (Cambridge: Cambridge University Press, 2009).

T. S. Eliot, "Autobiographical Note: *Harvard Class of 1910 Fiftieth Anniversary Report.*" In Jewel Spears Brooker and Ronald Schuchard (eds.), *The Complete Prose of T. S.*

Eliot: The Critical Edition, vol. 8, *Still and Still Moving, 1954–1965* (Baltimore: Johns Hopkins University Press, 2019), 419–22.

T. S. Eliot, "A Dialogue on Dramatic Poetry. With the Original Preface." In Frances Dickey, Jennifer Formichelli, and Ronald Schuchard (eds.), *The Complete Prose of T. S. Eliot: The Critical Edition*, vol. 3, *Literature, Politics, Belief, 1927–1929* (Baltimore: Johns Hopkins University Press, 2015), 396–412.

T. S. Eliot, "East Coker." In Christopher Ricks and Jim McCue (eds.), *The Poems of T. S. Eliot* vol. 1, *Collected and Uncollected Poems* (London: Faber & Faber, 2015), 185–92.

T. S. Eliot, "The Hollow Men." In Christopher Ricks and Jim McCue (eds.), *The Poems of T. S. Eliot*, vol. 1, *Collected and Uncollected Poems* (London: Faber & Faber, 2015), 81–84.

T. S. Eliot, "The Metaphysical Poets." In *Selected Essays* (London: Faber & Faber, 1999), 281–91.

T. S. Eliot, *Notes Towards the Definition of Culture*. In Iman Javadi and Ronald Schuchard (eds.), *The Complete Prose of T. S. Eliot: The Critical Edition*, vol. 7, *A European Society, 1947–1953* (Baltimore: Johns Hopkins University Press, 2018), 194–287.

T. S. Eliot, "Parliament and the New Prayer Book: To the Editor of *The New Adelphi*." In Frances Dickey, Jennifer Formichelli, and Ronald Schuchard (eds.), *The Complete Prose of T. S. Eliot: The Critical Edition*, vol. 3, *Literature, Politics, Belief, 1927–1929* (Baltimore: Johns Hopkins University Press, 2015), 431–4.

T. S. Eliot, "Religious Drama: Medieval and Modern." In Iman Javadi, Ronald Schuchard, and Jayme Stayer, *The Complete Prose of T. S. Eliot*, vol. 5, *Tradition and -Orthodoxy, 1934–1939* (Baltimore: Johns Hopkins University Press, 2021), 519–30.

T. S. Eliot, *The Rock: A Pageant Play Written for Performance at Sadler's Wells Theatre 28 May—9 June 1934 on Behalf of the Forty-Five Churches Fund of the Diocese of London* (London: Faber & Faber, 1934).

T. S. Eliot, *Sweeney Agonistes: Fragments of an Aristophanic Melodrama* (London: Faber & Faber, 1932).

T. S. Eliot, "T. S. Eliot on the Language of the New English Bible." In Jewel Spears Brooker and Ronald Schuchard (eds.), *The Complete Prose of T. S. Eliot: The Critical Edition*, vol. 8, *Still and Still Moving, 1954–1965* (Baltimore: Johns Hopkins University Press, 2019), 530–36.

Graham Elliott, *Benjamin Britten: The Spiritual Dimension* (Oxford: Oxford University Press, 2006).

Elizabeth English, "Orwell and Katharine Burdekin." In Nathan Waddell (ed.), *The Oxford Handbook of George Orwell* (Oxford: Oxford University Press, 2025), 560–76.

Jed Esty, *A Shrinking Island: Modernism and National Culture in England* (Princeton: Princeton University Press, 2004).

Ben Etherington, *Literary Primitivism* (Stanford: Stanford University Press, 2017).

Euripides, *Bacchae* (trans. John Davie). In *The Bacchae and Other Plays* (London: Penguin, 2005), 128–65.

Timothy H. Evans, "A Last Defense Against the Dark: Folklore, Horror, and the Uses of Tradition in the Works of H. P. Lovecraft." *Journal of Folklore Research* 42:1 (2005), 99–135.

Nicolai Evreinov, "The Storming of the Winter Palace: An Article by the Production's Director-in-Chief" (1920; trans. David Riff). In Inke Arns, Sylvia Sasse, and Igor Chubarov (eds.), *The Storming of the Winter Palace* (Chicago: University of Chicago Press, 2017), 23–25.

Marc Ferris, *Star Spangled Banner: The Unlikely Story of America's National Anthem* (Baltimore: Johns Hopkins University Press, 2014).

Erika Fischer-Lichte, *Theatre, Sacrifice, Ritual: Exploring Forms of Political Theatre* (Abingdon: Routledge, 2005).

Sheila Fitzpatrick, *The Russian Revolution*, 4th ed. (Oxford: Oxford University Press, 2017).

Monika Fludernik, "The Many in Action and Thought: Towards a Poetics of the Collective in Narrative." *Narrative* 25:2 (2017), 139–63.

Carolyn Fowler, *A Knot in the Thread: The Life and Work of Jacques Roumain* (Washington, DC: Howard University Press, 1980).

Richard France, preface to *Macbeth*. In Richard France (ed.), *Orson Welles on Shakespeare: The W.P.A. and Mercury Theatre Playscripts* (Westport: Greenwood Press, 1990), 29–36.

Nancy Fraser, "Rethinking Recognition." *New Left Review* 3 (May–June 2000), 107–20.

Nancy Fraser and Axel Honneth, *Redistribution or Recognition? A Political-Philosophical Exchange* (London: Verso, 2003).

Sigmund Freud, *Mass Psychology and the Analysis of the "I."* In *Mass Psychology and Other Writings* (trans. J. A. Underwood) (London: Penguin, 2004), 17–106.

Samba Gadjigo, *Ousmane Sembène: The Making of a Militant Artist* (trans. Moustapha Diop) (Bloomington: Indiana University Press, 2010).

Peter Garvie, "Plausible Darkness: *Peter Grimes* After a Quarter of a Century." *Tempo* 100 (1972), 9–14.

Henry Louis Gates Jr., "Criticism in the Jungle." In Henry Louis Gates (ed.), *Black Literature and Literary Theory* (New York: Methuen, 1984), 1–24.

Ernest Gellner, *Nations and Nationalism*, 2nd ed. (Oxford: Blackwell, 2006).

Simon Gikandi, *Reading the African Novel* (London: James Currey, 1987).

Paul Gilroy, "Black Fascism." *Transition* 81–82 (2000), 70–91.

Paul Gilroy, *The Black Atlantic: Modernity and Double Consciousness* (London: Verso, 2022).

Ted Gioia, *Work Songs* (Durham: Duke University Press, 2006).

Simon Goldhill, "The Greek Chorus: Our German Eye." In Joshua Billings, Felix Budelmann, and Fiona Macintosh (eds.), *Choruses, Ancient and Modern* (Oxford: Oxford University Press, 2013), 35–52.

Lewis R. Gordon, *Fear of Black Consciousness* (London: Penguin, 2022).

David Graeber and David Wengrow, *The Dawn of Everything: A New History of Humanity* (London: Penguin, 2021).

Shane Graham, "'It Cancels the Slave Ship!': Africa, Slavery, and the Haitian Revolution in Langston Hughes's *Emperor of Haiti* and Aimé Césaire's *The Tragedy of King Christophe.*" *Modern Drama* 62:4 (2019), 458–82.

Antonio Gramsci, *Selections from the Prison Notebooks* (ed. and trans. Quintin Hoare and Geoffrey Nowell Smith) (London: Lawrence and Wishart).

Nicholas Grant, "Patriotism and Black Internationalism." *Modern American History* 6 (2023), 322–40.

Ahmad Greene-Hayes, "'A Very Queer Case': Clementine Barnabet and the Erotics of a Sensationalized Voodoo Religion." *Nova Religio: The Journal of Alternative and Emergent Religions* 26:4 (2023), 58–84.

Thomas S. Grey, "Wagner's 'Lohengrin': Between *Grand Opéra* and *Musikdrama.*" In Richard Wagner, *Lohengrin* (opera guide) (London: Overture, 2011), 15–32.

Josef Gugler, "Wole Soyinka's Kongi's Harvest from Stage to Screen: Four Endings to Tyranny." *Canadian Journal of African Studies/La Revue canadienne des études africaines* 31:1 (1997), 32–49.

Hans Ulrich Gumbrecht, *Crowds: The Stadium as a Ritual of Intensity* (Stanford: Stanford University Press, 2021).

H. Rider Haggard, *King Solomon's Mines* (London: Penguin, 2007).

Edith Hall, "Christopher Caudwell's Greek and Latin Classics." In Henry Stead and Edith Hall (eds.), *Greek and Roman Classics in the British Struggle for Social Reform* (London: Bloomsbury, 2015), 235–55.

Edith Hall and Henry Stead, *A People's History of Classics: Class and Greco-Roman Antiquity in Britain and Ireland 1689 to 1939* (Abingdon: Routledge, 2020).

Stuart Hall and Tony Jefferson, *Resistance Through Rituals: Youth Subcultures in Post-war Britain* (Birmingham: University of Birmingham, Centre for Contemporary Cultural Studies, 1976).

Dan Hancox, *Multitudes: How Crowds Made the Modern World* (London: Verso, 2024).

Michael Hardt and Antonio Negri, *Assembly* (Oxford: Oxford University Press, 2017).

Ben Harker, *The Chronology of Revolution: Communism, Culture, and Civil Society in Twentieth-Century Britain* (Toronto: University of Toronto Press, 2021).

Ben Harker, "'Communism Is English': Edgell Rickword, Jack Lindsay and the Cultural Politics of the Popular Front." *Literature and History* 20:2 (2011), 16–24.

Ben Harker, "'Workers' Music': Communism and the British Folk Revival." In *Red Strains: Music and Communism Outside the Communist Bloc* (Oxford: Oxford University Press, 2013), 89–104.

Stefano Harney and Fred Moten, *The Undercommons: Fugitive Planning and Black Study* (Wivenhoe: Minor Compositions, 2013).

Jane Harrison, *Ancient Art and Ritual* (Bradford-on-Avon: Moonraker Press, 1978).

Jane Ellen Harrison, *Reminiscences of a Student's Life* (London: Hogarth Press, 1925).

Saidiya Hartman, "Intimate History, Radical Narrative." *Black Perspectives* (May 2022), https://www.aaihs.org/intimate-history-radical-narrative.

Dick Hebdige, *Subculture: The Meaning of Style* (London: Routledge, 2003).

Georg Wilhelm Friedrich Hegel, *The Phenomenology of Spirit* (trans. Terry Pinkard and Michael Baur) (Cambridge: Cambridge University Press, 2018).

Benjamin Hilb, "Afro-Haitian-American Ritual Power: *Vodou* in the Welles-FTP *Voodoo Macbeth.*" *Shakespeare Bulletin* 32:4 (Winter 2014), 649–81.

Eric Hobsbawm, "Introduction: Inventing Traditions." In Eric Hobsbawm and Terence Ranger (eds.), *The Invention of Tradition* (Cambridge: Cambridge University Press, 1983), 1–14.

Eric Hobsbawm, "Mass Producing Traditions: Europe, 1870–1914." In Eric Hobsbawm and Terence Ranger, *The Invention of Tradition* (Cambridge: Cambridge University Press, 1983), 263–307.

Friedrich Hölderlin (trans. By David Constantine), *Hölderlin's Sophocles: Oedipus and Antigone* (Northumberland: Bloodaxe Books, 2001).

Bonnie Honig, *A Feminist Theory of Refusal* (Cambridge: Harvard University Press, 2021).

Michel Houellebecq, *H. P. Lovecraft: Against the World, Against Life* (trans. Dorna Khazeni) (London: Gollancz, 2008).

Justin Hughes, "Group Speech Acts." *Linguistics and Philosophy* 7:4 (November 1984), 379–395.

Langston Hughes, *Emperor of Haiti.* In Leslie Sanders and Nancy Johnston (eds.), *The Collected Works of Langston Hughes,* vol. 5, *Plays to 1942: Mulatto to the Sun Do Move* (Columbia: University of Missouri Press, 2002), 278–332.

Langston Hughes, *I Wander as I Wander: An Autobiographical Journey* (New York: Hill and Wang, 1964).

Langston Hughes, *Scottsboro, Limited: A One Act Play.* In Leslie Sanders and Nancy Johnston (eds.), *The Collected Works of Langston Hughes,* vol. 5, *Plays to 1942: Mulatto to the Sun Do Move* (Columbia: University of Missouri Press, 2002), 116–29.

Zora Neale Hurston, "Art and Such." In Henry Louis Gates Jr. (ed.), *Reading Black, Reading Feminist: A Critical Anthology* (New York: Meridian, 1990), 21–26.

Zora Neale Hurston, *Dust Tracks on a Road.* In Zora Neale Hurston, *Folklore, Memoirs, and Other Writings,* ed. Cheryl Wall (New York: Library of America, 1995), 557–809.

Zora Neale Hurston, *Dust Tracks on a Road: An Autobiography* (London: Virago, 1986).

Zora Neale Hurston, *Jonah's Gourd Vine* (London: Virago, 1987).

Zora Neale Hurston, *Mules and Men* (New York: Harper Perennial, 1990).

Zora Neale Hurston, "Spirituals and Neo-Spirituals." In Nancy Cunard (ed.), *Negro: An Anthology* (London: Wishart & Co., 1934), 359–61.

Zora Neale Hurston, "Spunk." In *Spunk: The Selected Short Stories of Zora Neale Hurston* (Berkeley: Turtle Island, 1985), 1–8.

Zora Neale Hurston, "Spunk." In Jean Lee Cole and Charles Mitchell (eds.), *Zora Neale Hurston: Collected Plays* (New Brunswick: Rutgers University Press, 2008), 227–68.

Jeanne-Marie Jackson, *The African Novel of Ideas: Philosophy and Individualism in the Age of Global Writing* (Princeton: Princeton University Press, 2021).

Jeanne-Marie Jackson, "Against Ethnography: On Teaching Minority Literature." In Ato Quayson and Ankhi Mukherjee (eds.), *Decolonizing the English Literary Curriculum* (Cambridge: Cambridge University Press, 2023), 200–213.

Alan Jacobs, *The Book of Common Prayer: A Biography* (Princeton: Princeton University Press, 2013).
C. L. R. James, *The Black Jacobins: Toussaint L'Ouverture and the San Domingo Revolution* (London: Penguin, 2001).
C. L. R. James, *Every Cook Can Govern: A Study of Democracy in Ancient Greece, Its Meaning for Today*. In *A New Notion: Two Works by C. L. R. James* (Oakland: PA Press, 2010).
Fredric Jameson, "Criticism and Categories." *PMLA* 137:3 (2022), 563–67.
Fredric Jameson, "Schematizations, or How to Draw a Thought." *Critical Inquiry* 50:1 (2023), 31–53.
J.M.D.P., "Art in Nazi Germany," *Manchester Guardian*, 16 March 1937, 11.
Guy B. Johnson, *John Henry: Tracking Down a Negro Legend* (Chapel Hill: University of North Carolina Press, 1929).
Joseph "Chinaman" Johnson and Group, "This Old Hammer Killed John Henry." In Bruce Jackson (ed.), *Wake Up Dead Man: Afro-American Prison Worksongs from Texas Prisons* (Cambridge: Harvard University Press, 1972), 238–39.
Jean Jonassaint, "Le cinéma de Sembène Ousmane, une (double) contre-ethnographie: (Notes pour une recherche)." *Ethnologies* 31:2 (2010), 241–86.
Celucien L. Joseph, "The Religious Philosophy of Jean Price-Mars." *Journal of Black Studies* 43:6 (September 2012), 620–45.
Celucien L. Joseph, *Thinking in Public: Faith, Secular Humanism, and Development in Jacques Roumain* (Eugene: Pickwick Publications, 2017).
S. T. Joshi, *A Dreamer and a Visionary: H P Lovecraft in His Time* (Liverpool: Liverpool University Press, 2001).
Eileen Julien, "African Literature." In Phyllis M. Martin and Patrick O'Meara (eds.), *Africa*, 3rd ed. (Bloomington: Indiana University Press, 1995), 295–312.
Derek Kahn, "Theatre Notes." *Left Review* 2:15 (1936), 833.
Jomo Kenyatta, *Facing Mount Kenya: The Tribal Life of the Gikuyu* (London: Secker & Warburg, 1938).
Brendan Kibbee, "Black Labor and the Deep South in Hurston's *The Great Day* and Ellington's *Black, Brown, and Beige*." *Current Musicology* 101 (Fall 2017), 81–97.
L. C. Knights, *The Wheel of Fire: Essays in Interpretation of Shakespeare's Sombre Tragedies* (London: Oxford University Press, 1930).
Benjamin Kohlmann, *British Literature and the Life of Institutions: Speculative States* (Oxford: Oxford University Press, 2021).
Anna Kornbluh, *Immediacy, or The Style of Too Late Capitalism* (London: Verso, 2024).
Anthea Kraut, *Choreographing the Folk: The Dance Stagings of Zora Neale Hurston* (Minneapolis: University of Minnesota Press, 2008).
Gustave Le Bon, *The Crowd: A Study of the Popular Mind* (New York: Macmillan, 1896).
Peter Leman, "African Oral Law and the Critique of Colonial Modernity in The Trial of Jomo Kenyatta." *Law & Literature* 23:1 (2011), 26–47.
V. I. Lenin, *The State and Revolution* (trans. Robert Service) (London: Penguin, 1992).

Caroline Levine, *Forms: Whole, Rhythm, Hierarchy, Network* (Princeton: Princeton University Press, 2015).

Caroline Levine, "Literary Studies and Collective Life." *New Literary History* 54:1 (2022), 693–720.

Claude Lévi-Strauss, *Structural Anthropology* (trans. Claire Jacobson and Brooke Grundfest Schoepf) (New York: Basic Books, 1963).

Jack Lindsay, "The Fullness of Life" (unpublished autocriticism), https://jacklindsayproject.com/the-fullness-of-life/.

Jack Lindsay, introduction to *Ancient Art and Ritual*, by Jane Harrison (Bradford-on-Avon: Moonraker Press, 1978), v–xii.

Jack Lindsay, "The May-Day Tradition." *Left Review* 3:16 (May 1938), 963–66.

Jack Lindsay, *A Short History of Culture from Prehistory to the Renascence* (London: Studio Books, 1962).

A. L. Lloyd, *Folk Song in England* (New York: International Publishers, 1967).

A. L. Lloyd, "Sing Out, America!" *Keynote: The Progressive Music Quarterly* 1:1 (Autumn 1945), 18–19.

Eric G. Lorentzen, "'This Schoolroom Is a Nation': Subverting the Catechistic Method in Dickens." *Dickens Studies Annual* 49:2 (2018), 279–329.

H. P. Lovecraft, "The Call of Cthulhu." In *The Complete Cthulhu Mythos Tales* (New York: Barnes & Noble, 2016), 36–61.

Georg Lukács, *The Historical Novel* (trans. Hannah and Stanley Mitchell) (Harmondsworth: Penguin Books, 1976).

Georg Lukács, *The Theory of the Novel: A Historico-Philosophical Essay on the Forms of Great Epic Literature* (trans. by Anna Bostock) (Cambridge: MIT Press, 1971).

Steven Lukes, "Political Ritual and Social Integration" *Sociology* 9:2 (1975), 289–308.

Yunn-Shan Ma, "The Chorus as a Dramatic Force in Wagner's Operas." *Choral Journal* 60:11 (2020), 20–33.

Colin MacCabe, *T. S. Eliot* (Liverpool: Liverpool University Press, 2006).

Alasdair MacIntyre, *A Short History of Ethics: A History of Moral Philosophy from the Homeric Age to the Twentieth Century* (London: Routledge Classics, 2002).

John Maiden, *National Religion and the Prayer Book Controversy, 1927–1928* (Woodbridge: Boydell & Brewer, 2009).

Laura Marcus, *Rhythmical Subjects: The Measures of the Modern* (Oxford: Oxford University Press, 2023).

Peter Marks, "Art and Politics in the 1930s: *The European Quarterly* (1934–5), *Left Review* (1934–8), and *Poetry and the People* (1938–40)." In Peter Brooker and Andrew Thacker (eds.), *The Oxford Critical and Cultural History of Modernist Magazines*, vol. 1, *Britain and Ireland 1880–1955* (Oxford: Oxford University Press, 2013).

Karl Marx, *The Class Struggles in France, 1848–1850* (New York: New York Labor News Company, 1924).

Karl Marx and Friedrich Engels, *The Communist Manifesto* (trans. Samuel Moore) (London: Penguin, 1985).

Bim Mason, *Street Theatre and Other Outdoor Performance* (London: Routledge, 1992).

Clifford Mason, *Macbeth in Harlem: Black Theater in America from the Beginning to Raisin in the Sun* (New Brunswick: Rutgers University Press, 2020).

Tomoko Masuzawa, *The Invention of World Religions: Or, How European Universalism Was Preserved in the Language of Pluralism* (Chicago: University of Chicago Press, 2005).

Mary McCarthy, *Ideas and the Novel* (London: Weidenfeld and Nicholson, 1981).

Adam McGee, "Haitian Vodou and Voodoo: Imagined Religion and Popular Culture." *Studies in Religion / Sciences Religieuses* 41:2 (2012), 231–56.

Anthonie Meijers, "Collective Speech Acts." In Savas L. Tsohatzidis (ed.), *Intentional Acts and Institutional Facts: Essays on John Searle's Social Ontology* (Dordrecht: Springer, 2007), 93–110.

Elizabeth Carolyn Miller, *Slow Print: Literary Radicalism and Late Victorian Print Culture* (Stanford: Stanford University Press, 2013).

John Milton, *Eikonoklastes.* In Merritt Y. Hughes (ed.), *The Complete Prose Works of John Milton,* vol. 3, *1648–1649* (New Haven: Yale University Press, 1962), 335–601.

Donald Mitchell, "Montagu Slater (1902–1956): Who Was He?" In Philip Brett (ed.), *Benjamin Britten:* Peter Grimes (Cambridge: Cambridge University Press, 1983), 22–46.

Esther Mombo, "Anglican Liturgies in Eastern Africa." In Charles Heffing and Cynthia Shattuck (eds.), *The Oxford Guide to the Book of Common Prayer: A Worldwide Survey* (Oxford: Oxford University Press, 2006), 277–86.

Fred Moten, *Black and Blur (Consent Not to Be a Single Being)* (Durham: Duke University Press, 2017).

Fred Moten, *In the Break: The Aesthetics of the Black Radical Tradition* (Minneapolis: University of Minnesota Press, 2003).

Fred Moten, *The Universal Machine (Consent Not to Be a Single Being)* (Durham: Duke University Press, 2018).

Chantal Mouffe, *For a Left Populism* (London: Verso, 2018).

Chantal Mouffe, "Hegemony and Ideology in Gramsci." In Chantal Mouffe (ed.), *Gramsci and Marxist Theory* (trans. Denise Derôme), 169–205.

Lupenga Mphande, "Ngugi and the World of Christianity: A Dialectic." *Journal of Asian and African Studies* 39:5 (2004), 357–78.

Mpalive-Hangson Msiska, *Wole Soyinka* (Plymouth: Northcote House, 1998).

Kornél Mundruczó (interviewed by Malte Krasting), "Die Imagination des Helden: Ein Gespräch vor Probenbeginn mit dem Regisseur Kornél Mundruczó." In *Lohengrin: Oper in drei Acten* (concert program, Bayerische Staatsoper, München, Spielzeit 2022–23), 50–63.

David Murphy, "Fighting for the Homeland? The Second World War in the Films of Ousmane Sembene." *L'Esprit Créateur* 47:1 (2007), 56–67.

David Murphy, *Sembene: Imagining Alternatives in Film & Fiction* (Oxford: James Currey, 2000).

Scott Reynolds Nelson, *Steel Drivin' Man: John Henry, the Untold Story of an American Legend* (New York: Oxford University Press, 2006).

William T. Nettlefold, "Song for a Choir of Agricultural Workers to Sing at Covent Garden," *Poetry and the People* 9 (1939).

Wallace Nichols, *The Speaking of Poetry* (1937; London: Dennis Dobson Ltd., 1949).

Friedrich Nietzsche, *The Birth of Tragedy out of the Spirit of Music* (trans. Shaun Whiteside) (London: Penguin, 1993).

Sean O'Neill, "The Boasian Legacy in Ethnomusicology: Cultural Relativism, Narrative Texts, and the Role of Comparison." In Regna Darnell, Joshua Smith, Michelle Hamilton, and Robert L. A. Hancock (eds.), *The Franz Boas Papers*, vol. 1, *Franz Boas as Public Intellectual—Theory, Ethnography, Activism* (Lincoln: University of Nebraska Press, 2015), 129–60.

Ngũgĩ wa Thiong'o, *A Grain of Wheat* (London: Penguin, 2002).

Ngũgĩ wa Thiong'o, *The River Between* (London: Penguin, 2002).

Jeremy Noel-Tod, "Eliot as Public Intellectual." In Megan Quigley and David E. Chinitz (eds.), *Eliot Now* (London: Bloomsbury Academic, 2024), 51–63.

Walter J. Ong, *Orality and Literacy: The Technologizing of the Word* (London: Routledge, 2002).

José Ortega y Gasset, *The Revolt of the Masses* (authorized translation) (New York: Norton, 1993).

Fernando Ortiz, *Cuban Counterpoint: Tobacco and Sugar* (trans. Harriet De Onís) (New York: A. A. Knopf, 1947).

George Orwell, *Animal Farm: A Fairy Story* (London: Penguin, 1989).

George Orwell, *The Lion and the Unicorn: Socialism and the English Genius*. In Peter Davison (ed.), *The Complete Works of George Orwell*, vol. 12, *A Patriot After All* (London: Secker & Warburg, 1998), 391–432.

Ben Page, "'And the Oscar Goes to . . . *Daybreak in Udi*': Understanding Late Colonial Community Development and its Legacy through Film." *Development and Change* 45:5 (2014), 813–68.

Ian Patterson, "Two Librettists: Montagu Slater and Ronald Duncan." In Vicki P. Stroeher and Justin Vickers (eds.), *Benjamin Britten in Context* (Cambridge: Cambridge University Press, 2022), 232–40.

Gerald Peary and Patrick McGilligan, "Ousmane Sembène: An Interview (1972)." In Annett Busch and Max Annas (eds.), *Ousmane Sembène: Interviews* (Jackson: University of Mississippi, 2008), 41–51.

Imani Perr, *May We Forever Stand: A History of the Black National Anthem* (Chapel Hill: University of North Carolina Press, 2018).

Amanda T. Perry, "Becoming Indigenous in Haiti, from Dessalines to *La Revue Indigène*." *Small Axe* 21:2.53 (2017), 45–61.

Alasdair Pettinger, "'Eh! eh! Bomba, hen! hen!': Making Sense of a Vodou Chant." In Diana Paton and Maarit Forde (eds.), *Obeah and Other Powers: The Politics of Caribbean Religion and Healing* (Duke University Press, 2012), 80–102.

Alasdair Pettinger, "From Vaudoux to Voodoo." *Forum of Modern Language Studies* 40:4 (2004), 415–25.

Françoise Pfaff, "Myths, Traditions and Colonialism in Ousmane Sembène's Emitai." In *CLA Journal* 24:3 (1981), 336–46.

Rachel Potter, "International PEN: Writers, Free Expression, Organisations." In Benjamin Kohlmann and Matthew Taunton (eds.), *A History of 1930s British Literature* (Cambridge: Cambridge University Press, 2019), 120–33.

Rachel Potter and Matthew Taunton, "Introduction: The British Novel of Ideas." In *The British Novel of Ideas: George Eliot to Zadie Smith* (Cambridge: Cambridge University Press, 2025), 1–25.

Eugène Pottier, "L'Internationale." In *Chants révolutionnaires* (Paris: Dentu, 1887), 13–15.

Jean Price-Mars, *Ainsi parla l'oncle* (Ottawa: Lemeac, 1973).

Jean Price-Mars, *So Spoke the Uncle: Ethnographic Essays (Ainsi parla l'oncle)* (trans. Magdaline W. Shannon) (Washington, DC: Three Continents Press, 1983).

David Punter and Glennis Byron, *The Gothic* (Oxford: Blackwell, 2004).

Albert J. Raboteau, *Slave Religion: The "Invisible Institution" in the Antebellum South* (1978; Oxford: Oxford University Press, 2004).

Adolph L. Reed Jr., *The South: Jim Crow and Its Afterlives* (London: Verso, 2022).

Paul Rekret, *Take This Hammer: Work, Song, Crisis* (London: Goldsmiths Press, 2024).

The Revised Psalter: The First Report of the Commission to Revise the Psalter appointed by the Archbishops of Canterbury and York (London: S.P.C.K., 1961).

David Richards, "At Other Times: Modernism and the 'Primitive.'" In Vincent Sherry (ed.), *The Cambridge History of Modernism* (Cambridge: Cambridge University Press, 2017), 64–82.

Marguerite H. Rippy, *Orson Welles and the Unfinished RKO Projects: A Postmodern Perspective* (Carbondale: Southern Illinois University Press, 2009).

Douglas Robinson, *Translation and Empire: Postcolonial Theories Explained* (London: Routledge, 2014).

Jacques Roumain, "Filthy Negroes" (trans. Joanne Fungaroli and Ronald Sauer). In *When the Tom-Tom Beats: Selected Prose and Poems,* by Jacques Roumain (Washington, DC: Azul Editions, 1995), 84–97.

Léon-François Hoffman and Yves Chemla (eds.), *Jacques Romain: Œuvres complètes.* Critical ed. (Paris: CNRS Éditions, 2018).

Jacques Roumain, "Poetry as a Weapon" (trans. Joanne Fungaroli and Ronald Sauer). In *When the Tom-Tom Beats: Selected Prose and Poems,* by Jacques Roumain (Washington, DC: Azul Editions, 1995), 105–9.

Jacques Roumain, *Masters of the Dew* (trans. Langston Hughes and Mercer Cook) (London: Heinemann, 1978).

Jacques Roumain, *Le Sacrifice du tambour-assoto®* (Port-au-Prince: Imprimerie de L'État, 1943).

Edward Sackville-West, "The Musical and Dramatic Structure." In Eric Crozier (ed.), Peter Grimes: *Essays* (London: John Lane the Bodley Head, for The Governors of Sadler's Wells, 1945), 27–55.

Glyn Salton-Cox, "Katharine Burdekin: Self and Not-Self." In Rachel Potter and Matthew Taunton (eds.), *The British Novel of Ideas: George Eliot to Zadie Smith* (Cambridge: Cambridge University Press, 2025), 180–91.

Amelia Saunders, "Not Just Talk: The Politics of Enunciation in *BlacKkKlansman.*" *Black Camera* 13:2 (2022), 234–54.

Robert Sawyer, "'All's Well That Ends Welles': Orson Welles and the 'Voodoo' Macbeth." *Multicultural Shakespeare: Translation, Appropriation and Performance* 13:28 (2016), 87–103.

Murray Schafer, *British Composers in Interview* (London: Faber & Faber, 1963).

Friedrich Schiller, "Über den Gebrauch des Chors in der Tragödie / On the Use of the Chorus in Tragedy" (trans. by Guido Avezzù). In "The Chorus in Drama," special issue, *Skenè: Journal of Theatre and Drama Studies* 1:1 (2015), 193–66.

Augustus Wilhelm Schlegel, *A Course of Lectures on Dramatic Art and Literature* (trans. John Black), 2nd ed., vol. 1 (London: J. Templeman, 1840).

Bill Schwarz, "Breaking Bread with History: C. L. R. James and *The Black Jacobins*" (interview with Stuart Hall). *History Workshop Journal* 46:1 (1998), 17–32.

David Scott, *Conscripts of Modernity: The Tragedy of Colonial Enlightenment* (Durham: Duke University Press, 2004).

Eve Kosofsky Sedgwick, *Touching Feeling: Affect, Pedagogy, Performativity* (Duke University Press, 2003).

Ousmane Sembène, *God's Bits of Wood* (trans. Francis Price) (London: Heinemann, 1976).

Robert Sencourt, and Donald Adamson (ed.), *T. S. Eliot: A Memoir* (London: Garstone Press, 1971).

Richard Sennett, *The Craftsman* (London: Penguin, 2009).

William Shakespeare, *Macbeth.* In Stephen Greenblatt et al. (eds.), *The Norton Shakespeare* (New York: Norton, 1997), 2555–2618.

William Shakespeare, *The Tragedy of Julius Caesar.* In Stephen Greenblatt et al. (eds.), *The Norton Shakespeare* (New York: Norton, 1997), 1525–89.

Magdaline W. Shannon, introduction to *So Spoke the Uncle: Ainsi parla l'oncle,* by Jean Price-Mars (trans. Magdaline W. Shannon) (Washington, DC: Three Continents Press, 1983), ix–xxvi.

Nikola Shubski, "On Uritski Square (Impression of a Muscovite)" (1920; trans. David Riff). In Inke Arns, Sylvia Sasse, and Igor Chubarov (eds.), *The Storming of the Winter Palace* (Chicago: University of Chicago Press, 2017), 143–47.

George Shulman, "Fred Moten's Refusals and Consents: The Politics of Fugitivity." *Political Theory* 49:2 (2021), 272–313.

Carol Sicherman, "Ngugi's Colonial Education: 'The Subversion . . . of the African Mind.'" *African Studies Review* 38:3 (1995) pp. 11–41.

Montagu Slater, *The Trial of Jomo Kenyatta* (London: Secker and Warburg, 1955).

"Soviet Day." *The Listener* 30:773 (4 November 1943), 520.

Gerald Stanton Smith, *Songs to Seven Strings: Russian Guitar Poetry and Soviet "Mass Song"* (Bloomington: Indiana University Press, 1984).

Rosaleen Smyth, "Grierson, the British Documentary Movement, and Colonial Cinema in British Colonial Africa." *Film History* 25:4 (2013), 82–113.

Rosaleen Smyth, "The Post-War Career of the Colonial Film Unit in Africa: 1946–1955." *Historical Journal of Film, Radio and Television* 12:2 (1992), 163–77.

N. A. Soboleva, "The Composition of State Anthems of the Russian Empire and the Soviet Union." *Russian Social Science Review* 50:2 (2009), 67–94.

Wole Soyinka, *The Bacchae of Euripides*. In *Collected Plays 1* (Oxford: Oxford University Press, 1973), 233–307.
Wole Soyinka, *The Climate of Fear: The Reith Lectures 2004* (London: Profile Books, 2004).
Wole Soyinka, "Drama and the Revolutionary Ideal." In Karen L. Morrell (ed.), *In Person: Achebe, Awoonor, and Soyinka at the University of Washington* (Seattle: University of Washington African Studies Programme, 1975), 61–88.
Wole Soyinka, *Kongi's Harvest*. In *Collected Plays 2* (Oxford: Oxford University Press, 1974), 59–141.
Wole Soyinka, *Myth, Literature and the African World* (Cambridge: Cambridge University Press, 1978).
Barry Spurr, *Anglo-Catholic in Religion: T. S. Eliot and Christianity* (Cambridge: Lutterworth Press, 2010).
Lindsey Stewart, *The Politics of Black Joy: Zora Neale Hurston and Neo-Abolitionism* (Evanston: Northwestern University Press, 2021).
Carol Summers, "Education and Literacy." In John Parker (ed.), *The Oxford Handbook of Modern African History* (Oxford: Oxford University Press, 2013), 319–37.
Randall Swingler, *Soviet Airmen's Song: Unison Song with Piano Accompaniment*, words adapted by Randall Swingler, tune arranged by G.M.S. and J.T. (London: Worker's Music Association, 1939).
Randall Swingler and Edgar Criddle, "Spain: A Drama of Modern History," in Simon Breden (ed.), *El Unity Theatre y la Guerra Civil española: Propaganda literaria y teatral en el Reino Unido* (Madrid: Guillermo Escolar Editor, 2020), 269–89
Ramie Targoff, *Common Prayer: The Language of Public Devotion in Early Modern England* (Chicago: University of Chicago Press, 2001).
Matthew Taunton, "Chorus and Agon in the Political Novel: Staging Left-Wing Arguments in H. G. Wells, Iris Murdoch, and Doris Lessing." *MFS: Modern Fiction Studies* 67:2 (2021), 247–71.
Matthew Taunton, "Katharine Burdekin and Collective Speech: Politics, Chorus and Liturgy." *Women: A Cultural Review* 31:4 (2020), 384–400.
Elinor Taylor, "Experiments in Left Populism: British Literature Between the Wars." In Benjamin Kohlmann and Matthew Taunton (eds.), *"The People" and British Literature: Belonging, Exclusion, and Democracy* (Cambridge: Cambridge University Press, 2025), 141–56.
Elinor Taylor, "'The Voice Speaking, Desired, Awaited': Jack Lindsay's *1649*, Textual Form and Communist Historiography." *Twentieth Century Communism* 12 (2017), 15–36.
George Thomson, *Marxism and Poetry* (New York: International Publishers, 1946).
Mark Christian Thompson, *Black Fascisms: African American Literature & Culture Between the Wars* (Charlottesville: University of Virginia Press, 2007).
Michael Thurston, "Black Christ, Red Flag: Langston Hughes on Scottsboro." *College Literature* 22:3 (1995), 30–49.
Steven Tracey, *John Henry: Roark Bradford's Novel and Play* (Oxford: Oxford University Press, 2008).

Sarah Trimmer, *A Companion to the Book of Common Prayer of the Church of England: Containing a Comment on the Service for Sundays; Including the Collects, Epistles, and Gospels* (London: T. Longman, 1791).

Sarah Trimmer, *Reflections on the Education of Children in Charity Schools with the Outline of a Plan of Appropriate Instruction for the Children of the Poor Submitted to the Consideration of the Patrons of Schools of Every Denomination Supported by Charity* (London: T. Longman, 1792).

Sarah Trimmer, *The Teacher's Assistant: Consisting of Lectures in the Catechetical Form, Being Part of a Plan of Appropriate Instruction for the Children of the Poor* (London: F.C. and J. Rivington, 1812).

Edward Venn, "*Benjamin Britten: The Spiritual Dimension.* By Graham Elliott." *Music and Letters* 89:1 (2008), 143–48.

Richard Wagner, *Opera and Drama* (trans. Edwin Evans), vol. 1 (London: W. M. Reeves, 1913?).

Clare Warden, *Migrating Modernist Performance: British Theatrical Travels Through Russia* (Basingstoke: Palgrave Macmillan, 2016).

Don Watson, "Jack Lindsay: Poetry and the Spanish Civil War." Occasional Seminar Paper No. 4. In Robert Mackie (ed.), *Jack Lindsay: The Thirties and Forties* (London: University of London Institute of Commonwealth Studies Australian Studies Centre, 1984), 61–72.

Jini Kim Watson, *Cold War Reckonings: Authoritarianism and the Genres of Decolonization* (New York: Fordham University Press, 2021).

Ian Watt, *The Rise of the Novel: Studies in Defoe, Richardson and Fielding* (London: Pimlico, 2000).

Max Weber, *The Protestant Ethic and the Spirit of Capitalism* (trans. Talcott Parsons) (London: Routledge, 2001).

Judith Weisenfeld, "'A Rare Human Document': LoBagola's African American Humbug Religion." *American Religion* 1:1 (October 2019), 27–48.

Raymond Williams, *Culture & Society: Coleridge to Orwell* (London: Hogarth Press, 1993).

Raymond Williams, "Culture Is Ordinary." In *Resources of Hope: Culture, Democracy, Socialism* (London: Verso, 1989), 3–18.

Raymond Williams, *Marxism and Literature* (Oxford: Oxford University Press, 1977).

Raymond Williams, *Modern Tragedy* (London: Chatto & Windus, 1966).

Peter Womack, "Pronouns: We/Us/Our." *Critical Quarterly* 64:2 (2022), 93–99.

Richard Wright, *Twelve Million Black Voices: A Folk History of the Negro in the United States* (London: Lindsay Drummond Ltd., 1947).

ARCHIVAL MATERIALS

Henry W. and Albert A. Berg Collection of English and American Literature, New York Public Library.

Alan Bush Papers, British Library.

Federal Theatre Project Materials Collection, George Mason University. Available at https://hdl.handle.net/1920/3478.

Fisher Papers, Lambeth Palace Library.

Herbert Halpert 1939 Southern States Recording Expedition, Library of Congress. Available at https://www.loc.gov/search/?fa=partof:herbert+halpert+1939+southern+states+recording+expedition.

House of Commons, Hansard's Parliamentary Debates: The Official Report. Available at https://hansard.parliament.uk/commons.

Langston Hughes Papers, James Weldon Johnson Collection in the Yale Collection of American Literature, Beinecke Rare Book and Manuscript Library.

Papers of the Archbishops' Commission to Revise the Psalter, Church of England Record Centre, Bermondsey.

Unity Theater records, Special Collections Research Center, Southern Illinois University Carbondale.

University of Warwick Archives, Warwick Digital Collections.

Welles mss., 1930–1950, Lilly Library, Indiana University, Bloomington, Indiana.

FILM AND MEDIA

Terry Bishop (dir.), *Daybreak in Udi* (1949).

John Fahey, "Nine Pound Hammer," *The Voice of the Turtle* (Takoma, 1968).

John Fahey, "John Henry Variations," *Death Chants, Breakdowns, and Military Waltzes* (reissue; Takoma, 1999).

Shannon Furman, Jay Jackson, Terrell Riley, and Steve Trout (dirs.), *All or Nothing*, season 3, episode 2, *The Writing on the Wall* (Amazon Prime Video, 2018).

"Kamala Harris shuts down 'Lock him up!' chant about Trump," YouTube video, https://www.youtube.com/watch?v=BSoU2-zpAco.

Spike Lee (dir.), *BlacKkKlansman* (2018).

"Orson Welles, Sketch Book—Episode 2: Critics," YouTube video, https://www.youtube.com/watch?v=NL3ZoUJ-Tek.

"Premier League Statement: Players to Take the Knee Again in 2024/25," https://www.premierleague.com/news/4089060.

Senghor et les arts, réinventer l'universel, RFI podcast, 8 February 2023, https://www.rfi.fr/fr/podcasts/vous-m-en-direz-des-nouvelles/20230208-senghor-et-les-arts-r%C3%A9inventer-l-universel.

Jean Rouch (dir.), *Yenendi: Les hommes qui font la pluie* (1951).

Ousmane Sembène (dir.), *Camp de Thiaroye* (1988).

Strange Beliefs: Sir Edward Evans-Pritchard, TV documentary first screened 1986, YouTube video, https://www.youtube.com/watch?v=hXyoOyEcQnk.

Luke Turner, "HEWILLNOTDIVIDE.US," digital video, color, sound, 3:15. Displayed at *Milk,* Wellcome Collection, London, 30 March–10 September 2023.

INDEX

The authorized representative in the EU for product safety and compliance is:
Mare Nostrum Group
B.V Doelen 72
4831 GR Breda
The Netherlands

www.ingramcontent.com/pod-product-compliance
Ingram Content Group UK Ltd.
Pitfield, Milton Keynes, MK11 3LW, UK
UKHW042225200926
475760UK00003B/93

* 9 7 8 1 5 0 3 6 4 8 4 9 4 *